The Business of
Value Investing

The Business of Value Investing

SIX ESSENTIAL ELEMENTS TO BUYING COMPANIES LIKE WARREN BUFFETT

Sham Gad

WILEY

John Wiley & Sons, Inc.

Published by John Wiley & Sons, Inc., Hoboken, New Jersey.
Published simultaneously in Canada.

For general information on our other products and services or for technical support, please
contact our Customer Care Department within the United States at (800) 762-2974, outside
the United States at (317) 572-3993 or fax (317) 572-4002.

Wiley also publishes its books in a variety of electronic formats. Some content that appears in
print may not be available in electronic books. For more information about Wiley products,
visit our web site at www.wiley.com.

Library of Congress Cataloging-in-Publication Data

Gad, Hesham, 1978—
    The business of value investing: six essential elements to buying companies like Warren
Buffett / Sham Gad.
        p. cm.
    Includes index.
    ISBN 978-0-470-44448-1
    1. Value investing.   2. Corporations-Valuation.   3. Stocks.   I Title.
HG4521.G16   2010
332.63'22—dc22

                                                                    2009025052

10 9 8 7 6 5 4 3 2 1

To my mom and dad,
Seham and Moustafa Gad, and my wife,
Maggie Allen Gad.
You are the best.

Contents

Acknowledgments   xiii

Introduction   xvii

Chapter 1   Invest in the Business, Buy the Stock   1

Stock Prices Are More Noise Than
Information   4

A Businesslike Approach to Valuing
the Business   6

The Making of a Legend   11

A Simple Idea, Really   14

Chapter 2   The Only Three Types of Investments You
Need to Know   15

Stocks Prices Aren't Always Rational   16

The Business Side of Investing   17

Three Buckets: Undervalued, Overvalued,
and Fairly Valued   21

Price Determines Value   24

Key Takeaways   31

Chapter 3   The Six Elements of Intelligent Investing   33

All Investing Is Value Investing   35

Learn from the Masters   38

The Sum of Its Parts: A Fundamental
Framework   39

A Mental Latticework   42

Overview of the Six Elements   43

Emphasize the Process, Not the Outcome   46

Key Takeaways   46

Chapter 4   Establish a Sound Investment Philosophy
The First Element   47

Preservation of Capital Is the Name
of the Game   49

Price Paid Determines Value Received   52

The Starting Point Matters   54

Avoid Using Margin   61

Focus on Absolute Returns   64

Key Takeaways   66

Chapter 5   Develop a Search Strategy
The Second Element   67

Ignore the Media   69

Imitation Is the Sincerest Form of Flattery   72

Basic Search Strategies   75

Advanced Search Strategy   85

Key Takeaways   89

Chapter 6 Effective Business Valuation
The Third Element   91

Value Investing 101: Margin of Safety   92

Value Investing 201: Intrinsic Value   95

Value Investing 301: Seek Businesses
with a Wide Moat   101

Value Investing 401: Calculating a
True Intrinsic Value   106

The Value of Management   111

Understanding Return on Equity:
Microsoft Corporation   121

Key Takeaways   124

Chapter 7 Have the Discipline to Say No
The Fourth Element   125

In Investing, Discipline is Everything   126

Discipline Affects the Price Paid,
Which Determines the Value You Get   128

Be Prepared to Look Stupid   132

Don't Split Hairs   137

Unveiling Investor A: Warren Buffett   139

Discipline Is Simple but Rarely Easy   145

Key Takeaways   146

Chapter 8 Practicing the Art of Patience
The Fifth Element   147

Swimming against the Current   150

The Benefits of Waiting for a Good Pitch   151

Ignorance Can Be Bliss 158

The Benefits of a Buy-and-Hold Approach 162

Conservative Tests of Safety a Must 171

Key Takeaways 172

Chapter 9 Invest Significantly at the Maximum
Point of Pessimism
The Sixth Element 173

Putting It All Together 174

Pessimism Leads to Value 179

Avoid That Which Is Most Valuable 181

Remain Flexible in the Approach 186

All or Nothing 192

Key Takeaways 193

Chapter 10 More Than One Way to Find Value
*Case Studies Showing the Approach
at Work* 195

A Reminder: Process First, Outcome
Second 197

Case Study #1: Finding Value in an
Unloved Industry
Sunrise Senior Living (SRZ) 198

Case Study #2: Money Machine South
of the Border
Ternium Steel 205

Case Study #3: A Tale of Two Shares
Mueller Water Products 214

	Fertile Hunting Ground	216
	Conclusion	219
	Key Takeaways	220
Chapter 11	Avoiding Common Stumbling Blocks	221
	Growth and Value: Two Sides of the Same Coin	225
	Book Value: More Than Meets the Eye	232
	What Matters Most	240
	Key Takeaways	242
Chapter 12	Starting an Investment Partnership	243
	Two Key Considerations	244
	Service Providers	245
	Quality Matters Most	247
Notes		**249**
About the Author		**253**
Index		**255**

Acknowledgments

As I began writing this book, it very quickly became evident that this project would not be possible without the aid of many people. As this is a book about investing, specifically value investing, substantial credit goes to the late Ben Graham, the educator and practitioner who formulated the fundamental concepts of what is now commonly referred to as value investing. It was Ben Graham who taught Warren Buffett, and it was Warren Buffett who sparked my investment passion as early as high school.

When I was an MBA student at the University of Georgia (UGA) in 2006, three accomplishments occurred during that year that I consider akin to winning the Triple Crown. My first victory came in Omaha, when, after writing a letter to Warren Buffett, he invited my classmates and me to visit him. Mr. Buffett typically hosts the students for a morning Q&A session followed by lunch. However, as luck would have it, we also got to spend over three hours with Mr. Buffett the night before. Getting two days of face time with Mr. Buffett was like winning the grand prize. The golfing equivalent would be showing up to play 9 holes with Tiger Woods and instead playing 36. Thank you, Mr. Buffett.

The visit to Omaha would not have been possible had it not been for Geoffrey Cole, M.D., whom I met at the University of Georgia's Terry College of Business. Jeff is one of the smartest guys I've met and a walking encyclopedia on Warren Buffet. I'm fortunate to have him around to pick his brilliant brain. Thanks, Jeff.

A special thanks to Peter Shedd, the MBA director at the time, who gave me his and the university's full support to make the visit with Mr. Buffett an unforgettable experience. Thank you, Peter.

The second victory came in Memphis. Not many people know this, but Mason Hawkins got his MBA at the University of Georgia. In May 2007, Mason invited me to attend the Longleaf Partner's Funds Annual Shareholders Presentation. I have always felt that Mason is one of the most underrated investors of our time. After meeting him, I understood why: Mason's shrewdness as an investor is hidden by his humbleness. But most of all, he is extremely generous with his time to those who seek his assistance. His accomplishments both as an investment fund manager and as a philanthropist set the finest standards of excellence. In Memphis, it is considered an honor and privilege to be invested in the Longleaf Funds. Spend a few minutes with Mason or read Longleaf's Governing Principles, and anyone would feel the same.

I was blown away at the annual presentation, and the knowledge I picked up helped inspire a major portion of this book. Although I expected to go home after the meeting, Mason invited me to dinner, where I was introduced to all of the wonderful people at Southeastern Asset Management, Inc. Thank you, Mason.

And no modern book on value investing isn't influenced by the work of Columbia Business School professor Bruce Greenwald, one of the most respected and accomplished professors in the arena of value investing today. Professor Greenwald's work has influenced countless value investors and his teachings helped inspire this book.

The final victory was by far the best one and came at home in Athens. After meeting Messrs. Buffett and Hawkins, it's hard to think of anything to top it. But I did when I met Maggie Allen, who at the time was working for the Terry College of Business. Through a combination of creativity and charm (at least I think so), Maggie and I developed a wonderful relationship that ultimately led to our marriage in March 2009. I've always felt that the most important decision anyone will ever make in life is deciding who to marry. I could go on and on about the value Maggie has added to my life, but no amount of words can fully describe what she means to me. She is my best friend, and I can't imagine my life without her. I am a better person because of her, and the world is a much better place because she is in it. If I was given the chance to create the perfect lifelong partner, no one would compare to what Maggie has done for me. I do nothing for her—but she does everything for me. Maggie, I love you more than you will ever know. Thank you for choosing me.

This book wouldn't have been possible without Vitaliy Katsenelson, who suggested that I contact John Wiley & Sons about my thoughts for this book. Thanks, Vitaliy.

When you write a book, you realize the enormous value an editorial team has on creating a book. Pamela Van Giessen, thank you for taking my thoughts and turning them into a book. I appreciate your willingness to make this happen. Emilie Herman cannot be thanked enough for editing my chapters and being a wonderful sounding board for ideas. And Kate Wood, thank you for all you've done to ensure that this tome is not just another book on investing. A special thanks goes to Rose Lugtu for all she did to make sure that this book is what it is today. I couldn't be more fortunate to work with such a first-class organization as Wiley.

And there are two people who are never appreciated enough: Mom and Dad. I have never met two people as selfless as my mother and father. Both have sacrificed tremendously in order for their children to succeed. It's not until you get a little older and wiser that you truly begin to appreciate the enormous role that your parents play in your life. Thank you, Dad, for making me the man I am today. As for my mother, I really lucked out. I will always cherish the moments we have together. The devotion she showers on her children is rare in today's world, and it's impossible for me to fairly quantify the values she has given me. I love you both.

My two sisters, Imann and Asmaa, thanks for putting up with your big brother. I love you both.

One easily realizes that being successful in life is greatly due to the people that you meet along the way. I've always felt that to take sole credit for your achievements in life is an unappreciative way to lead your life. While I could easily devote countless paragraphs to each person, I am very thankful to these people: Mohnish Pabrai; John and Jennifer Allen (thank you for raising such a wonderful daughter!); Professor John Scruggs (the market isn't always efficient, Dr. Scruggs); Bahman Mossavar-Rahmani and Ali Granmayeh at UAS Asset Management; Shai Dardashti; Peter Lindmark; Cole Donley; Jim Donley; Joel Harber (thanks for subsidizing my golf, Joel); Michael Breaux; Nadim Kazi; Ajay Desai and his entire team at Smith Barney; Mark Sellers; and the countless others who I know have had a valuable influence on my life.

Introduction

This is a book about how to think about investing intelligently. Due to the unrivaled success of investor Warren Buffett, value investing has become the only intelligent manner in which to approach investing. The philosophies of value investing emphasize an approach that focuses on preservation of capital, risk aversion, discipline, and avoidance of crowd psychology. Contrary to the academic belief that greater return can only be achieved by taking on greater risk, value investing confirms that returns can be maximized by taking on very little relative risk.

Reciting the value investing rhetoric is one thing, but doing it is something else entirely. Value investor Seth Klarman of the Baupost Group suggests that the philosophies of value investing may very well be genetically determined: "When you first learn of the value approach, it either resonates with you or it doesn't."[1] My interpretation of Klarman's assessment is that the foundations of value investing—patience, discipline, and risk aversion—aren't subjects that are taught in school. You either possess them or you don't. Business schools can teach how to analyze a business and how to value a business, but they can't teach you patience or discipline to say no to a popular security. More so, business schools can't teach you to have the courage to make a significant investment during the maximum point of pessimism. Education is invaluable and certainly aids in investment success, but it's not the sole determinant of investing acumen.

The aim of this book is to define and examine the essential framework that encompasses the foundation of value investing. Like a golf swing, value investing is most effective when mastery of the essential elements come together to produce a consistently reliable result.

This book centers on the concept that successful value investors have an ingrained mental framework through which all investment decisions are contemplated. This framework stems from Benjamin Graham, who told us in *The Intelligent Investor* that "investment is most intelligent when it is most businesslike."[2]

When examining the performance and method of operation for today's most successful investors—Warren Buffett, Mason Hawkins, Seth Klarman, Bruce Berkowitz, and others—their results stem from their ability to consistently apply the same fundamental approach to investing time and time again. In analyzing such an approach, the central concepts of value investing come down to six fundamental elements.

Use of the word "element" is deliberate. In science, chemical elements are combined to create the foundation of human existence. Water is comprised of two elements, hydrogen and oxygen. You must have both to make water.

Similarly, for value investing to be intelligent and successful, six essential elements are required. Analyze the investment approach of any successful value-oriented investor and you will observe that, like water, the basic elements exist. While these elements can be identified individually, it's critical to understand that all six elements come together to form a complete mental framework. Of even greater value, they can serve to spot any faults or mistakes that were made in making an investment. Find an investment mistake that you made and odds are that one of these elements was compromised. These six elements in order are:

1. Develop a **sound investment philosophy.**
2. Have a **good search strategy.**
3. Know how to **value a business and assess the quality of management.**

4. Have the **discipline to say no.**
5. Practice the **art of patience.**
6. Have the **courage to make a significant investment at the point of maximum pessimism.**

Successful investors take the above six elements and incorporate them in their investment decision making. The order is significant. Potential investors should not even attempt to seriously invest without first developing a sound investment philosophy. Developing such a sound philosophy—loss avoidance, risk aversion, avoidance of crowd psychology, and staying within one's circle of competence—is the fundamental building block for everything going forward. A successful and fruitful search strategy won't succeed unless it incorporates a sound investment philosophy. Going down the list, it becomes apparent that one element cannot be successfully applied without the one preceding it.

But as a whole, these elements come together to create the essential mental framework that is found inside the most successful minds in investing.

In Chapters 1 and 2, the focus is on the two ways to approach any investment opportunity. First, investors should look at stocks as a fractional interest in an entire business. The stock is the instrument that is bought; the business is the entity you own and will determine your long-term investment outcome. Investors often confuse this distinction, the result of which leads to expensive and unnecessary investment mistakes.

Chapter 3 gives an overview of the six elements, with Chapters 4 through 9 each devoted to a single element. Chapter 10 crystallizes the thesis of the book by examining three investment case studies, and Chapter 11 concludes with reasons for why many investors stumble time and time again. Finally, I conclude with a chapter on how to create an investment partnership. I thought long and hard about adding this chapter to the book but decided to write it after remembering the wonderful help I received that enabled me to go into business for myself.

For the new student of value investing, this book aims to provide a clear and concise illustration of the fundamental tenets of value investing, which are ingrained in the mind and psyche of every successful value investor. For the more advanced student and the active professional, *The Business of Value Investing* endeavors to add to the never-ending process of constant learning and application.

In the investment management business, eating one's own cooking should be the standard not the exception. The investment manager who has his own capital invested alongside his clients' is a powerful sign of alignment of interests. I see no reason why this viewpoint should not spill over to an author who is recommending an investment approach in a book. Thus, as you go over the case studies presented in this book, they were, at one time or another, all actual investments made by me.

1

Invest in the Business, Buy the Stock

Investment is most prudent when it is most businesslike.
—Benjamin Graham, *The Intelligent Investor*

Mention Ben Graham's quote to investors, and they all nod their heads in agreement. But for most people, that's where the understanding ends. In practice, most individuals approach investing in a very unbusinesslike fashion; they just don't realize it at the time. Often they give more attention to the stock price and what it does than to what the business itself is doing. When markets are in an upswing, this perspective might not matter much. Then again, a value-oriented investment approach is not geared toward bull markets but at bear markets. Riding out the storm relatively unscathed is the name of the game. To invest at sensible prices, it is wise to think first about the business and understanding it and its industry.

I know firsthand the value of investing in the business versus the stock because I thought this was the approach I was taking when I first starting investing in my late teens. Yet years later, I decided to go back and look at some of my investment decisions, and what I found surprised me.

I realized that while I was buying good businesses that I understood, I was letting a moving stock price instruct me as to when to buy and sell. One specific deal that crystallized these thoughts was my 2002 investment in a company called Meridian Medical Technologies. It was a good profitable business, but unfortunately, I was not around to reap the benefits of those profits. Rather, I gave in to Mr. Market at the first sign of trouble. I wrote about this experience in one of my first letters to my limited partners.

> Meridian is a manufacturer and supplier of auto-injectors, or ready to use drug delivery systems used by emergency personnel throughout the world. At the time, Meridian owned the auto-injector market—no other company had FDA approval. The company had no debt, a fair P/E multiple, and large market all to itself.
>
> Meridian was a good business with a very strong competitive advantage at the time in the form of FDA approval. And the valuation implied a decent investment price.
>
> I bought shares around $33 or so. Within a couple of months the stock was down to $27 . . . the next earnings announcement showed that Meridian had posted "moderate" top and bottom line growth. The stock tanked that day to $22, and I sold out. Less than a year later, Meridian was trading over $40 a share, and shortly after that, it was bought out at an even higher price by King Pharmaceuticals.

This experience taught me two very important lessons immediately. The first was to accept the fact that investment decisions should be made based on the value of the underlying business, not according to the short-term movements in the stock price. Investors have to learn to come to terms with their decisions. If you can, then assuming you understand and have properly valued the business, you aren't swayed when the stock price of your investment declines

20 percent. Business valuation is both art and skill; I go over valuing a business in greater detail later in this book. Financial markets constantly quote prices others are willing to pay on any given day for a business, usually to the detriment of most investors. Ninety percent of the time, market prices are useless. They serve to distract investors from looking at the whole business and instead lead them to focus on the day-to-day price movements of a ticker symbol. As a result, investors often confuse market value with business value, leading to poor decision making and expensive mistakes. All too often, the terms "luck" and "skill" are tossed around the investment field inaccurately. The truth is that investment skill will always lead to certain moments of luck, but in the long term, luck alone simply cannot last long enough to produce a consistent, profitable result.

The second important lesson I learned is to think independently and rely on your own data. My mistake in Meridian was very fundamental: I let the crowd dictate my decision making. My mistake was not that I was wrong but that I decided that the stock price decline implied that I was wrong. I thought I had invested in the business, but I was really invested in the stock. My analysis was sound: a good business with a good product and a market leader with a strong operating performance. But my approach toward the business was far from sound; I let the noise from the market weaken my conviction of the business value.

Warren Buffett has often said that "investing is simple, but not easy to do." I believe that one of the things he was referring to was the difficulty many people have separating the value of the business from the price of the stock. I remember a few years back, I was sitting in a hotel restaurant having a cup of coffee when I struck up a conversation with a gentleman who had spent years on Wall Street. He shared some wonderful (and not so wonderful) stories about his experiences there. At the time, I was still an undergrad student at the University of Georgia, so I was asking this gentleman as many questions as I could. When we got to the topic of the stock markets, the last thing

I expected to hear was what he said: "Stock markets are essentially obsolete places. We don't need them. They only exist to serve the needs and self-interests of the big Wall Street banks."

What he was referring to, of course, was the existence of the actual floor exchanges like the New York Stock Exchange. With the advent of electronic exchanges like the Nasdaq Stock Exchange, having a floor exchange is essentially unnecessary.

I've always remembered that conversation, because it came from an individual who worked for one of the big Wall Street banks that supported having the floor exchanges. I include this encounter not to say that we should shut down the New York Stock Exchange but to add my own spin: You should not equate the value of businesses with the daily volatility of stock prices. For the most part, the market gets it right and generally values businesses fairly. As a value investor, you are not interested in buying fairly valued businesses; you are focused only on selecting undervalued businesses. The stock market should exist only for you to buy an undervalued business and to sell a fairly valued business. Aside from those situations, you too should consider the stock market nonexistent.

Stock Prices Are More Noise Than Information

The majority of the time, daily stock prices are simply random noise movements. Warren Buffett has said that he invests as if stock markets would be closed for years. The truth is, most investors—and their portfolios—would be a lot better off if stock markets were closed throughout the year.

Imagine if the stock market were open only once during the year. Every year on one day, investors would have the chance to buy and sell any investments they wanted. Then they would have to wait until the next year to do the same. What do you think would happen? For one thing, many people would probably cease to participate. Those are the individuals who participate in the market for more speculative reasons.

If you were looking to buy a small business, I doubt that you would buy it with the intention to sell it in a few months unless you were offered a most attractive offer. At the same time, it's doubtful you would sell it at the first hint of bad news. Stock investing should be handled the same way. If you invest and the market decides to reward you immediately, you can choose to sell a short-term investment if you feel the price reflects the company value. Conversely, don't jump to sell because you see a decline in the stock price without first determining if the business has been permanently impaired.

Most important, if markets were only open annually, investors would get really serious about which securities they would want to own. They would spend a lot more time understanding the businesses they invest in, because they would want to be absolutely sure that they were allocating their capital in the most intelligent fashion. In other words, they would invest in the business, not the stock.

Since markets are open every day with willing buyers and sellers, market participants often try to shortcut their way to investing. The shortcuts usually lead to a lot of short-term losses. One of the most "advantageous" aspects of the stock market—its liquidity—is actually also one of the worst. Knowing that you can sell your securities any time the mood strikes you is more of a detriment than a benefit. Equity markets do a great job of making smart people do some really dumb things. The idea that a security should be sold after three weeks or three months because the stock price has declined seems rather foolish. The greatest business success stories—Coca-Cola, McDonald's, General Electric—evolved over decades with plenty of periods of temporary decline. Any investor who abandoned these companies at the first sign of trouble missed out on some extraordinary returns that were to come.

It's hard for most people to ignore the useless noise that the market produces day in and day out. Even if today you gave someone a copy of the *Wall Street Journal* two years into the future, most still wouldn't profit from the information. Why not? Because even knowing with 100 percent certainty that XYZ Corp. would be worth twice what is today, people would still jump ship if the price collapsed on them in the interim.

True value investors ignore such meaningless noise. To the value investor, stock markets have one sole purpose: to allow the purchase of undervalued securities and to facilitate the sale of fairly valued securities. Security prices are there to inform, not instruct. Security prices allow investors to determine whether bargain opportunities exist once the business has been analyzed and appraised. Conversely, when the mood is euphoric, security prices offer the opportunity to dispose of an investment at prices equal to or above fair value.

A Businesslike Approach to Valuing the Business

Contrary to popular belief, most sound investments are made on the basis of very few rational decisions. The most illustrative example is the investment in the Washington Post Company made by Warren Buffett. Back in 1973, Berkshire Hathaway's Buffett began accumulating shares in the Washington Post Company. At the time, the Post owned a top-tier collection of media assets—including *Newsweek,* the *Washington Post* newspaper, and several television stations in major markets—and the entire market capitalization was approximately $80 million. Buffett concluded that the Post's assets could easily fetch some $400 million or more if they were auctioned off.

While I am certain that Buffett was armed with a lot more information on the company, the major compelling reason for making the investment was that the assets were worth a whole lot more than the current price. Buffett made the investment based on the merits of the business; the stock price informed him that the current valuation was way too low. Interestingly, the market value of the Post continued to decline after Buffett's investment. Looking at the company through the mind-set of a businessman enabled Buffett to ignore the noise of the declining stock price. So what was the end result? Buffett's company, Berkshire Hathaway, still owns its shares in the Washington Post and considers it one of its "permanent equity holdings." The $11 million investment was worth $1.367 billion at the end of 2007.[1]

Investing in the business is a simple task that gets complicated as the focus shifts away from the business's performance and fixates on the day-to-day fluctuating stock price. Investors should approach buying a single share of stock using the same process they would apply to buying the entire business. A simple example illustrates my point. It demonstrates the businesslike approach of investing in a business; it is not necessarily indicative of an actual business with actual numbers.

Suppose you are interested in buying your hometown bicycle shop that is up for sale. The owner is selling the business for $100,000. Is this price a good value?

Your first approach is very general in nature to allow you to get a feel for the place. This would be akin to reading the annual report of a public company. You look at the location of the shop, find out how long it has been in business and if there are any other competitors in the area.

After this general investigation, you want to determine if the business is a worthy investment based on the sales price. You start looking at the numbers. Sales figures are nice, profits are even better, but at the end of the day, you want to know how much cash is left over after paying the bills. In other words, how much free cash flow does this bicycle shop produce? Looking over the last five years of operation, you see these figures for free cash flow:

Year	Free Cash Flow
1	$10,000
2	$11,000
3	$12,500
4	$13,500
5	$15,000

Based the on the past five years, the business appears to be doing well. It's growing its free cash flow at a nice rate, but that was the past. You are buying the business based on the future antici-pated cash flows. And when it comes to predicting future results, there is always an element of uncertainty involved. Looking back at the past five years, you realize that the business has increased cash flow by approximately 10 percent a year.

Going forward, you might be inclined to think that this same rate of growth will occur for the next five years, but I don't think most rational individuals would buy a business based solely on the past. For one, as businesses expand, the law of large numbers kick in. It's a lot easier to grow from $100,000 to $110,000 than to go from $1,000,000 to $1,100,000—although both figures represent a growth rate of 10 percent.

So, you decide to assume that over the next five years, the business will grow its cash flow by 6 percent a year. A bicycle shop is generally a local business, so at some point market saturation will cause a decline in sales level as the number of bike owners increases in your city. However, the business generates revenue doing repairs and selling accessories, so you can expect to make up for slowing sales growth. You predict that, over the next five years, the business will deliver these numbers:

Year	Free Cash Flow	Present Value at 10% Discount Rate
1	$15,900	$14,450
2	$16,850	$13,930
3	$17,860	$13,420
4	$18,940	$12,940
5	$20,000	$12,400
Total		$67,140

Remember that money earned in the future is not worth the same as it would be in your hand today, so we have to discount the future sum back to the present. Why use 10 percent? I used it simply for illustrative purposes. The discount rate should be customized to the specific business. If you are buying a start-up, then you would use a much higher discount rate to account for the higher degree of uncertainty involved in the business's future operating performance. A higher discount rate will, of course, decrease the present value of the future cash flows, implying a lower business valuation. Conversely, a more established business—which might have lower rates of cash flow growth—will command a lower discount rate to account for the relative consistency of the cash flows and its more established competitive position. (Think of Coca-Cola or the Procter & Gamble Company.)

The total value of discounted cash flows comes to $67,140. Of course, the business is also worth something as well as it will continue to exist and operate beyond five years. You figure you can easily sell it for five to seven times the free cash flow in year 10, or around $60,000 to $85,000. This sales figure is referred to as the terminal value of a business, a very important concept that is used hand-in-hand with the discounted cash flow analysis to assess the present value of a firm. The terminal value calculation is used to determine the value of the firm for all the years beyond which one can reliably project cash flow using the discounted cash flow. The terminal value can be calculated in several ways. One calculation assumes the liquidation of the firm's assets in the final year of the discounted cash flow analysis. This method estimates what the market would pay for the firm's assets at this point. The other two methods assume the firm will continue operations for an indefinite time period. The terminal value is determined either by applying a multiple to earnings, revenues, or book value, or by assuming an indefinite, constant growth rate. Add this figure to the sum of the discounted cash flows ($67,140) and you get a value for the business of approximately $127,000 to $150,000. With this information, you can make an intelligent decision on whether to purchase the business, negotiate a lower price, or simply walk away.

Notice what you don't do. You don't spend much time trying to forecast the individual price of bicycles and basing your decision on lots of moving inputs. The more moving parts you add to your analysis, the more complex and likely inaccurate your valuation will become. Stick to what counts: cash generation.

Apply the same general approach to buying shares in public companies. Get a general feel for the business by reading its annual reports. Understand the business, get a feel for the competitive landscape, and assess the quality of the folks running the ship. Then go over the numbers and see if they offer you a potential investment. Then you can decide to invest, wait for a lower market price, or simply move on.

If you end up deciding to invest, and you've looked at the business in the way I've explained, chances are slim that you will have any concern about the short-term movement in the stock price. Similar to buying the bicycle shop, you won't dump the business because you experience a few months of lower sales. Another way to think about it using the bicycle shop example is this: Suppose you bought the bicycle business for $100,000 and, a year later, you experienced a slow selling season due to the weather. The next day, someone walks into your shop and offers to buy your business for $75,000. Would you simply hand over the keys and take the check? I doubt it. You are not going to justify a lowball offer based on a few months of slow results. Why not wait until you have a prosperous period and sell to the guy who offers you $150,000?

Unfortunately, many investors do the exact opposite. They invest in a company and then, a few months later, when the stock is down 25 percent, they can't sell quick enough. They can't handle "looking" at the lower market price. Instead, they sell the stock so they no longer have to see a lower stock price. Such investors throw any consideration regarding the underlying business out the window. To make matters worse, once market conditions improve and the market price begins to climb, they eagerly jump back in without any discipline or analysis for fear of missing any climb in stock price. Without realizing it, these investors have just sold their "bicycle shop" for $75,000 only to by it back later for $150,000. The price they pay for a happy consensus is very steep indeed.

The value-seeking investor, however, is looking through the lenses of a businessperson. One of my all-time favorite quotes from Warren Buffett is "I am a better investor because I am a business-man and a better businessman because I am an investor."[2] There's tremendous wisdom in this concept. A successful long-term inves-tor must be able to grasp the main value drivers for a business and have the discipline to ignore the remaining noise. Conversely, by going through the process of investing—learning about businesses and industries, analyzing the competitive landscape, assessing the quality of management—you develop a more astute mind-set for running and operating a business.

The stock market is just like any other market. It is a place where you can show up when you feel like it to buy or sell items; in this case, ownership interests in a business. Yet instead of being treated like a market that exists to serve you, many people view the stock market as a place of instruction. True, the thousands of mar-ket participants provide information in the form of prices, but this information is not perfect, and it should not be relied on exclu-sively as the sole determinant of value. When you visit the grocery store, you don't go there looking for someone to tell you what to buy. You also don't go there looking to pay full price for groceries because everyone else is. You visit the grocery store when you need to and seek out items on sale. Approach the stock market with the same perspective. Use it only when it affords you bargains.

The Making of a Legend

Many readers of this book are familiar with the Buffett Partnership, but it nonetheless deserves a mention. Buffett's phenomenal investment track record from 1956 to 1969 is why most are familiar with the success of the Buffett Partnerships, but that success had as much to do with *what Buffett didn't do as much as with what Buffett did do.* I will explain what I mean shortly, but first a brief background on the Buffett Partnership so we are all on the same page.

In 1956, Warren Buffett started an investment partnership with capital from family and friends. Over the next 13 years, the annualized return clocked in at over 30 percent a year. More amazing, in the 13 years of operation, Buffett never recorded a down year. The length and consistency of this performance makes it one of the best performances by any investor. In 1969, Buffett closed down shop and walked away. Instead of taking in the loads of additional capital that would surely follow such a performance, Buffett instead wrote a letter to his partners telling them he no longer felt it was prudent to participate in the market:

> The investing environment . . . has generally become more negative and frustrating as time has passed. Maybe I am merely suffering from lack of mental flexibility . . . ,
>
> However it seems to me that: (1) opportunities for investment that are open to the analyst who stresses quantitative factors have virtually disappeared, after rather steadily drying up over the past twenty years; (2) our $100 million of assets further eliminates a large portion of this seemingly barren investment world, since commitments of less than about $3 million cannot have a real impact on our overall performance, and virtually rules out companies with less than about $100 million of common stock at market value; and (3) a swelling interest in performance has created an increasingly short-term oriented and (in my opinion) more speculative market.
>
> Therefore before year end, I intend to give all limited partners the required formal notice of my intent to retire . . .
>
> Quite frankly . . . I would continue to operate the Partnership in 1970, or even 1971, if I had some really first class ideas.

Some of you are going to ask, "What do you plan to do?" I don't have an answer to that question.[3]

In this modern age of money management, no money manager walks away after a year in which his performance beat the market and leaves all new potential capital on the side. Instead, many fund managers are forced to shut down after poor results made even worse by excessive use of leverage. But Buffett felt that market valuations were vastly exceeding business values, so he put his money into bonds and walked away. While I'm sure Buffett was keeping up with markets, he didn't seriously reappear until 1974. For five years, he simply ignored the stock market. He probably spent a lot of time playing bridge, his favorite card game. Bridge, much like investing, requires making bets based on odds. It's a fun and intellectually challenging game enjoyed by many investors.

The key point is this: Sometimes success from investing comes from the fact that you are not investing at all. It's a true sign of discipline to avoid the market if it doesn't provide you with favorable risk/reward bets. Being an investor does not mean always being invested. Being an investor means taking action if and when your data and analysis tell you of quality businesses selling at valuations that, with a high degree of probability, will result in satisfactory returns over a period of years. The most expensive lessons in investing are typically a result of making too many investments, not too few.

Value investors know how to be at peace with their decisions. Trying to invest through the rearview mirror is unproductive. In hindsight, everything to everyone seems obvious. Value investors understand that they will rarely invest at the absolute bottom price, nor will they sell at the absolute top price. As will be detailed in the next chapter, value investors seek to invest in a business only when it is undervalued and to sell it when it exceeds fair value. Any other approach is speculative in nature and often leads to expensive consequences.

Case in point: Between 2001 and 2003, shares in Apple traded between $7 and $13 a share. Yet during those years, sales were slowly climbing, the company was paying off its debt, and cash flow was growing. In addition, Steve Jobs was introducing the iPod and revamping the product line with a slick, modern computer. Restless investors who were frustrated with the dormant stock price or, worse, sitting on paper losses, abandoned ship. They were blinded by the stock price movements. As a result, they failed to see the progress *that the business was making.* Businesses cannot control the economy; all they can do is keep operating soundly during the good and bad cycles. Over the next four years, shares in Apple leapt to a high of $203 a share. Frustrated investors paid an expensive price indeed.

A Simple Idea, Really

It's going to sound redundant, but if you look at investing as buying a piece of a business, then the task of prudently investing your money is not that difficult. Avoid what you do not know and pay a sensible price. As Buffett quips, "Invest like you're buying groceries, not perfume."

The rest of this book articulates the notion that to be a successful investor, whether professionally or individually, you need to do only a few things right. It begins with the most important thing, developing a sound investment philosophy. Once you have truly developed a mental framework that seeks to buy good businesses at low prices, you are significantly ahead of the pack. The notion that the stock market is the place to get rich quick causes a lot of grief for investors and leads to sloppy results.

The value investing approach has been tried and tested for decades. It works. For those who are willing to exert the effort and patience, the stock market offers the greatest forum for wealth accumulation. The chapters to come illustrate the framework and approach to participating in equities in a logical, businesslike fashion.

The late Ben Graham, widely regarded as the creator of the school of thought that is value investing, astutely remarked in *The Intelligent Investor:* "Investment is most prudent when it is most businesslike." I would add a corollary to Graham's statement: Investment is most foolish when it is unbusinesslike.

CHAPTER 2

The Only Three Types of Investments You Need to Know

The third-rate mind is only happy when it is thinking with the majority. The second-rate mind is only happy when it is thinking with the minority. The first-rate mind is only happy when it is thinking.

—A. A. Milne

The beauty of investing is that there is enough room for many participants to succeed. In the U.S. markets alone, there are thousands of publicly traded businesses from which to choose. Add in Europe, Latin America, and the Asian markets, and the pool of opportunity is vast.

Yet many investors fail to outperform the average indexes. John Bogle, founder of the Vanguard Group of mutual funds, once observed that nearly 85 percent of active money managers fail to outperform the broad market indexes.[1] Part of this result can be explained by elementary statistics. With a sample size (market participants) so large, it is impossible for everyone to beat the average. For one, investing is a zero-sum game: Someone is buying what you're selling and selling what you're buying. When someone is realizing a gain, someone is taking a loss somewhere down the line. For every winner there has to be a loser somewhere in the chain. When Tiger Woods wins a golf tournament, he does so at the expense of the entire field.

Stocks Prices Aren't Always Rational

When it comes to stocks, this zero-sum characteristic might not happen immediately. Consider the Internet boom. For years, it seemed that stock prices would only go up. Someone could buy shares in a dot-com, sell them after they doubled (or even tripled) in price, and the new buyer would experience the same pleasure. When the euphoria ended, the losses were just as severe on the way down as the joy was on the way up. Buy shares at a $100 and sell them at $50. The new buyer would see the purchase price halved, and on the cycle went. While some people made out with fortunes, the proportion is very small when compared with the overall participant pool. Make no mistake: There is a winner and a loser on every side of the trade.

However, there are scores of successful long-term investors who have found themselves more on the winning side of the transaction. Besides Buffett, these include guys like Bill Miller at Legg Mason who beat the Standard & Poor's (S&P) index for 15 consecutive years; Bruce Berkowitz at the Fairholme Funds; and Mason Hawkins at the Longleaf Funds. Their long-term success rate is a result of more than just mere luck. In 1982, Warren Buffett wrote a wonderful essay titled "The Super Investors of Graham and Doddsville," where he defended the success of a value investing approach over long periods of time. Rebuttals were posited that Buffett's performance was a six sigma type of event (an event so rare that it could probabilistically occur only once every 2.5 million days). Yet all the recent market slumps, including the 1987 stock market crash, the Asian currency crisis, and the Internet bubble, have been six sigma types of events. All have occurred in the past two decades. To those who considered Buffett's results a six sigma event and that "looking for value [investments] with a significant margin of safety" was an outdated method, Buffett delivered this powerful argument:

> In this group of successful investors . . . there has been a common intellectual patriarch, Ben Graham. But the children who left the house of this intellectual patriarch have called their "flip" in very different ways. They have gone to different places and bought and sold different stocks and companies, yet they have had a combined record that simply can't be explained by random chance.[2]

Benjamin Graham is considered the father of the value investing approach. His two great works, *The Intelligent Investor* and *Security Analysis*, created the foundation for investing in businesses that were selling for less than their true value. The general idea behind Graham's approach was to look at the fundamental, concrete variables in the business, namely profits and cash generation. Find those businesses that were selling in the market for less than total value of the discounted future cash flows and invest in them. Graham defined his approach to investing as "an operation . . . which, upon thorough analysis, promises safety of principal and a satisfactory return. Operations not meeting these requirements are speculative."[3]

The Business Side of Investing

What Ben Graham did was take stock market participation and suggest that it too could be approached in a logical scientific-like manner. Before Graham's value-oriented approach took hold, the stock market was viewed as a speculative arena for the wealthy. The idea of buying a share of stock based on the business's future earnings potential, asset values, or balance sheet strength was virtually unheard of. Instead, speculators were buying shares of businesses hoping for the next great oil field or gold mine discovery. Investors did not understand or even consider the concept of looking for cheap businesses that had high margins of safety. Graham provided an almost scientific formula characterized by intense analytical effort toward approaching stocks. The underlying premise was that a stock represents a piece of a business, and the investment approach should be rooted on that concept.

Notice the three underlying characteristics of an investment operation: thorough analysis, safety of principal, and a satisfactory return. An investment must encompass all three. Interestingly, the order of the three conditions is very important. Obviously, you first must analyze the business and figure out what it is you are buying. You can achieve this goal only through deep, rigorous analysis. Then, before you should consider how much money you stand to make, you first should rule out any possibility of a substantial loss in capital. One of the cornerstones of value investing is understanding that capital preservation comes first; only afterward should you think about capital appreciation. You see this devotion toward capital preservation in various sayings by many of today's most successful value investors: "Preserve the downside and let the upside take care of itself" or "Heads I win, tails I lose little." No matter how you word it, the idea is the same: Preserving your capital ensures a very high degree of long-term investment success.

Some very simple math will bring this point home. Consider two investors. During the first year, a tough time for stocks, both investors suffer a down year. Investor A is down 10 percent while B is down 25 percent. The next three years are more favorable market environments, and both investors do well. Their performance results are:

Year	A	B
1	−10%	−25%
2	10%	15%
3	12%	15%
4	12%	15%

At the end of year 4, $100 invested with A is worth $124.18 while the same $100 invested with B is worth $114.06. Clearly this is a very simple example and in no way is intended to imply that one investor is more skilled than the other, especially after only four years of data. But the point is that a huge loss in one year can overshadow magnificent results for quite some time. Investor B outperformed A by a substantial margin in years 2 to 4, but Investor A had nearly 10 percent more in capital at the end. B's annualized return was around 3.4 percent while A delivered an annualized return of approximately 5.6 percent.

Warren Buffett realized this significance when, in 1961, he wrote to his limited partners: "I would consider a year in which we decline 15% and the [Dow Jones] Average 30%, to be much superior to a year when both we and the Average advanced 20%."[4]

Graham's teachings relied more on the quantitative attributes of a business than on the qualitative factors. He focused on analyzing the balance sheet, income statement, and statement of cash flows to get an idea of the quality of the business and of whether it was worthy of investment. Today, this approach is commonly referred to as fundamental analysis—aptly named, because it's the fundamentals of the business that count the most. Without understanding the numbers, you cannot understand the business, no matter how well you think you know it. You wouldn't purchase a home without first knowing your mortgage payments, taxes, anticipated utilities, and general cost of upkeep; similarly, never invest in a business without understanding its financial framework.

Although Graham focused his investment activities primarily on quantitative aspects, *qualitative* attributes sometimes can be very valuable when supplemented by a sound quantitative foundation. Brand recognition is the most obvious of qualitative considerations. The Coca-Cola Company has the most recognized brand in the world; that recognition is extremely valuable. The Coke brand allows the company to operate and compete anywhere in the world. Coke has spent decades and hundreds of millions of dollars in marketing and advertising to make its name the most dominant in the soft-drink industry. When is the last time you heard of an entrepreneurs looking to start a soft-drink company? Even with $1 billion, it would be virtually impossible for even the cleverest of entrepreneurs to dent Coca-Cola's worldwide dominance. The brand is a very valuable quality, and it has created billions of dollars in value for Coke shareholders over the years.

What can explain the long-term success of a value-based approach, since luck obviously can't be the reason for so many different investors who follow the same intellectual philosophy? Piggybacking isn't one of them, as many value investors hold strikingly different portfolios. In his essay, Buffett compared the results of several Ben Graham–schooled investors. While all of them had market-beating track records, their portfolios were not strikingly similar to one another. In fact, Walter Schloss, who, like Buffett, was an original student of Graham, was widely diversified, unlike many value investors who prefer a higher degree of concentration. During the 28 years that Schloss ran WJS Partners investment partnership (1956–1984), he typically held over 100 securities. Yet his annual compounded rate came in at 16.1 percent versus 8.4 percent for the S&P. And Schloss never went to college. Schloss did, however, focus on the cold hard numbers of the business and could calculate if a business was selling at a market price that was significantly below its value to a private buyer. He didn't worry whether he was buying the business in January, December, or any other month that pundits claim is better for equity performance.[5]

Another example is the Sequoia Fund, run by another Graham student, Bill Ruane. Ruane started the fund in 1970, the beginning of one of the worst down markets in U.S. history. The Sequoia Fund was begun to take the money of the investors of the Buffett Partnership because Buffett was closing shop. What did Ruane do? Over the next 14 years, he delivered a 17.2 percent annual compounded rate versus 10 percent for the S&P.[6]

So if every value approach is different with respect to its investment makeup, what is the underlying common theme? The answer is simple: Value investors are seeking discrepancies between business value and the stock price of those businesses in the market. That's all they do.

So the next logical question is: How do we determine whether a business is cheap and an attractive investment? Although investing is part art and part science, thanks to the foundation laid out by Ben Graham and expanded on by Warren Buffett and others, determining the value of a stock is a fairly straightforward concept. Ironically, most investors stumble because they make the process more difficult than it needs to be. Let's be clear: Successful investing requires intense analytical effort. Nonetheless, if you can understand that what really matters in determining the value of a business is usually a few data points, you are less likely to make an expensive mistake.

Three Buckets: Undervalued, Overvalued, and Fairly Valued

Value investors look at businesses through a very simple construct. Businesses come in only three flavors: undervalued, overvalued, or fairly valued. Every single business will fall into one of these three buckets.

Let me first start with an important caveat. In determining which bucket of valuation a business falls into, you must first be able to value the business. And to be able to value it, *you must first understand the business.* And to understand a business, you should really know it. Simply reading the annual report is the beginning. In order to understand the business, you should also be familiar with the industry the business operates in, the competitive forces within the industry, and how any external business threats could affect the business going forward. If you can't understand the business, you can't make intelligent assumptions about its future cash flows or anything else that might be meaningful to assessing the value of the business.

Realize that you do not need to understand every industry in the business world; it's far better and more rewarding in the long run if you can understand a few industries exceptionally well. Develop a core competency in a few areas, and you will find plenty of opportunities to make money. Buffett's core competency is the insurance industry; he understands all the ins and outs of the insurance business and has used his expertise to great success. Also remember that Buffett has been investing for over 50 years, so developing an investment acumen does take time and it's an ongoing process. Focus on what you can understand, and read as much as you can. Over time, the competency will develop and serve as building blocks for different investment opportunities.

What exactly do I mean when I call a business undervalued, overvalued, or fairly valued? As the goal of investment success hinges on finding discrepancies between market value and business value, it is more precise to refer to an investment as *underpriced, overpriced,* or *fairly priced.* An undervalued business is one in which the underlying stock price is underpriced. Why get so technical with the wording?

Just because a stock price is cheap does not mean that the underlying business is undervalued. Conversely, an undervalued business does not have to be a cheap stock. When seeking to define value-oriented investments, many academics and professional investors focus on two valuation metrics: the price-to-earnings ratio (P/E) and the price-to-book ratio (P/B). The P/E ratio is simply a number that shows the relationship between a stock price and the earnings per share of the business. For example, for a business with a stock price of $20 with earnings per share of stock of $2, the P/E ratio is 10. You are paying 10 times for the earnings of the business. Another way to look at is by flipping the ratio and looking at the earnings yield. In this case, you are paying $20 for a share of stock that earns $2 per share; your earnings yield is 10 percent. Obviously, the lower P/E ratios are characteristic of value investments. It would seem intuitive that if you could buy a share of stock for $20 and get $5 in earnings per share (P/E of 4), you are getting a better value than a business with a P/E of 10.

Similarly, a lower P/B often is viewed as more indicative of a value investment. The book value, or net assets, of a business is akin to the net worth of a household. Start with your assets (home, savings, and investments) and deduct your liabilities (credit cards, loans). What you are left with is your net worth or value on the books. The same goes for a company. Take its assets (cash, inventory, receivables, property) and deduct the liabilities (debt, payables); you are left with the book value of the business. It stands to reason that if a business is selling for a lower price relative to book value, you are getting more of a value. Paying $100 million for a business with net assets of $75 million (P/B = 1.33) seems much more conservative than paying $100 million for a company with net assets of $40 million (P/B = 2.50).

Generally speaking, studies have shown that businesses with lower P/E and P/B values (value stocks) have performed better than businesses with high P/E and P/B values (growth stocks). A well-known academic study by Professors Eugene Fama and Kenneth French has shown that value stocks outperform growth stocks over longer periods of time.[7] Essentially, Fama and French took all the stocks on the New York Stock Exchange, American Stock Exchange, and NASDAQ that had reliable data and grouped them into 10 groups based on the book-to-price ratio (B/P; the flip of the P/B ratio, thus making a higher book-to-price stock an indicator of value). The first group contained the most extreme value stocks (lowest P/B or highest B/P [both are the same]) while the tenth group contained the most extreme growth stocks. Analyzing the returns over 27 years that included both up and down markets, they found that the Group 1 extreme value stocks went up nearly seven times in price (~600 percent) in 10 years, or nearly a 21 percent annualized gain, while the Group 10 extreme growth stocks doubled in price over 10 years, or about an 8 percent annualized rate of return.

Although I find the P/E and P/B values useful, unless you decide to buy hundreds of low P/B stocks and hold them for 27 years, I wouldn't bank on them completely in making investment decisions. One of the greatest investors, Sir John Templeton, bought $100 of every stock trading below $1 on the New York and American Stock exchanges in 1939 on the heels of World War II. This well-known trade gave Templeton a basket of 104 companies for a total investment of $10,400. Thirty-four went bankrupt, but four years later, Templeton sold his holdings for more than $40,000. Again, unless you want to go out today and buy the thousand of stocks trading for less than $1, I wouldn't count on many penny stocks as being undervalued businesses.

Price Determines Value

The most common cause of low prices is pessimism—sometimes pervasive, sometimes specific to a company or industry. We want to do business in such an environment, not because we like pessimism but because we like the prices it produces. It's optimism that is the enemy of the rational buyer.

　　　　　　　　—Warren Buffett, 1990 Berkshire Hathaway
　　　　　　　　Letter to Shareholders

As I mentioned earlier, prices exist to inform investors. Any business is undervalued at one price, fairly valued at another price, and overvalued at yet another price. A value investor is looking for the first type of business. The price you pay determines the value you will get. By all accounts, Google is a fantastic business run by some first-rate individuals. But when Google's stock price started trading for $600 a share, that price failed to make Google a good investment value. This has nothing to do with the numerically high dollar price of the stock. As of June 2009, Berkshire Hathaway class A shares traded for approximately $90,000 per share but this is arguably a much better value than Google, based on the underlying value of the assets of the two respective businesses.

In looking for undervalued securities, you should focus on price only to the extent that it provides you with information to determine whether the quoted stock price is less than the value of the business. Merely looking at the stock price doesn't do much; you have to determine what you are getting for the current price being quoted. For example, how much in earnings does the business generate in relation to the current market price of the company? How much cash is being generated each year? Has the book value of the company been rising or sitting still? Above all, is this a good strong business with future growth opportunity ahead? Chapter 5 discusses searching for such investment opportunities in greater detail, but for now, let's keep the focus on how to determine whether a business is undervalued or not.

Let's look at a simple, boring business: carpets and flooring. This industry is dominated by two players: Mohawk Industries and Shaw Carpet. At the end of 2008, they commanded over 45 percent of the market. Shaw is privately held (coincidentally by Berkshire Hathaway). As I write this chapter in the late summer of 2008, here is what I find on Mohawk.

In the most recent full year, 2007, Mohawk sold $7.6 billion worth of flooring and earned $435 million in net income. Looking

back over several years, I see that Mohawk has done exceptionally well:

Year	Sales ($ billions)	Net Profits ($ millions)
2004	$5.8	$371
2005	$6.6	$387
2006	$7.9	$456

When looking at the cash flows, the picture looks even better:

Year	Operating Cash Flow
2004	$242 million
2005	$561 million
2006	$782 million
2007	$875 million

In analyzing the strength of a business, you want to focus more
of your attention on cash flows, as they truly represent the cash
being generated by the business. A company can boost its sales, and
hence its profits, by extending a lot of credit to its customers. As
a result, the profits rise, but no cash has come in the door. Until
the customers pay off their credit bills, you don't have the cash.
Operating cash flow, however, accounts for all these adjustments
and reveals just how much cash is coming into the door. As you can
see from Mohawk, the picture looks very good.

To take this one final step further and see what cash is left
over for the investors, we examine *free cash flow*. Free cash flow
is simply the cash left over after the company pays its bills, or
expenditures. Mohawk's expenditures for 2004, 2005, 2006, and
2007 were $106 million, $247 million, $166 million, and $163 million respectively.

Mohawk's free cash flow picture looks like this:

Year	Free Cash Flow
2004	$136 million
2005	$314 million
2006	$616 million
2007	$712 million

As you can see without doing any math, the rate of growth in free cash flow has been exceptional, averaging well over 20 percent a year. The company has generated tremendous cash for the shareholders.

But the past is the past, and looking at the company today, you have to extrapolate from the past performance and see if the future operations of the business coupled with today's market value indicate that Mohawk is indeed undervalued. It's time to start looking at the business.

Mohawk is one of the top two suppliers of flooring products in the United States, which includes carpets and rugs, ceramic tile, laminate, and hardwoods. The three markets that Mohawk supplies are new residential construction, commercial real estate, and residential replacement. As of late 2008, the real estate industry was deteriorating rapidly, and Mohawk's business was feeling the pain in declining home sales. Nonetheless, the company's bulk business comes from replacement flooring, and the commercial segment remained stable. While sales volume was slowing, Mohawk still was doing respectable business. But because the market was so sour on the economic environment, the stock price was getting hit.

In addition, Mohawk operates a state-of-the-art distribution system with over 300 locations across the country serviced by a fleet of over 1,000 trucks. The chief executive, Jeff Lorberbaum, has been with the company since day one when it was formed to acquire the business he previously ran. He and his family own over 17 percent of the company, so he definitely has skin in the game. Unless you think office buildings, houses, schools, and hospitals are disappearing, the need for Mohawk's products is soundly assured. And its duopolistic position in the industry gives the company a strong competitive advantage.

So what is the intrinsic value of Mohawk based on the present value of the future cash flows? Let's make some quick yet conservative assumptions. For the 2008 year free cash flow came in at $253 million, $450 million less than 2007. (The year 2008 was a disaster for housing related businesses.)

It looks like 2009 won't be much better for the housing/construction industry, so let's assume there is no free cash flow growth from 2008. Given Mohawk's dominance and anticipated industry recovery in 2010 or 2011, it's not unreasonable for the company to earn $500 million in free cash flow in 2010. For the next two years as the industry recovers from all-time lows, I'll assume a 15 percent increase in free cash flow.

Because money received in the future is worth a lot less than money in hand today, future cash flows need to be discounted back to the present at an appropriate rate. A very common rule of thumb is to take the current yield on a U.S 10-year Treasury note and add a premium to compensate added risk of the business. Let's assume a discount rate of 10 percent. For a business as strong as Mohawk, 10 percent might be a notch too high, but the goal is to get a very conservative valuation. The numbers are:

Year	Free Cash Flow	Present Value of FCF @10% discount rate
2009	$253 million	$230 million
2010	$500 million	$413 million
2011	$575 million	$432 million
2012	$661 million	$451 million
Total		$1.53 billion

The sum of the present value of the cash flows is $1.53 billion. Given that Mohawk has grown its profits and cash flow in the high teens for some time, the company's terminal value could easily be worth 10 to 12 times the free cash flow of year 2012. Discounted back to the present, you get a value of $4.5 to $5.4 billion ($4.51 million × 10 or 12), or a total company value of approximately $6 to $7 billion ($4.5 or $5.41 $+.8).

Assume shares outstanding increase by 5 percent over the four years to 72 million from 68.5 million today. Since 2004, diluted shares outstanding rose by only 1 million shares (less than 2 percent). A $6 to $7 billion market cap over 72 million shares equals a share price of $83 to $97 in 2012, up from $35 in June of 2009.

This is an effective yet simplified analysis of the potential intrinsic value of Mohawk. In Chapter 10, I present more detailed case studies of valuing a couple of distinct businesses. For now, however, the analysis allows you to determine whether Mohawk is a good investment *at the current price*. We already know that Mohawk is a great business with a dominant market position. The analysis suggests that Mohawk could be worth at least twice as much in a few years at the then current price of $35 a share based on some very realistic if not conservative cash flow assumptions. It is thus prudent to conclude that Mohawk is currently an undervalued business because it is underpriced.

Most investors prefer to use a 10-year discounted cash flow model in determining the true value of a business. Generally, I agree with this approach, but sometimes I am reluctant to rely on numbers beyond 5 years from today. A lot can happen to a business over 10 years; specific operating or general economic conditions can skew results for a year or two. The result is that you would have to reassess your assumptions anyway, so I find that a 5-year model is a good starting point. Again, the important thing is to consider the business. A company like Coca-Cola generally can be counted on to sell its product in all environments. But there are few businesses in the world like Coke. For years, it seemed as if financial institutions could continue to deliver solid, consistent results, but the financial funk that began in 2006 and has thus far not let up in late 2008 proves otherwise.

Notice the meaningful gap between the current price of Mohawk shares and the intrinsic value derived from my assumptions. This gap is meaningful because it offers a strong cushion for any errors or overtly wrong assumptions in my analysis. In value investing circles, this safety net is known as the margin of safety, a concept developed by Ben Graham in Chapter 20 of *The Intelligent Investor*. Two investors will never arrive at the same value for a business, because no two investors will have the identical set of assumptions. For this reason, any intrinsic value figure for a business always will be an approximation, never a precise number. Requiring a margin of safety is a necessity if an investor demands preservation of capital. Ben Graham succinctly summed it up: "Confronted with a challenge to distill the secret of sound investment into three words, we venture the motto, Margin of Safety."[8]

What is an adequate margin of safety? No set rule of thumb defines how wide a gap should exist between market price and the true value of a business. Some investors look for a margin of safety equal to twice the current market price. Again, it's most beneficial to think in a businesslike manner. A superior business with a dominant competitive position should not require as high a margin of safety as a smaller, less dominant business. It is much easier to accurately forecast the cash flows of businesses such as Mohawk, Kroger, or Home Depot than it would be for businesses such as Pacific Sunwear or Bare Escentuals. While no cash flow forecasts will be spot-on accurate, your probability for a wide margin of error is smaller when looking at stronger, well-established businesses. For Mohawk, if my assumptions had led to an intrinsic value figure of $50 per share instead of $83, I would consider that an inadequate margin of safety. If they had led to a figure of, say, $70 to $75,

I would accept it, given the underlying qualities of this business. As you can see, the scenario in this case is very favorable, even if your assumptions turn out to be slightly off.

Key Takeaways

- In the short run, stock prices do not have to behave rationally. Don't allow short-term market gyrations to cloud your judgment about the quality of the business.
- While the majority of professional money managers fail to outperform the broad market, numerous investors deliver consistent market-beating returns. A common thread is the businesslike orientation of their investment selections.
- Remember to view stocks as little pieces of a whole business. Your goal is to determine whether that business is undervalued, fairly valued, or overvalued.
- The value of most businesses usually is based on several key variables; any other information is typically noise and doesn't add significant value.

CHAPTER

The Six Elements of
Intelligent Investing

*One of the many unique and advantageous aspects of value
investing is that the larger the discount from intrinsic value, the
greater the margin of safety and the greater the potential return
when the stock price moves back to intrinsic value. Contrary to
the view of modern portfolio theorists that increased returns can
only be achieved by taking greater levels of risk, value investing is
predicated on the notion that increased returns are associated with
a greater margin of safety, i.e., lower risk.*

—The Partners of Tweedy Browne

Imagine for a moment that you're a real estate investor and that
a series of tropical storms has caused beachfront houses in Hawaii
that were once selling for $2 million to now sell for $400,000 apiece.
How many would you buy?

After you determined that the construction was solid and that
the land doesn't sit on a toxic dump, you probably would jump in
and buy as many as you could afford. While the threat of another
tropical storm exists, it's also expected and factored into the cost

of construction and insurance. Even if the houses only were to get back to a value of $1 million in a couple years, you would still do very well. The process behind this purchase is completely rational. You paid $400,000 for an asset that was selling for $2 million. Because the discount was so wide, you weren't concerned with whether the price would ever again reach $2 million. Your margin of safety was so high that even at a sales price of $1 million two years later, your total return would have exceeded 100 percent, or a return on investment of over 25 percent a year. The numbers are quite good even if the final sales price was $750,000.

The key point is that in a situation like this you wouldn't just buy one property if you had the means to buy more. Seeing the tremendous discount between market price and fair price, you would seize the opportunity to make a substantial investment. But you would also want to seize the opportunity in a sensible manner. You're not going to lever yourself up to a point where you don't give yourself ample time for the market to correct and attract buyers. This is your margin of safety in this investment. This is Hawaii, where everyone dreams of owning beachfront property and it is a matter of when, and not if, the values rise back to normal.

You should have a similar mindset when investing in businesses via the stock market. If your analysis suggests that a quality business is selling for a bargain price and that sooner or later the price will rise to catch up with value, you should be excited at the opportunity to bet big, as such opportunities (like buying a $400,000 beachfront Hawaiian house) are very rare. At the same time, you don't want to invest with money you don't have by using funds borrowed on margin. The instant you make slam-dunk investments using proceeds from your broker, the rules of the game have changed. You give up any margin of safety the minute you expose yourself to redemption calls from your broker. Similar to our real estate analogy, it may take many months for the market to agree with your investment analysis, but if you're forced to sell in the interim in order to satisfy broker demands for the borrowed money, then any short-term fluctuations in the stock price may force you to sell at the absolute worst moment.

While investors find value in different places, in my examination of all investing greats—beginning with the teachings of Ben Graham—I've discovered that any successful investing approach rests on a sound fundamental framework, or mindset. Most of us are familiar with the names of successful investors: Warren Buffett, Charlie Munger, Seth Klarman, Peter Lynch, Mason Hawkins, Eddie Lampert, and Bruce Berkowitz to name just a few. These are some of the most highly regarded and recognized value investors due to their superior long-term performance.

All Investing Is Value Investing

During the early days of stock market activity, investing was commonly perceived as a speculative activity practiced only by the rich or by those with wild dreams of striking it rich. Many of the publicly traded companies at the time were oil companies with nothing more than land and hopes of striking oil and all the riches that came with it.

It wasn't until a professor by the name of Benjamin Graham came along that investing became a more scientific process that could be understood and applied analytically to producing long-term profits. In 1934, while a professor at Columbia University, Graham coauthored a book with colleague David Dodd titled *Security Analysis*. This 700-plus-page work provided a blueprint for fundamental analysis of both stocks and bonds. In other words, Graham instructed readers to focus on the business's assets and liabilities, profits, and cash generation. Graham often took a pair of common stocks in alphabetical order from the stock tables and analyzed them based on earnings multiples, growth rates, and balance sheet composition. Then he would illustrate why one business was a more sensible investment than the other.

Later, in 1949, Graham published the *The Intelligent Investor*, a much shorter yet equally effective text on the practical principles of sound investing. It was *Security Analysis* for a more general audience, although the book became much more than that. The core theme of *The Intelligent Investor* hinged on the distinction between investment and speculation that was provided in *Security Analysis:*

> An investment operation is one which, upon thorough analysis, promises safety of principal and an adequate return. Operations not meeting these requirements are speculative.[1]

Notice the three conditions that must exist for an investment: thorough analysis, safety of principal, and an adequate return. I think most investors would agree that satisfying these three conditions is the cornerstone of all investing activity, regardless of what you invest in. In Chapter 11, I will discuss why growth investing and value investing are merely two sides of the same coin. Part of the value in any investment is the growth potential of the business. Ben Graham came along and taught us how to value this future growth and use those principles in paying sensible prices for the stock today. As you will read throughout this book, a major determinant between a successful investment and an unsuccessful investment is the price you pay.

Ben Graham's most famous disciple was Warren Buffett, who today is undeniably considered as the world's most successful and accomplished investor. Beginning in 1965, when Buffett assumed control of Berkshire Hathaway—at the time a Massachusetts textile business—to 2007, Berkshire Hathaway's book value per share grew at an annual compounded gain of 21.1 percent.[2] Buffett took the fundamentals that Graham had taught him and adapted them over the years to produce the most successful long-term track record in modern-day investing. It should come as no surprise that many professional investors who want to follow Graham's philosophies and teachings look to Warren Buffett and his activities over the past 40 years.

People who are notable in value investing include:

- **Seth Klarman.** Klarman is founder of the hedge fund Baupost Group. Klarman keeps a very low profile, and it's hard to follow his progress without keeping tabs on his Securities and Exchange Commission filings. Since 1983, Klarman has averaged annual returns of approximately 20 percent. While this figure might not be precise, what is beyond dispute is that Klarman's multiyear performance has vastly exceeded that of the general market. Today, Klarman manages over $1 billion (up from less than $30 million when he started in the early 1980s). Widely regarded as a student of Graham and Buffett and the value approach, Klarman has done exceedingly well during both bull and bear markets.
- **Eddie Lampert.** Lampert started a hedge fund in his 20s after a successful career at Goldman Sachs. His earliest investors included Michael Dell and David Geffen. His fund, ESL Investments, produced annualized returns of over 30 percent since 1988. His investment approach is best characterized as concentrated value, as Lampert typically makes a handful of big investment bets. Lampert is currently the chairman of Sears Holding, the product of a merger between Sears and Kmart that Lampert orchestrated earlier this decade. Currently ESL Investments owns 50 percent of Sears Holdings. As a retailer, Sears has been struggling, but Lampert's loyal followers see Sears as a new Berkshire Hathaway, which was once a textile mill before becoming Buffett's investment vehicle.
- **Peter Lynch.** While no longer actively managing money, Lynch is widely considered one of the greatest mutual fund managers of all time. Rarely referred to as a value investor according to the rigid definition of the term, Lynch nonetheless created enormous value for his investors as manager

of the Fidelity Magellan Fund. During his 13 years atop the Magellan Fund, from 1977 to 1990, the fund's value rose 28-fold per share, making it the best-performing fund in the world.

- **Mason Hawkins.** Hawkins founded Southeastern Asset Management, which runs the Longleaf mutual funds, in 1975. Hawkins read Ben Graham's *Intelligent Investor* while a high school senior, and his investment approach has followed Graham's teachings ever since. Collectively the Longleaf funds manage over $20 billion and are one of the most shareholder-oriented investment funds in the world. All employees have their money invested in the Longleaf funds and nowhere else.

- **Bruce Berkowitz.** Berkowitz is portfolio manager of Fairholme Capital Management, which he founded in 1997. He is an avid disciple of Warren Buffett and the value-inspired approach. His investment philosophy, which has proven very successful, is to invest in businesses with talented managers (or jockeys, as he likes to call them) and in businesses that spin off a ton of cash. Since 1997, the Fairholme funds have handily outperformed the markets, and Berkowitz is widely considered as one of the most talented money managers around today.

Learn from the Masters

Fortunately, we don't all have to be like Buffett and be "wired at birth" for investing. We *do* need to understand that successful value investing hinges on activities that you are trained *not to pursue* and often requires that you do the exact opposite of what the majority is doing. As Buffett often says, "You pay an expensive price for a cheery consensus." Some of the best bargains usually are found in industries that are currently under distress, where investment dollars are exiting and not entering. If you want to invest in the cocktail party stock of the year, the idea won't come cheap.

For example, we are taught that a highly diversified portfolio is the soundest approach. For the general individual, this might be an intelligent way to go. But if you're a serious investor and are devoting serious time to stock selection, then concentration makes the most sense. The wealthiest people on the planet have derived their wealth from a single business: Warren Buffett from Berkshire Hathaway; Bill Gates from Microsoft; Lakshmi Mittal from ArcelorMittal; and on it goes. It's silly to think that just having a few eggs in your basket is riskier than having more. If you know the business cold, why put money in something else that you don't know as well? As Buffett suggests, it is better to have a few eggs in your basket and watch them closely than to have many and risk some breaking.

The Sum of Its Parts: A Fundamental Framework

In observing great investors, I've discovered that their investing approach hinges on six elements that comprise the entire investment process. These six elements always go together in selecting investment candidates; in other words, you can't have a good search strategy (Element 2) without first having a sound investment philosophy (Element 1). Just like crawling before walking, you need to know what you're looking for before beginning to look. Jumping ahead and investing without understanding what it is you're looking for often will send you into a crash.

At first, the framework looks obvious; all of the individual pieces have been discussed and dissected in other investing literature. Here, it's the total framework that counts, not the individual components. This is not a checklist that you go through every time you want to pick an investment but rather six essential elements that should truly exist if you are a value-seeking investor.

It is surprising how few "value investors" actually invest with this mental framework in mind. Referring back to Graham's definition of an investment operation, relatively few investors truly take the time to analyze the business and determine whether the price is right so *that a satisfactory return is achieved.* Investing in this manner is not easy to do. It requires discipline and no emotional attachments. Emotions are the enemy of the disciplined investor. Maintaining discipline minimizes the severity of mistakes. The key to successful investing is not to eliminate mistakes, which are inevitable, but to minimize their impact on the overall investment portfolio.

Investors should not take this viewpoint to mean that investing is a rigid science. On the contrary, investment is part art and part science with a little luck thrown in on the side. The framework to be outlined hardly suggests that investing is a rigid discipline. Rather these elements are essential fundamentals that enable each unique investor to succeed in his or her own way. All golf swings are different, but attention to the essential elements of a pure golf swing—keeping your head still, a good shoulder turn, and maintaining plane—all serve to keep the ball flying accurately. Similar to golf, the essential elements in investments all work together to produce a consistent and effective selection strategy.

True value investing often requires that you look stupid in the short run. Often you will own shares in businesses that are hated by the majority. With each passing month that goes by without anything positive happening, the criticisms will get louder. You must have complete faith in your decisions or else you will be guided by the crowd. And most important, value investing requires total and complete independence of thought. The ability to sit still for months while your investments do nothing *and* have all the "smart money" berate you for having completely missed the boat requires a very independent and emotionless state of mind. As Ben Graham states in *The Intelligent Investor:*

> You are neither right nor wrong because the crowd disagrees with you. You are right because your data and reasoning are right.[3]

During the Internet boom of the late 1990s, Berkshire Hathaway's stock price was tested as never before under Buffett's watch. Reporter after reporter was quick to criticize Buffett for not having participated in the Internet boom. In December of 1999, *Barron's* ran a cover story titled "What's Wrong Warren?" The first sentence of the article was "After more than 30 years of unrivaled investment success, Warren Buffett may be losing his magic touch." What sparked such an opinion? Shares in Berkshire were set to decline for the first time since 1990. Thankfully for Berkshire investors, Buffett spends no time paying attention to what the media thinks about his investments.[4] So for Buffett, his aversion to the Internet companies was simply an exercise in discipline. With billions of dollars at his disposal, he could have easily allocated tens of millions of dollars to a basket of Internet stocks and not affected Berkshire's performance if they all lost money. But he didn't do that because doing so would have taken him outside of his circle of competence. This is a very important lesson and one Buffett has alluded to over and over. If you're not willing to risk millions in an endeavor you don't fully understand, then you shouldn't be willing to risk thousands. An intelligent investor seeks to avoid all losses and does not differentiate between a "small" and a "big" loss.

Just as Tiger Woods adheres to a concise and disciplined set of steps for each and every golf swing, so does the value investor in selecting stocks. In order, these six essential elements are:

1. Commit to a sound investment philosophy.
2. Find a good search strategy.
3. Effectively value a business.
4. Have the discipline to say no.
5. Be patient.
6. Be willing to make a significant bet at the point of maximum pessimism.

This framework—ingrained in the minds of Warren Buffett, Charlie Munger, Mason Hawkins, Seth Klarman, and others—provides a complete mental approach to investing that, if rigorously applied, will eliminate many unforced errors in investing. All investors make mistakes, but the most successful investors are those who are best able to avoid the unnecessary mistakes and to avoid making the same mistakes twice. Also, when investors apply and commit to pursuing investing based on the six elements, they are conditioning their minds to be more disciplined in making investment decisions, and a disciplined approach is a much more focused approach.

A Mental Latticework

As I mentioned earlier, many value investors have come across the individual components of this process. Warren Buffett's annual reports are littered with references to a sound investment philosophy, patience, and discipline. Buffett's partner Charlie Munger often extols the virtues of patience. The key to this framework is viewing it as a series of building blocks, or—to borrow a term from Charlie Munger—a latticework within investing. It's a latticework because you can't have one without the other. It's ineffective to develop a good search strategy without first having a sound approach and philosophy. Similarly, you won't be able to make a big bet during moments of maximum pessimism if you don't have patience or the ability to value a business. Successful investing is not a rigid science defined by one exact formula; it is a continuous, evolving process of constant learning. The framework can't be learned in mere months or years but rather applied over and over again over decades. Warren Buffett has been developing a sound investment philosophy his entire life. The foundation of that philosophy began with Graham's *Intelligent Investor*, but Buffett has been perfecting it for decades. Charlie Munger often has praised Buffett as one of the "greatest learning machines."

A rational approach to value investing will deliver the desired outcome over a meaningful period of time. All too often, investors begin searching for the next great investment without giving serious consideration to what it is they actually are trying to accomplish. Every investor's goal is to buy a security at one price and sell it later at a much higher price. But this goal rarely happens in an orderly fashion, and if your mental approach is not defined by a sound investment philosophy, the odds of costly mistakes are greatly enhanced. The path between buying low and selling high is often littered with bumps, and a patient, businesslike approach to investing makes a huge difference.

Overview of the Six Elements

The next six chapters dig deeper into this fundamental framework beginning with the foundation of any investing approach: a sound investment philosophy (Chapter 4). There can be no dispute that after nearly a century of practice, which began with Ben Graham in the 1920s and has been carried on by Buffett and many other value investors, a sound investment philosophy centers around the principles of value investing: thorough analysis, margin of safety, and satisfactory returns. In this book, the term "value investing" is used to describe this type of investment philosophy.

With a sound investment philosophy, an effective and productive search strategy can begin (Chapter 5). One of the most popular questions investors get asked is: So what's the next great stock? Unfortunately, there is no one definitive answer and no easy formula; Warren Buffett went through 10,000 pages of a dry Moody's stock manual searching for stocks. Finding investment opportunities will require work and there are no shortcuts, but knowing what to look for will make your search much more effective and productive.

Next, you need to take the raw data from the search results and turn them into meaningful facts and figures through the process of valuation. Valuing a business (Chapter 6) is part art and part science; no two investors will ever value a business equally. Regardless, you have to understand the business to value it appropriately. Without coming up with a value, you won't be able to decide whether to walk away, invest, or sit still. One chapter cannot teach you everything you need to know about valuing a business. Businesses are evolving creatures, and all valuations hinge on numerous assumptions. Understanding the limitations of those assumptions is a vital component of evaluating the worth of a business. The focus of Chapter 6 is not only on how to value a business but *why the process of valuation is critical.*

Once you've valued the business, the next critical step is to detach all emotion from businesses and make all buy-and-sell decisions on facts (Chapter 7). The discipline to say no is as important as any quantitative skill that you may possess. Success in investing rests on more than simply a high IQ or razor-sharp mathematical skills. Without discipline to hold you back and resist the short-term temptation of market gyrations, the best analytical work still can lead to poor results.

Maintaining the discipline to say no requires two abilities.

1. You have to separate any emotional attachment to stocks.
2. You have to always have a clear distinction between value and price.

One of my favorite businesses is Chipotle, a fast-casual gourmet Mexican food restaurant chain. The quality of the food is excellent, and I eat at Chipotle any chance I get. (As of this writing, Chipotle has yet to open up shop in my hometown of Athens, Georgia. Steve Ells, if you are reading this, please look at the Athens market!) Every time I visit a Chipotle, the lines are deep, the restaurants are clean, the service is friendly, and the food is always tops. Without a doubt, Chipotle is a wonderful business with a fantastic future. Unfortunately, this success has not gone unnoticed: Shares in Chipotle, like the food quality, continue to command a premium valuation. As much as I would love to own a stake in Chipotle and ride the success of this company for many many years to come, I can't let my love for the food cloud a rational business decision. For now I will have to continue enjoying the food and wait for a compelling opportunity. All businesses are undervalued at one price, fairly valued at another price, and overvalued at yet another price.

Patience (Chapter 8) is arguably the hardest quality for many investors to develop. Wall Street, with its fixation on quarterly performance numbers, has defined patience as a period of months. Hedge funds, with their rapid-fire trading programs, have made monthly returns the standard reporting metric. A business doesn't succeed or fail based on the results of a single month or quarter. Stock prices, in the short term, typically behave in a way that may not resemble the underlying value of the business. A businessperson doesn't buy or start a business with the intent of selling next month (unless offered a much higher price). As an investor in a business, your buy-and-sell decisions should also not hinge on monthly or quarterly expectations. I've been waiting for Chipotle for years; until I'm comfortable with the price, I'll have to continue to wait. A great business is not a great investment if the price is too high.

Once you have found a compelling investment opportunity, *act on it* (Chapter 9). Mr. Market hates bad news and uncertainty. An intelligent investor should use this knowledge to the maximum advantage. Many of the best bargains occur when businesses are experiencing a period of uncertainty or difficult operating environment. The underlying business remains sound, but the stock price continues to go down, causing the gap between market price and business value to widen. Having the conviction to make a big investment during the point of maximum pessimism requires the highest degree of independent thought and analysis. Very few investors do it, and very few investors reap the huge rewards that arise from betting big against the crowd.

Emphasize the Process, Not the Outcome

If you carefully observe the best investing minds today, you can see this mental model applied over and over. The best investors are much more concerned with developing a sound, effective process and letting the outcome follow as a result. Each investor's approach is different, but the mental process is generally the same from beginning to end. Great investors:

- Ignore 90 percent of the market information that is noise.
- Invest independently without any regard for the general consensus.
- Understand that time works to the benefit of the investor.

Key Takeaways

- The best value investors always work within a fundamental framework that emphasizes the process first and the outcome second.
- Developing a sound investment philosophy is the basic foundational element for all investment activity.
- The best value investors all commit to an investment philosophy that emphasizes capital preservation, patience, discipline, and avoiding crowd psychology.

Establish a Sound
Investment Philosophy

THE FIRST ELEMENT

Value investing is actually a comprehensive investment philosophy that emphasizes the need to perform in-depth fundamental analysis, pursue long-term investment results, limit risk, and resist crowd psychology.

—Seth Klarman

The vast majority of information about any particular investment is merely noise. Successful businesses usually are identified by a handful of meaningful variables or data points; everything else is secondary to the success or failure of the business. Warren Buffett has often remarked that he never uses a spreadsheet or calculator when making investment decisions. It is also true that Buffett has a gifted mind for numbers and remembering data. The point is not against the use of spreadsheets (or a calculator). Spreadsheets and calculators are tools that can add value to any analysis. The point is that elaborate spreadsheets with hundreds of formulas and ratios have so many built-in assumptions that most likely offer no additional value to the investment analysis. After the first several major pieces of data, any additional variables offer very little significant value to the analysis.

Consider Buffett's 1973 investment in the Washington Post Company. An often cited example by value investors, the investment illustrates the elegance of a straightforward, businesslike approach to investing. In a 1984 speech at Columbia University, Buffett discussed his attraction to the company: "The Washington Post Company in 1973 was selling for $80 million . . . at the time, you could have sold the assets to any one of ten buyers for not less than $400 million."[1]

While Buffett had been keenly familiar with the operations of the Post Company through his friendship with *Post* publisher Katherine Graham, he made his ultimate investment decision based on facts, not hundreds of bits of information about newspaper subscriptions, advertising revenue, and so on. He determined that you could buy approximately $1 worth of assets for 20 cents and that, over time, that was a very good bet to make. Any time you can buy $1 worth of assets for substantially less, it's generally a good bet to make.

I discussed in Chapter 1 why approaching any particular investment as if purchasing an actual piece of a business as opposed to a share of stock leads to a more intelligent investment process. Attempting to invest in stocks or any other security without first defining and understanding the reasoning behind your investment considerations is like jumping into the ocean without first having learned to swim in a pool. Likely you will succumb to emotion and fear at the slightest sign of troubles, and your chances of long-term survival are slim. Most, if not all, of your market activities would be speculative but mistaken for an investment operation because no fundamental intellectual framework exists behind the decision-making process. This chapter lays out the foundation of value investing, which is to have a sound investment philosophy. Successful value investing does not rely on advanced intellectual capability but hinges on understanding the value investing approach. The philosophies of the value investing approach either will take hold with an investor or they will not. It's that simple. This doesn't mean that you must be born with a value investing orientation; it does mean that once you understand the philosophies of value investing, it immediately clicks in your brain or it doesn't.

And the philosophies underlying value investing are straightforward. Value investors focus on capital preservation first and capital appreciation second. The main focus of value investing is avoiding permanent losses of capital. Value investors understand that buying a stock at $20 per share and holding it until it declines to $10 is not a permanent loss of capital but a mere move in the stock price. Value investors distinguish between risk—the probability of a permanent capital loss—and volatility—the mere movement in stock price. They also understand that the price paid for an investment ultimately determines the future investment results. But value investors don't worry over whether to pay $15 or $15.50 for a share of stock; instead they focus on whether $1 of assets can be bought for substantially less. Also, value investors seek to eliminate as much risk as possible from investing by seeking out only those investments selling at valuations that create a very comfortable margin of safety.

The value investing approach is an all-or-none proposition. You don't choose to be risk averse yet pursue the popular investments of the day without any regard to margin of safety. Without the foundation of a sound investment philosophy, an attempt at investing based on the risk-averse tenants of value investing is lost.

Preservation of Capital Is the Name of the Game

Value investing, by its nature, is a highly contrarian approach. The aim of every investor is to sell an asset at a higher price than that at which it was bought. However, value investors have one aim that comes before realizing a capital gain. First and foremost, value investing focuses on avoiding losses. Although loss aversion may indeed be the goal of every market participant, it seems absent in the decisions of many market bets. By investing at undervalued prices, value investors avoid losses. Often undervalued securities are found in areas unloved by the overall market, thus requiring value investors to zig when most zag. Before making any investment, value investors consider and analyze not how much money can be made but how much money can be lost. Mohnish Pabrai sums it up succinctly when he remarks: "Heads I win big, tails I don't lose much."[2]

Buffett has immortalized value investors' aversion to capital losses with his two top rules of investing:

Rule One: Don't lose money.

Rule Two: Refer to Rule One.

The focus on capital preservation is of paramount importance to the value investor. Value investors are not interested in situations where the odds of a capital loss or gain are 50/50 or even 40/60. The goal is to find opportunities where the probability of loss is minimal and there is a probability of a very high upside. Attention to capital preservation requires that you pay attention to the value of the business and ignore stock price fluctuations, unless they provide an opportunity to buy at cheap prices or sell at fully valued prices.

Focusing on the underlying business and not the stock price allows you to understand the fine line between preservation of capital and capital at risk of permanent loss. If you buy shares in a business for $50 that you determine to have an intrinsic value of $100, you shouldn't panic if you see the stock price decline to $30.

Assuming you have analyzed the business and determined its operations sound and its management able, the 40 percent decline in the *price* of the shares is meaningless in the long run relative to the *value* of the business. The movement in the stock price has not permanently eroded your capital. If you succumb to emotion because you can't stomach watching the stock price decline and sell the stock, you have made a temporary decline in the stock's price lead to a permanent loss of capital.

I can't overemphasize the tremendous importance of separating the activity of the stock price from the activity of the business. Stock prices tend to overreact in both directions. If a company reports quarterly results that are a few pennies less than the estimates analysts had in place, the price of the stock can go down by double digits in no time at all.

Consider this statement made by William Ruane and Richard Cuniff of the Sequoia Fund in 1987. I preface by adding a little color to the market environment of the time: Until August 1987, the stock market had surged. This surge was followed by a stock market crash in October 1987, when the Dow Jones declined by nearly 23 percent in a single day. Cuniff and Ruane astutely commented:

> Disregarding for the moment whether the prevailing level of stock prices on January 1, 1987 was logical, we are certain that the *value* of American industry in the aggregate had not increased by 44% as of August 25. Similarly, it is highly unlikely that the value of American industry declined by 23% on a single day, October 19.[3]

Investors should ponder this thought when stock prices fluctuate widely. At the time of this writing, the U.S. Treasury has spent over $150 billion to aid American International Group (AIG) and over $1 trillion on rescuing the financial sector. As a guest writer for investing sites, I recently got an e-mail from an investor who was concerned about the precipitous decline in one of his investments. This e-mail stood out because of the timing. The man writes about a particular security and remarks, "The stock . . . is being hammered . . . I am very fearful and thinking about selling it tomorrow." This note came on the evening after a near 500-point drop in the Dow.

Such fears run rampant during periods of market turmoil. It is very easy to surrender to your emotions and exit in a state of panic. The human brain is not designed to tolerate or ignore pain, and financial loss is arguably one of the most painful experiences a human can face. Emotional pain can surpass physical pain in terms of severity and longevity. This behavior often is responsible for most capital losses many investors, both individual and professional, realize. Selling at a loss is not the problem; as investors, we will all make mistakes and must realize that, at times, the most prudent course of action is to cut our losses and move on. The key point is to differentiate between deterioration in the economics of the business and a drop in share price. Several days of stock price declines usually have nothing to do with the quality of the business but more with the general mood of the market. Usually more than a week is necessary to determine if the underlying business has lost some of its economic advantages or earning power.

Price Paid Determines Value Received

Before investing, it is vital to understand the function the markets play. Stock markets are important only because they allow you to buy and sell ownership interests in businesses. Everything else is just noise. I like to say that the best investors are pretend investors: those who can pretend that the stock market does not exist.

One of the best advantages of a stock market, liquidity, also happens to be one of the worst. Being able to buy and sell stock at the click of a mouse causes most investors more harm than good. Of course, if you find yourself in a financial bind and need access to capital, the liquidity of the stock market helps you, but I assume that you are investing capital that will not be needed for meaningful periods of time. In this case, the liquidity of the stock market is not as beneficial as you might think. Paying constant attention to the daily fluctuation in stock prices can influence you to make very poor investment decisions.

As an investor, your goal is to let the market give you the opportunity to buy and sell at attractive prices, not instruct you on when to buy and sell. It is not uncommon for two investors investing in the same security to have materially different investment results, even to the extreme where one result is gain and the other is a loss. The reason is due to the price paid for the investment. Value investors approach the market as a proxy for determining whether security prices are undervalued, fairly valued, or overvalued. They don't allow the market to formulate their investment decisions. This distinction between guidance and instruction is very subtle and often is blurred, especially when the market is experiencing periods of wide price fluctuations, or volatility. Referring back to the e-mail I received, it's obvious that this individual was being influenced by the rapid decline in the stock price although the business was doing just fine. He let the market volatility instruct him and make him feel that he had made a mistake. Make no mistake, it's not easy to watch your investment decline by 20 percent in a week or two and not feel like you have made a dumb move.

Between September 15 and 19, 2008, the Dow Jones experienced one of the most volatile trading weeks in history. The mess created by the excessive and irresponsible mortgage and securitization practices came very close to creating a financial catastrophe. Whether you agree with the government bailout or not, without it, the market contagion that would have resulted would have made the

1987 stock market look like a dress rehearsal. On September 15, the Dow dropped over 500 points, or 4.4 percent, on news that insurance titan AIG was facing collapse. On Wednesday, the Dow declined another 450 points, or 4.1 percent. The final two days of the week, the Dow gained nearly 800 points, or 8 percent, to leave the stock market average basically unchanged over the week. Had you let the price volatility instruct your decisions, you were selling during the drops out of fear and buying again at the end of the week when the mood became more optimistic. Without even realizing it, you were selling low and buying high.

In fact, most equity portfolios were worth more at the end of the week as the two-day surge in the market recaptured the declines earlier in the week and then some.

Investors would benefit tremendously if they would remember to echo the sentiments of Bill Ruane and Richard Cuniff during moments of great market turmoil. Before succumbing to your emotions and rushing to sell at moments of pessimism (or buying at moments of jubilant optimism), step back and ask yourself whether the movement in the stock price reflects the intrinsic or true value of the business. Absent some discovery of fraud or any other illegal activity, a quick decline in stock price should not persuade you to head for the exit. Instead, you need to look at the business. If your fundamental thesis remains intact, then do nothing or buy more of a good thing for less.

The Starting Point Matters

Value investors often are credited with espousing the buy-and-hold approach to investing. Warren Buffett is famous for saying "My holding period is forever." A buy-and-hold technique enables the greatest attribute of investing to play out: compounding. If you are constantly buying and selling stocks, the frictional costs—commissions, taxes, fees—will eat into your profits. Nothing is more valuable or sought after than a wonderful business that can deliver returns year in and year out. These investments allow you to sit back and enjoy the ride.

However, the concept of buy and hold is not without its caveats. The most crucial one is the starting point of the buy process. Whenever you hear any serious investor advocate the concept of buy and hold, take the phrase a step further to mean buy *at the right price* and then hold. In value investing, the stock price is of extreme importance when entering and exiting an investment. When prices indicate that a good business is cheap, use it to your advantage to make a good investment. Conversely, when prices indicate that business values have exceeded intrinsic value, use the opportunity to sell the overvalued business and once again buy an undervalued business. At any other time, the stock price fluctuation is a distraction.

To appreciate the significance of why valuation matters in choosing the right starting point, consider the 17-year period from 1964 to 1981. Had you bought the stocks in the Dow Jones Industrial Average at the beginning of 1965 and held until 1981, your returns would have been nonexistent. During those 17 years, the Dow Jones started and ended at the same point. At the beginning of 1965, the Dow stood at about 875 points. Seventeen years later, the Dow was at 875. A buy-and-hold approach over that period would have effectively delivered a zero percent return—a negative return when you factor in decline in purchasing power over that period.

Seventeen years is a significant amount of time. For many investors, it represents the bulk of their investment years and is certainly a long enough buy-and-hold period. Interestingly, the period from 1982 to 1999 turned into one of the greatest market periods in American history. The Dow Jones advanced more than tenfold, and a $100,000 investment in 1982 would have made you more than $1 million by the end of 1999.

The starting point matters. While you can never expect to buy at the exact bottom (say, in 1982) and sell at the peak (as in 1999), you can avoid doing the exact opposite, which is what many investors did by buying in the late 1990s at inflated prices. Excited by the quick and unsustainable rise in stock prices fueled by the Internet boom, investing turned into speculating motivated by greed rather than commonsense business principles. Very few individuals would pay $10 million to buy an entire business that had no customers, much less profits. Yet millions of well-educated people were buying shares of companies valued at billions of dollars without a single dollar of profits.

A very good rule of thumb and decades of data suggest that the best starting points occur when the price to earnings (P/E) ratios are lower rather than higher. The P/E ratio is simply the share price of stock divided by the per-share earnings of a business. It represents how much investors are willing to pay for the future earnings of a business based on future business expectations. If a company's shares trade at $20 and its earnings per share for the year are $2, then the P/E ratio is 10 (20/2). The inverse of the P/E ratio is known as the earnings yield or the percentage of earnings per share. In the example, the earnings yield is 10 percent (2/10). As you can see, the lower the P/E ratio, the higher the earnings yield.

Interestingly, you don't need decades of data to tell you that it is more prudent (and more likely profitable) to look for quality businesses that are trading at lower P/Es. Anyone would rather pay $1 million for a business that earns $200,000 in profits versus one that earns $100,000, all else being equal. Similarly, the odds of favorable market returns increase when the general market has a lower P/E ratio. In fact, decades of data confirm this logical assumption, as shown in Table 4.1 and Figure 4.1.

Table 4.1   20-Year Periods, 1919 to 2007, S&P 500 Stock Index: Net Total Return

Decile	Net Total Returns by Decile Range		S&P 500 Decile Average	Average Begin P/E	Average End P/E
	From	To			
1	1.2%	4.5%	3.2%	19	9
2	4.5%	5.2%	4.9%	18	9
3	5.2%	5.4%	5.3%	12	12
4	5.4%	6.0%	5.6%	13	12
5	6.2%	7.9%	7.0%	15	15
6	8.0%	9.0%	8.7%	16	19
7	9.0%	9.6%	9.3%	15	19
8	9.7%	11.0%	10.4%	11	20
9	11.5%	11.9%	11.7%	12	22
10	12.1%	15.0%	13.4%	10	29

Note: P/E ratio based on Shiller methodology; net total returns including market gains, dividends, and transaction costs of 2 percent.
Source: Copyright 2005, Crestmont Research (www.CrestmontResearch.com).

In business, you make money when you buy an asset, not when you sell it. By that I mean that if you buy low, odds are very strong that you will make money when it is time to sell. Occasionally there are periods when logic and discipline don't matter, and you can buy at any price and sell at a better price. The Internet boom of the late 1990s and the housing bubble that started earlier this century are two examples that come to mind. But blindly participating in periods of excessive speculation ultimately ends up doing more harm than good to most participants.

Employing a sound philosophy with regard to stock investing demands that you consider the price paid. In order to buy intelligently, you must know how to assess the value of the business. Valuation is explored in greater detail in Chapter 6. In addi-

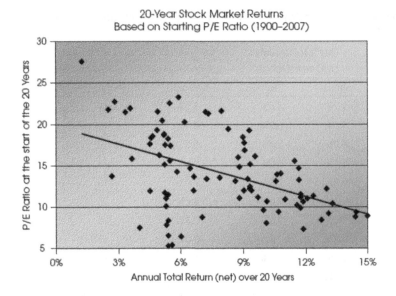

20-Year Stock Market Returns
Based on Starting P/E Ratio (1900–2007)

Figure 4.1   Starting Point Matters
Copyright 2005, Crestmont Research (www.CrestmontResearch.com).

tion to valuation, investors need to recognize another important part of buying securities that has more to do with temperament than valuation.

Recognize that very rarely will you make your purchase decisions at the very bottom. A true value-oriented investor doesn't try to time markets but instead focuses on pricing stocks. As such, you will rarely ever buy at the absolute bottom or even sell at the absolute top. If you are fortunate to buy at the bottom and sell at the absolute top, understand that doing so involves a big dose of lucky timing. Prudent investors who devote serious time and effort to understanding and valuing a business will be able to buy at an undervalued price and sell at a higher price. A businesslike investment approach characterized by a quantitative analysis of each individual company will significantly increase the probability that you buy at a low price and are thus able to sell later at a higher price.

Investors must learn to be at peace with their investment decisions. You can do this only if you have truly focused on paying cheap prices for your investments. If you have, any subsequent decline in the stock price will not cause you to make ill-timed sell decisions. Instead, most likely either you will sit still, knowing that the movement in stock price has nothing to do with the value of the business, or you will look to buy more of an even better bargain.

It should come as no surprise that a value-oriented investment approach looks to profit and capitalize during weak markets. Periods of market turmoil and uncertainty increase the likelihood of finding bargain investment opportunities. When the general mood is against equities, the likelihood of finding irrational valuations is greatest. Declining markets tend to create very fertile hunting ground for patient value investors. The biggest investment opportunities can arise during the direst market environments. Subsequently, investors often produce some of their best results from exploiting bear market opportunities, but they don't know it until the bear market passes.

Risk versus Volatility

As I wrote this book, the U.S. economy was experiencing one of the toughest pullbacks since the Great Depression. The substandard lending practices that were fueled by one of the greatest housing booms in history have virtually frozen the global credit markets. Once-storied financial powerhouses such as Bear Sterns and Lehman Brothers no longer exist as a result of excessive financial leverage and the inability to dispose of toxic assets in a timely fashion. The biggest bank collapse in the history of the United States took place when Washington Mutual had to dissolve in September 2008.

Making matters worse, the first proposed temporary assistance relief program, in which the U.S Treasury proposed a $700 billion line of credit to buy the troubled assets of the financial sector, failed to pass a vote by the U.S. House of Representatives (the vote later passed), which sent the Dow Jones down nearly 800 points, or 7 percent, on September 29, 2008. This represents the biggest point drop in Dow history and the second largest percentage fall after the October 1987 crash.

Stock prices in general have been declining for well over a year, but on September 29, 2008, stock prices went into a free fall. That day, $1.2 trillion in market value was wiped out (the first time over $1 trillion was lost in a single day). Aside from financial institutions—some of which declined by over 50 percent that day—perfectly sound (and often debt-free) businesses suffered single-day losses that in some instances exceeded 20 percent. In such times, markets can experience prolonged periods where valuations simply do not matter. In late 2007, plenty of strong nonfinancial businesses were selling for under 10 times earnings, with little or no debt, and producing gobs of free cash flow. Today some of these same businesses are now trading at two to three times forward earnings.

Yet these valuation metrics don't seem to matter when markets are in a state of turmoil. In the short run, the market moves on the votes of participants, not the quality of businesses. It's crucial for investors to understand the difference between a stock price decline as a result of an overall bear market versus a decline in the intrinsic value of a business. Global economic slowdowns will certainly reduce intrinsic values if future earnings are set to decline. But just as stock prices tend to overshoot during periods of endless optimism, they can also undershoot during periods of endless pessimism. And these periods can last several months or many years. Timing markets is a fool's errand while pricing stocks is an investor's goal. Nonetheless, even value investors must learn to respect the market and realize that bear markets can put you to the ultimate test of patience.

Determining whether the stock price indicates an undervalued or overvalued business is challenging. Consider a bond, which is relatively straightforward to value. If the bond currently pays $500 a year in interest and has a face value of $10,000, it yields 5 percent. If interest rates for similar bonds are 5 percent, investors will be willing to pay $10,000 for the bond. Since 5 percent is the current yield in the market for similar bonds, by paying $10,000, the investor is not overpaying for bond. However, if the price of the same bond is more than $10,000, then the investor will not be getting a 5 percent yield and should choose another bond. There is certainly more to bond pricing, but the general idea is that relative to stocks, bonds are relatively straightforward to value. And during environments of unprecedented financial turmoil, such as 2008, valuations simply do not seem to matter, so any attempt to value a business seems worthless. Still, the ultimate driver of value is the amount of cash produced by business after all other needs and bills are paid (the free cash flow). A business that continues to generate cash ultimately will become more valuable. But in the short term, stock market prices are affected by the votes of market participants, not by business fundamentals. Over time, the stock market becomes a weighing machine where valuations are influenced by business attributes. Unfortunately, when markets are in crisis mode, the market can vote for a very long time.

Avoid Using Margin

As a value investor, your goal is to participate in investment opportunities where the probability of a gain exceeds the probability of loss by the widest possible margins. You devote serious time to analyzing the business, assessing the quality of management, and rationalizing what the business will look like into the future. These efforts require time and painstaking effort. In short, the goal of value investors is to skew the odds very heavily in their favor toward the number-one goal: preservation of capital. This mentality often is referred to as focusing on the downside while letting the upside take care of itself.

Margin, or the use of borrowed money, takes all of these goals and renders them useless. For that reason, most value investors avoid the use of margin like the plague. To put it simply, using margin in an investment fund is much like using debt in a business. Although there are important differences, this much is certain: Too much debt can cripple, if not kill, your business. Another critical reason to avoid the use of margin is that it places the destiny of your investment returns in the hands of your broker or banker. And the only time you will ever get a margin call is not when your securities are up in value but when they have declined and your broker demands that you sell your investments to raise cash. Finally, more people should consider the cost of margin. Once you invest using margin, your returns are now influenced by the interest rate charged on that borrowed amount.

It seems rather silly to participate in a transaction where the disadvantages clearly outweigh the advantages. And that's exactly the kind of bet you make when you decide to use margin. Margin essentially involves you agreeing to sell securities at even lower prices and better valuations. Instead of buying more of a business at a cheaper price, margin can force to you sell perfectly sound businesses at fire-sale prices. The financial crisis that came to a head in 2008 illustrates the destructive nature of an overdose of borrowed money. Some of most respected names in finance and banking—Lehman Brothers, Washington Mutual, and Wachovia—have either collapsed or have been chopped up and sold off because they couldn't restrain themselves from binging on leverage.

Imagine a $1 million portfolio that juices its purchasing power to $1.5 million by taking on 50 percent margin. For every dollar of equity, you have taken on 50 cents of leverage, or debt. Assume your cost of debt is 6 percent a year. You invest in a collection of perfectly sound businesses at very sensible prices. For simplicity, we'll assume three outcomes:

Scenario 1: After one year, your holdings have declined by 33 percent, so your portfolio is now worth $1 million.

Scenario 2: You returns are flat, so your portfolio is worth $1.5 million.

Scenario 3: You are up 33 percent after one year, so your portfolio is worth approximately $2 million.

Table 4.2 illustrates the net returns in each of the three possible outcomes. When you have a good year, margin works as it amplifies returns, but it has the same effect on losses when performance is negative or even flat. However, what you don't see from the numbers is the added disadvantages when your performance is negative. As your portfolio holdings decline, your broker will require you to sell holdings to raise cash in order to protect the $500,000 loan. You have no choice but to sell or to somehow raise additional outside capital. Most often, the only option is to sell investments, thereby risking the chance that you are selling a security that was initially bought at an undervalued price at an even lower and more attractive price. Making matters worse, should the same security later have a price rebound, your lack of capital prevents you from participating from the upside. All in all, the juiced losses coupled with the loss of control when using margin far outweigh the benefits of juiced returns.

Table 4.2   Pitfalls of Margin Use

	Scenario 1	Scenario 2	Scenario 3
Starting capital	$1,500,000	$1,500,000	$1,500,000
Ending capital	$1,000,000	$1,500,000	$2,000,000
– Less margin	$500,000	$500,000	$500,000
– Less cost of margin	$30,000	$30,000	$30,000
Net equity capital	$470,000	$970,000	$1,470,000
Total gain/loss	(53%)	(3%)	47%

The key to successful stock market investing is being able to stay in the game for many years. Avoiding margin is a big step in avoiding a complete wipeout. Buffett said it best when he remarked, "If you depend on borrowed money, you have to worry about what the world thinks of you everyday."[4]

Focus on Absolute Returns

Value investing focuses on analyzing businesses and committing capital to those opportunities that are the most compelling. It should come as no surprise then that the focus for value investors is and should always be absolute returns.

An absolute return philosophy is one that has consistent profitability as its key objective. You may be reading this wondering, Don't all investment advisors and investment managers desire to consistently deliver profitable returns? While the clear answer is yes, the goal of most investment professionals suggests no. This is not because they don't want to generate profits but instead because the vast majority of the investment industry focuses on relative returns. A relative return approach accepts the notion that markets are risky in the short term but believes that, in the long term, investors will benefit from the general growth in the economy. As a result, the relative return approach focuses its efforts on allocating capital across various asset classes and industries. The ultimate effect is a broad portfolio that comes very close to mirroring the general stock market indexes. The vast diversification of the relative portfolio will greatly reduce volatility, which has the effect of creating returns that broadly mimic those of the overall stock market. Relative return investors accept these market-matching returns because the majority of individuals will be reporting the same or similar returns. You won't lose your job if you deliver a negative 15 percent in a year when the stock market declines by 12 percent. Economist John Maynard Keynes said it best when he remarked, "Worldly wisdom teaches that it is far better for the reputation to fail conventionally than to succeed unconventionally."[5]

If it's clear that one of the inherent weaknesses of relative return investing is that returns tend to run in tandem with general stock market returns, why do the vast majority of investment professionals practice relative return investing? The name of the game in investment management is to, first, keep your job and then, second, attract additional amounts of capital. To Wall Street, money managers are only as good as their latest year's results. So why not protect your job simply by using an approach followed by the vast majority? If 80 percent of active money managers all report declines in the same year, you can't single one out for being less skillful. It's far easier to hide among the masses than to stick out your neck and risk getting it chopped off.

Unlike the relative return approach, an absolute return approach aims to profit consistently regardless of market return. It should be clear then that absolute return investing relies more on the investor's skill to produce profits. Further, and as I mentioned earlier, an absolute return approach is obviously much more valuable during bear market periods. Bull markets can make the most novice of investors seem brilliant; it's not until the times get tough that you separate skill from luck. Most important, however, is the understanding that investment records start becoming meaningful after a period of years, not just one year. In the short run, a relative return approach can look extremely good during bear markets. Because value often is found in the most unloved industries, a concentrated value-oriented portfolio could easily find itself vastly underperforming the broad market during a bear market. Remember that in the short run, the market votes, and often those votes don't favor temporarily depressed businesses.

Value investors are by default oriented toward an absolute return approach. Rather than looking at the market as whole, they focus attention on individual businesses. Rather than invest in general asset classes, value investors invest in securities one by one, attempting to find those opportunities that have been temporarily tossed out by the market. And rather than needing to be invested at all times, if the valuations are not attractive, value investors recognize that the best investment option may at times be to make no investment at all.

Key Takeaways

- Before investing, develop a sound mental philosophy of what it is you are doing and understand that philosophy cold. Understand that you are investing in businesses, not stock prices.
- The stock market exists to afford you the opportunity to own a piece of a business at a sensible price. The volatility of the stock market should not instruct you in valuing a business. Remember in the short run, prices are determined by votes of the market participants.
- When you invest is just as important as how you invest. Focus on buying great businesses at sensible prices. The starting point matters.
- Avoid using borrowed money to make your investments. Leverage is the only way that a smart investor can go broke.

CHAPTER 5

Develop a Search Strategy

THE SECOND ELEMENT

A public opinion is no substitute for thought.

—Warren Buffett

There are thousands of publicly traded companies in the United States and thousands more throughout the world. Searching for stocks is both interesting and daunting. The quest for the "next great stock" has become the holy grail of investing. The truth is there are no great stocks, only great investments. What differentiates between the two? The price you pay. And how do you increase the likelihood of paying a sensible price for a share in a company? By making your investment decisions based on business fundamentals and nothing else.

A great business does not necessarily imply a great stock investment. Google is a fantastic business that generates tremendous profits. However, if you were buying Google at $700 a share and paying 42 times earnings, you weren't making a great investment. Remember the other way to look at the price to earnings (P/E) ratio is by inverting it to get the earnings yield. So for Google, a

P/E ratio of 42 means you are paying $42 for each dollar of earnings. The earnings yield is the return you get based on the price you pay. For $42 you are getting $1, implying a yield of 2.4 percent ($1/$42). When Google was trading at these valuations, ultra-safe U.S. Treasury bills yielded over 3 percent. In other words, investors were willing to take less return by paying more in hope of a continual rise the in share price. You have no margin of safety at such lofty valuations. The slightest hiccups and the share price begins to free fall.

Stocks are merely pieces of paper that fluctuate in price every Monday through Friday. Great investments, however, arise when sound business fundamentals dictate the investment decision. That's why it's imperative to have a sound grasp of what it is you are doing—buying businesses—and what that entails. As I alluded to in Chapter 4, you must approach the markets with an emotion-free, fundamentally based approach before beginning your search strategy. Searching the stock market without a sound investment philosophy is like trying to walk before learning to crawl: It's a painful experience.

There is only one Warren Buffett, and he devoted the time, passion, and intensity needed to go through the 10,000-page *Moody's Stock Manual* page by page, looking at every single stock, in order to develop a mental model of the markets. If you are a serious investor looking to participate in the investing game for many years, be prepared to roll up your sleeves and look at hundreds of stocks continuously. Fortunately, investors today have many more resources that aid in the search process than were available during Buffett's early years. Unfortunately, investors today have many more resources that also can lead to poor investment decisions. What I mean by this is that while it's great to have more resources, too much information or data begins to add noise to the meaningful information that you really need. In order to have a good search strategy, it's important to flip the concept around first.

In other words, instead of directly delving into how to develop a good search strategy by suggesting the best places to look, let's flip it around. It is far easier to develop a good search strategy if you first understand *where not to look.*

Ignore the Media

On August 13, 1979, *BusinessWeek* published the now-legendary issue titled "The Death of Equities." The synopsis for the headline article stated:

> The masses long ago switched from stocks to investments having higher yields and more protection from inflation. Now the pension funds—the market's last hope—have won permission to quit stocks and bonds for real estate, futures, gold, and even diamonds. The death of equities looks like an almost permanent condition—reversible someday, but not soon.[1]

On that same date, the Dow Jones Industrial Average (DJIA) closed at 875 points. By the end of the year, the Dow stood at 838, a decline of approximately 4.2 percent.[2] It seemed that readers of the magazine were saved by the warning that the "death of equities looks like an almost permanent condition."

Compiling data from the Dow Jones site (www.djindexes.com), I created a chart showing the DJIA performance over the next 10 years (see Table 5.1).

If you thought equities were dead, you might have missed out on what is now arguably one of the best performance decades in market history. Please note: I am by no means singling out *BusinessWeek* as having made a wrong call. All media outlets were in one way or another disregarding equities as a viable investment class. *BusinessWeek* is just known for having the most famous and sensational cover at a time when the markets were preparing to make a historic upward run.

Table 5.1 Dow Jones Industrial Average Annual Returns, 1980-1989

Year	DJIA Start	DJIA End	% Return
1980	838	964	15%
1981	964	875	-9.2%
1982	875	1046	19.5%
1983	1046	1258	20.3%
1984	1258	1211	-3.7%
1985	1211	1546	27.7%
1986	1546	1896	22.6%
1987	1896	1938	22.1%
1988	1938	2168	11.9%
1989	2168	2753	27%

Data source: Dow Jones & Company (www.djindexes.com).

One fundamental difference between the markets and the media makes the media a poor guidepost in security selection. The media tends to focus on the current state of affairs while markets are anticipatory creatures. While the media focuses on the current outlook of the economy, it is highly likely that markets begin to turn up just when investors are being told to exit the game. As Warren Buffett likes to quip, "If you wait for robins, spring will be gone."[3]

What the media failed to convey during its bleak assessment of the economy in the late 1970s was that equity valuations had reached decade lows and the stock market was as a cheap as it had been in a very long time. Over the past 100 years of market activity, the market historically has experienced cycles in which it advanced (bull market) or declined (bear markets). Table 5.2 illustrates the various market cycles of the twentieth century based on the performance of the DJIA.

While the media maintains its focus on the current situation, markets—and investors—tend to focus on the future. And when you have a situation like the 1970s, when equities were selling at

Table 5.2 Secular Bull/Bear Market Returns, 1900–Present

Market	DJIA Start	DJIA End	Starting P/E Ratio	Ending P/E Ratio
1901–1920 Bear	71	72	23	5
1921–1928 Bull	72	300	5	22
1929–1932 Bear	300	60	28	8
1933–1936 Bull	60	180	11	19
1937–1941 Bear	180	111	19	12
1942–1965 Bull	111	969	9	23
1966–1981 Bear	969	875	21	9
1982–1999 Bull	875	11497	7	42
2000–???? Bear	11497	????	42	14: ?

some of the lowest valuations in decades, the markets can start advancing before the slightest hint of good news from the media.

Investors should rely on the media as one source of information. Similar to the analogy regarding the stock markets, let the media inform but not guide you in what to do. As investors, we need accurate and honest journalism. We are fortunate to have many excellent sources, including *BusinessWeek*. But investors must remember the role of the media: to provide news commentary, not investment guidance. The media is staffed by journalists, not market analysts.

And lest we forget, by the time information reaches the front cover or front-page news, it's already well known by the market. Annual issues proclaiming next year's hottest mutual funds or hottest stocks are not new or original ideas. Investors are rewarded for finding value when everyone else is leaving the party. By the time the media gets hold of investment ideas, the smart money has already been there. Excitement is an investor's worst enemy; it leads to paying high prices to participate with the herd mentality. An effective search strategy relies on knowing where not to look just as much as where to look. Let the media do its job of providing up-to-date news analysis on the state of the world; don't rely on it to instruct you as to where to allocate your capital.

Imitation Is the Sincerest Form of Flattery

Unlike most other professions, where copying someone's work or using another's data could be illegal, in investing there are no penalties for copying others' ideas. In fact, seeing what other investors are buying is the greatest and most effective starting point for an effective search strategy. With thousands of publicly traded securities in the United States alone, it is an intelligent move to take that large pool of stocks and shrink it down to those owned by the most experienced and talented investors in the world. As far as I am concerned, there is no new secret formula waiting to be discovered in value investing, only the discovery of bargain investment opportunities.

Fortunately, our search is aided by the existence of many highly regarded value investors who have produced the long-term numbers to back up their reputations. Some names that stand out include Seth Klarman (the Baupost Group), Mason Hawkins (Longleaf Funds), Bruce Berkowitz (Fairholme Funds), Mohnish Pabrai (Pabrai Investment Funds), Marty Whitman (Third Avenue Funds), and of course Warren Buffett and his partner Charles Munger. These investors have been tried and tested over years and have demonstrated an ability to outperform the markets over meaningful periods of time. So why not begin your search for companies by leaning on the shoulders of great men?

Copying the Great One

In 2007, two professors published a study that analyzed the investment moves made by Warren Buffett between 1976 and 2000.[4] What they found was remarkable, not for the returns that Buffett has produced (which many of us are already familiar with), but for what those returns meant to the individual investor. Over the 31 years covered by the study, the Berkshire Hathaway equity portfolio beat the benchmark in 27 out of the 31 years, on average exceeding the Standard and Poor's 500 Index by 14.65 percent. This performance should come as no surprise. Here's the incredible part. If investors had simply bought the same stocks that Buffett was buying for Berkshire over the same period, they would have earned average returns of 24 percent during the 1976 to 2006 period. And this means buying the stocks *after Buffett had disclosed them in Securities and Exchange Commission (SEC) regulatory filings.* You didn't have to guess what Buffett was buying. You simply had to wait until his investments became public information and then make the same investments on your own. What's phenomenal here is the wide margin of outperformance. An average return of 24 percent versus 11 percent implies that you could have spent some time performing your own due diligence, and odds are you still would have done better than the index. Even more impressive, you would have done better than a vast majority of professional investors. A monkey could have beaten the socks off the market by copying Buffett!

Interestingly, the study concluded that Buffett's performance was confined to a very small number of carefully chosen investments. In fact, the study found that Berkshire's five top equity holdings averaged 73 percent of the portfolio's value. Buffett is obviously a unique individual and a brilliant investor without equal. But he is certainly not alone is delivering incredible performance numbers year in and year out. Aside from the names just mentioned, do some digging, and you will find some excellent candidates worthy of imitation.

Where to Look

Fortunately, SEC regulations today make it effortless to find out what other investors are buying and selling. According to SEC rules, any money manager with over $100 million under management is required to file a quarterly statement disclosing holdings. This quarterly report is referred to as a 13-F filing and is public information. It has to be filed 45 days following the end of each calendar quarter.

The four-step process of getting copies of 13-F filings is quick and simple:

1. Go to the SEC Web site, www.sec.gov, and click on the "Search for Company Filings" link under the Filings and Forms section.
2. Then click on the "Companies and Other Filers" link.
3. Under the search information, enter the name of the investment fund in the Company Name section.
4. Once there, scroll down and look for the most recent 13-F filing. (Typically the dates will be 45 days after each calendar quarter.)

Many investment firms have various funds or different legal names for the funds and the investment management company. Also, some companies share similar names, so do some research on the specific company and where it's based to be certain you are looking at the right one.

Once you have the 13-F, it's fairly simple to decipher. Figure 5.1 shows a section of the Fairholme Funds 2008 second-quarter 13-F, which was filed on August 14, 2008 (about 45 days from June 30, 2008).

You can use this search process over and over for numerous investors. Sometimes you might see similar investments across various investment managers. These common holdings should really grab your attention. For example, many value managers hold sizable positions in Berkshire Hathaway. It's not hard to understand why; many folks believe that at the current price of $90,000 per A share as of June 2009, Berkshire is significantly undervalued. Even more so, Buffett still keeps on increasing intrinsic value by an average of 10 percent a year, so even at its current size, Berkshire still represents a solid investment coupled with very little risk.

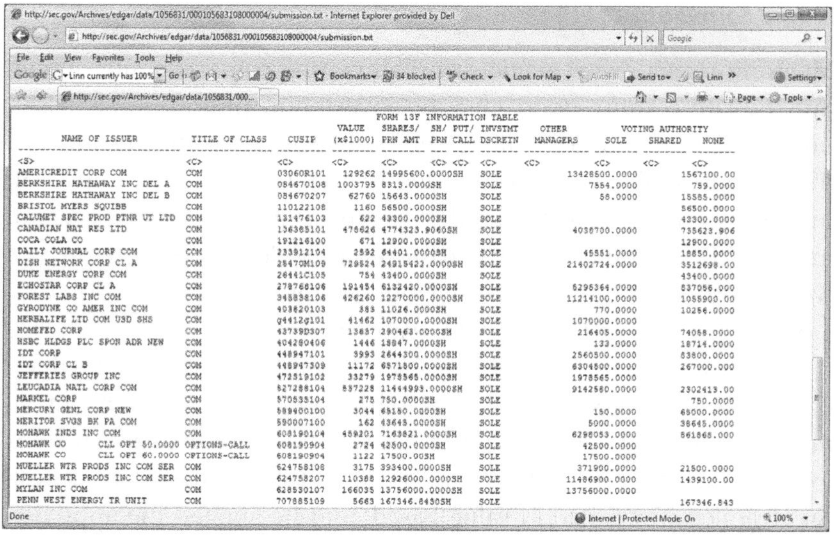

Figure 5.1   Fairholme Funds Filing for Second Quarter 2008 (filed August 14, 2008)

Source: SEC filings.

Aside from Berkshire and Buffett, value investors occasionally jump on the same wagon, whether it is for the same stock or a general industry that has been battered and offers value. The filings of several value investors will provide you with at least 100 ideas to research. I can't think of a better search filter than first to see what other smart successful investors are buying.

Basic Search Strategies

Researching what the smart money is buying is just the beginning. The next step in developing a good search strategy is to filter out the best resources and rely heavily on them. In no particular order of importance, the next resources offer valuable investment ideas for any value investor.

Magic Formula

Magic Formula (www.magicformulainvesting.com) is a silly name, but the site is quite good and the investment philosophy is based on sound fundamentals (and free, as are most of the resources I discuss here). The site was founded by Joel Greenblatt, an investor, professor, and author. Greenblatt began as a value investor in the mold of Ben Graham and Christopher Dodd. (Ben Graham was Buffett's mentor; Graham and Dodd coauthored *Security Analysis*, a book regarded without equal in value investing.)

Not much is known about Greenblatt's hedge fund Gotham Capital, as it operated very privately. What we do know is that the investment partnership began in 1985 and achieved annualized returns exceeding 40 percent until it shut down in 1995.[5] Greenblatt's investment philosophy is deeply value based, and he applied the approach rigorously in his investment fund. Like Buffett, Greenblatt focused on good-quality businesses that were selling for cheap in the market.

How did Greenblatt define "cheap"? He looked at the earnings yield of the business. The earnings yield is simply the stock price divided by the annual earnings per share of the business. So, for example, a stock that trades for $20 a share and earns $2 for the year has an earnings yield of 10 percent. Obviously, the higher the yield, the cheaper the stock as long it can continue to grow earnings.

The other variable was finding good businesses. And, like Buffett, Greenblatt defined "good businesses" as those that earn the highest returns on invested capital (ROIC). To keep it simple, think of ROIC as how much a business earns pretax for each dollar invested in the business. The concept is simple. If a business generates more than a dollar in pretax income from each dollar invested in the business, then it is creating value. The company is taking a dollar and earning more than a dollar. For example, a company is said to have a 20 percent ROIC if for every dollar it invests in the business, it earns 20 cents above that dollar. Over time, businesses that continue to generate strong returns on invested capital increase the value of the company and, ultimately, the stock price.

So Greenblatt took these two valuable pieces of data and created the Magic Formula list of stocks. The site is merely a list of stocks based on a minimum company market value that you choose. The list gives you the business name, its stock symbol, the earnings yield, and the return on capital. The intuitive concept behind the Magic Formula is brilliant; value investors should research and analyze its list of stocks. The site is updated daily so it remains a very useful tool for stock searches.

Value Line

Most investors are familiar with the Value Line Investment Survey (www.valueline.com). Value Line is one of the oldest and most respected investment research firms around. Most important, it is an independent research company, so its information is unbiased. Value Line covers over 3,000 securities in its research database. Each week, Value Line publishes an issue that covers a couple hundred stocks until the cycle is repeated again each quarter.

What I like about Value Line is the loads of data you get on each company. On one page, Value Line gives you 10 years of data on the company. It lists all the necessary fundamentals including sales, profits, margins, and return on capital. Over time, serious investors should become aware of the universe of Value Line stocks, much as Buffett did when he went through Moody's investment manuals. The businesses profiled in Value Line cover all the major industries and sectors; just knowing them will give you an excellent mental model of the market.

While the weekly publications are great for general investment ideas, the Value Line Web site offers a powerful search tool. Each week along with the publication, Value Line produces preset screen filters according to certain categories. Based on the category, Value Line screens its own database and lists the 50 to 100 stocks that fall under that classification. So instead of initially going through all the securities in the database, you can look at the areas that would likely contain bargain investment opportunities. For instance, each week Value Line produces a list of stocks under these categories, plus many others:

- Biggest "Free Cash Flow" Generator
- Highest Dividend Yielding Non Utility Stocks
- Lowest P/E's
- Widest Discounts from Book Value
- Bargain Basement Stocks

Each category filters through the Value Line database and provides fertile hunting ground for potential investments. You get the same detailed one-page Value Line report for each business. This is an excellent resource base for initial investment ideas.

Unfortunately, Value Line's data is proprietary and thus is not free. An annual subscription to the print manuals will set you back several hundred dollars a year. Unless you need the print manuals, however, the online service is the way to go. You don't have to wait for your issue in the mail plus you get the added search and data features. Most local libraries have both print and online subscriptions to Value Line, so if you don't want to shell out the money, you can head over to your local library. Purchasing your own subscription is definitely worth the investment.

52-Week Low Lists

Numerous sources can provide lists of stocks that are trading at their lowest prices of the year. Again take these lists as wonderful starting points, but also be careful of value traps. While the markets are never 100 percent efficient, today's marketplace is much more efficient than it was when Buffett was getting started. Occasionally you have periods of extreme pessimism, where all rationality ceases to exist. The 1974 market decline comes to mind, where tons of great businesses were trading at low single-digit P/E ratios. As I write these pages in the fall of 2008, the implosion of the credit crisis, steep housing declines, and global economic recession are providing a similar 1974-type market environment.

You can find lists of stocks hitting new annual lows in various places. The Yahoo! stock screener allows you to search for stocks trading at new low prices. My favorite source is Barchart (www.barchart.com). Each day it provides a comprehensive list of 52-week lows, highs, and everything in between. It's a valuable list of stocks and should be a part of any sound investment strategy.

Value Investors Club

Value Investors Club (www.valueinvestorsclub.com) is a site created by Joel Greenblatt. It's a membership site; the only way you can become a member is by submitting an investment idea so compelling that it selected for the club. As a member, you have real-time access to the ideas posted by other members. The membership is capped at 500, so the emphasis is truly on the quality, not quantity of ideas. Many of the members are widely known in the value investing community.

Fortunately, the heads at the Value Investors Club (VIC) graciously allow guest access to nonmembers to see ideas that are at least 45 days old. You get the same information as members, except that the ideas have already been up for 45 days. In many cases, a 45-day-old idea is still very current, as many value investment ideas take some time to play out. In any case, each investment idea is usually a two- to four-page write-up on why the investment is a compelling one at the time. The neat concept behind VIC is that all ideas are rated by the other members on a scale of 1 to 10, so you have a peer evaluation system going on. A good place to start would be the highest-rated ideas, but with only 500 members contributing two ideas a year, you can easily keep up with them all.

Without question, you can find some phenomenal investment ideas on VIC. The idea write-ups can include some unique analysis that you can't find anywhere else. Nearly all the investment write-ups are owned by the writers themselves, so you get the most compelling reasons why the investment should be made. And since these are ideas are obviously biased from the writer's point of view, they can come off as quite convincing. Ultimately, it is up to you to decide whether to pursue the investment idea; some ideas can be so compelling that a mere due diligence of the facts and figures presented is all that is needed.

However, I would urge investors to take the ideas presented on VIC just as any other source: as fertile hunting ground for great investments. Unlike other sources, it is quite easy to get wrapped up in the analysis presented from the contributors; you can see the substantial work that was done to present the idea. The best write-ups do an excellent job of demonstrating a clear understanding of the business, its history, the industry landscape, and a sound, conservative valuation. In fact, one of my major reasons for recommending VIC is not only because of the ideas but because of the wonderful education you can get simply by reading the write-ups. There's no better way to learn how to value a business than to read and understand how other investment minds are doing it.

Nonetheless, because the ideas on VIC are so detailed, it is easy to substitute VIC's analysis for your own. This is the last thing you want to do. One of the central tenets of successful investing—and a big theme in this book—is to invest in what you understand. Regardless of how sound an investment may be, it's always wise to perform your own diligence to the point where you are confident in the analysis provided. The last thing you want to do is buy based on someone else's work, even if it's Warren Buffett doing the analyzing. I say this not because I don't advocate copying Buffett but to emphasize that in order to be an effective and successful investor, you have to have discipline. You have to be disciplined enough always to perform due diligence, even if you're absolutely confident that your efforts will confirm someone else's thesis. The last thing you want to do is make mistakes that could have been avoided easily with some basic research. As with any of the resources mentioned, use VIC for its insights and recommendations, but do your own work.

Your Own Common Sense

One of the most underrated and underappreciated sources for good investment ideas is your own common knowledge. Use your own advantages or those of the people around you to discover new investment ideas. Odds are almost 100 percent that you will be looking at business where the most important factor—understanding the business—is virtually guaranteed. In other words, using your interest and lifestyle habits to find those businesses that fit within your lifestyle guarantees that you will always be looking within your circle of competence.

While I admire Warren Buffett a great deal and give him credit for the great bulk of my investment philosophy, one area he and I differ on is our dietary habits. While Buffett usually begins his day with a Cherry Coke, I usually start my day off with a mango smoothie or some other type of fresh-squeezed fruit juice. I enjoy eating lots of fresh fruits, generally avoid soft drinks (herbal tea is my choice for a pick-me-up, although I do enjoy a good root beer or cola), avoid eating meat on a daily basis, and pay close attention to food ingredients. As with my investment habits, if I can't understand what I'm eating, I do my best to avoid it.

So, it should come as no surprise that I am very fond of and familiar with Whole Foods. Whole Foods is a phenomenal company.

It's the largest organic and natural foods grocer in the United States. The company sells the highest-quality foods, such as grass-fed beef, organic fruits and vegetables, and chemical-free health and beauty care products. Its products command premium prices, but consumers pay it knowing that are getting the highest-quality foods. We don't have one yet in my hometown of Athens, Georgia, but if I'm in a city with one, I usually stop by. Even if I don't need anything, I like to stop in to check out the store. I am constantly impressed with the merchandising, the abundant variety of fresh produce and meats, and the impeccable cleanliness. Among retail grocers, Whole Foods is unique.

For years my favorable views on Whole Foods have been shared by Mr. Market. The stock has always traded a premium price; sales and earnings growth climbed rapidly each year. So while I loved the company and followed the business each year, it was easy for me to sit back and wait for a better entry point into the investment. I understood the business very well and while I knew that its long-term prospects were strong, no business can continue to grow at such a rapid pace forever. Eventually the business would experience a temporary growth rate plateau and the market would react quickly. Like the Google example at the beginning of the chapter, Whole Foods was a fantastic business but not a fantastic investment at $65 a share with a P/E of over 32. (Note: In late 2008 with the economy in a recession, Whole Foods has been hit hard as consumers cut back on spending, and sales growth has virtually stalled. As a result, shares now trade around $10 and a more digestible P/E of 12. You can rest assured I am very excited at these levels.)

Because I know Whole Foods both as an investor and a customer, I have a very clear understanding of both the benefits and the risks of this business. As such, I am able to value the business and handicap my odds of permanent capital loss with greater accuracy and greater confidence.

Investors too often underestimate the power of common knowledge in providing excellent investment ideas and opportunities. Many people believe that it is too good to be true that a company or product you like so much could turn out to be a wonderful investment opportunity. Such thinking is very one-sided and ignores a central tenet of successful investing: staying within your circle of competence. For example, I do not believe that Whole Foods will be less profitable five years from now. If and when the stock price starts trading at levels that completely discounts any future growth, I get excited because I now have the opportunity to own part of a business that I am confident will be more valuable in the future. Further, this confidence and conviction supersedes emotions in the investment-making process. As a result, the investment is made based on rational considerations. When this mental process occurs, you can easily ignore short-time gyrations in stock price and instead focus on the long-term picture.

Peter Lynch, the legendary mutual fund manager at Fidelity's Magellan Fund between 1977 and 1990, made some of his most spectacular investments just by using a little common knowledge and nothing more. He invested in Taco Bell after being impressed with the food; he invested in Apple after seeing his kids and their friends own an Apple computer; La Quinta Motor Inns after a friend at Holiday Inn told him about it. In fact, Lynch praises his wife as being one of his best investment sources. She led him to L'eggs, which turned out to be one of the most successful consumer products of the 1970s. Before working at Fidelity, Lynch was a securities analyst and studied the textile business extensively. Yet all his work failed to uncover L'eggs. Instead, his wife discovered it at the grocery store.

For those of us too young to remember, L'eggs are women's panty hose sold in plastic egg packaging, usually positioned in grocery stores near the checkout counter. When Lynch discovered them, they were being test marketed by Hanes. Lynch came to find out that women absolutely loved L'eggs for their superior comfort and durability. This plus the convenience of not having to make a special trip to a department store to purchase them led Lynch to believe that L'eggs was a blockbuster product for Hanes. He followed up his theory by doing lots of research: visiting grocery stores and observing how many women had plastic eggs in their shopping carts. I'm sure Lynch pored over the financials, but the idea of Hanes and the blockbuster L'eggs panty hose came from his wife who tried them and loved them. Lynch, with all his fancy Quotron machines, brokers, and analysts, was finding his best ideas by eating a burrito and listening to his wife and kids.

Search Far and Wide

In searching for stocks, value investors naturally lean toward the lowest P/E stocks, lowest price-to-book (P/B) stocks, stocks trading at or near new low prices, and other indicators of "cheapness" or value. On the whole, I think this is a generally prudent approach, as some very fantastic opportunities can be found in unloved areas. However, finding the diamonds in the rough requires that investors navigate through minefields.

While it is a great idea to look for bargain investments among such categories, understand that Mr. Market generally has it right and many investments trading at new lows or uncharacteristically low P/E or P/B ratios are there for a reason. A business that earned $4 a share and trades for $20 and has a P/E of 5 is only the beginning. If such earnings power can't grow or be sustained, then the seemingly low P/E might not be low at all; in other words, the investment is not as cheap as you might think. Similarly, a business that trades for $20 a share but has book value of $30 looks very appealing until you find out that the $30 of book value is really worth $10. This was the case with many financials in 2008. Generally, book value is a very valuable metric in valuing financial companies because their primary assets are money, and $1 is worth $1. Unfortunately, when banks overdosed on asset-backed securities and then used leverage to add more potency, the comedown was deadly. We found out very quickly that book value was not as solid as it once was.

The key when looking in unloved areas for bargains is to approach the task with a healthy dose of skepticism. Realize that a "low" stock price is not an indicator of value. The market proved this in 2008, when stocks of seemingly invincible businesses that were down 70 percent fell another 50 percent!

Falling stock prices and low valuation ratios are an excellent source of ideas, but understand that among the value buys lie many more value traps.

Advanced Search Strategy

I use the heading "Advanced Search Strategy" reluctantly. The search sources I outlined earlier are all used by the most sophisticated and advanced investors in the business. Buffett, Lynch, and hundreds of other pros use the Value Line Investment Survey. And searching other investors' quarterly SEC filings has been a tried and true practice for decades.

The difference between a basic and an advanced search strategy has nothing to do with the quality of the source or the level of difficulty in finding investments. Rather the difference between the two can be explained by one word: time. The advanced search strategy is nothing more than the devotion of countless hours to looking at thousands of public companies and everything in between. When asked how to find stocks, Buffett once remarked begin with the letter A and work your way down.[8] As humorous as Buffett can be, he was not kidding in this instance. At the end of the day, the only way you're going to find more investment opportunities is to look at more stocks. And there's no shortcut to doing it; you start with a list and go through it all. Ironically, the most advanced search strategy is the most basic mundane strategy you can think of.

In 2004, Warren Buffett began investing in Korean stocks. Most value investors and Buffett fans are familiar with the now-famous story of how he received a manual on Korean stocks, spent some time looking through it, and then picked a handful of stocks that did remarkably well over the next couple of years. The real story of Buffett's Korean investment is much deeper and clearly illustrates the time and intensity required when selecting securities.

To begin with, the famous "Korean stock manual" that Buffett received from his broker was as thick as several phone books put together.[7] Buffett went to work. Each night he leafed through the manual, page by page, in much the same way he pored over 10,000 pages of Moody's manuals. Buffett realized he was dealing with foreign numbers and nomenclature that confused him, so he learned everything he could about Korean accounting. Once he had a firm grasp of how Korean securities were traded, he went back to the manual and shortened the list of thousands of Korean stocks to a workable number based on fundamental valuation metrics. When he was done, he had reduced the oversize manual to a couple dozen stocks. Buffett's account of the process is an excellent illustration of his rational, disciplined approach:

> . . . this is how I do it. They are quoted in won. If you go to the Internet and look them up on the Korean stock exchange, they have numbers instead of ticker symbols. . . . Every night you can go to the Internet at a certain time and look up some issues and it'll show you the five brokerage firms that would have been the largest buyers and the five that would have been the largest sellers that day. . . . That's not easy to do. I'm learning as I go along. . . .

These are good companies, and yet they're cheap. The stocks have gotten cheaper than five years ago, and yet the businesses are more valuable. . . . They make basic products like steel and cement and flour and electricity, which people will still be buying in ten years. They have a big market share in Korea which isn't going to change, and some of these companies are exporting to China and Japan too. . . . I could end up with nothing but a bunch of Korean securities in my personal portfolio.

The main risk, and part of why the stocks are cheap, is North Korea. And North Korea is a real threat. . . . But I would make the bet that the rest of the world, including China and Japan, are simply not going to let the situation get to the point that North Korea makes a nuclear attack on South Korea anytime soon.

When you invest, you have to take some risk. The future is uncertain. I think a group of these stocks will do very well for several years. . . . I could end up owning them for several years.[9]

Read, Read, Read

There was no secret trick to Buffett's success in Korea. He simply put pen to paper and took the necessary time to satisfy his objectives. And above all, he continued to read and read until he had developed a satisfactory core competency to invest in South Korea.

Reading, and lots of it, is the final clue to a successful search strategy. When you find a company you like, don't just read the latest annual report. Go back and read the annual reports for several years. Assess what the business was like then, and evaluate management's goals and objectives then. Did they accomplish, exceed, or fail to meet those objectives? Read the annual reports of competitors. You may discover that your initial idea has led to an even better business competitor within the same industry. Read up on industry data so you understand the underlying dynamics going on within the business. It's true that value investors ignore the macro picture and focus on the underlying business. But there's a big difference between ignoring something and being ignorant of the facts. In fact, astute investors are very well aware of the macroeconomy. For example, you might discover a wonderful oil company that looks cheap but realize that with oil trading at $150 a barrel, most of the future value comes from oil prices remaining at those levels. By understanding industry fundamentals, you will avoid such elementary mistakes. Instead, you want a business that is still growing when oil is at $60 a barrel and everything in between. Or you may decide to wait it out until a temporary setback brings oil prices down and place your bet then. The point is that by arming yourself with more and more information, you are less likely to make mistakes of commission.

If you're serious about business and investing, these publications, listed in no order of importance, should be mandatory reading:

- *Financial Times*
- *Wall Street Journal*
- *Intelligent Investor* by Benjamin Graham
- *Security Analysis* by Benjamin Graham
- *The Economist* (excellent global journalism)
- *Fortune* (excellent business journalism)
- The Value Line Investment Survey
- Berkshire Hathaway Annual Letters
- *Barron's*

Suggested readings include:

- *Outstanding Investor Digest*
- *New York Times*
- *The Shanghai Daily*
- This book . . . ;)

Key Takeaways

- Start your search with the lowest-hanging fruit first—the investments of other successful value investors. Imitation is truly the sincerest form of flattery.
- Like the markets, let the media inform you, not instruct your investment decision. The world benefits from great journalism; let journalists be journalists, not stock pickers.
- Start your search for stocks in places where fundamentals are the driving force behind the ideas. Remember, these are idea lists, not buy lists.
- The more time you spend, the more ideas you can come up with.
- Remember that plenty of value traps surround cheap bargain investments.
- Read as much as you can about businesses, the economy, and industries.
- *Always, always do your homework.*

CHAPTER 6

Effective Business Valuation

THE THIRD ELEMENT

If you have to go through too much investigation, something is wrong.

—Warren Buffett

I don't think investment is that hard. It's doing the simple things on a regular basis.

—Paul Clitheroe,
Australian financial writer

You might find it silly to title a chapter "Effective Business Valuation," implying that one *chapter* can do what Ben Graham and David Dodd did in 700-plus pages of *Security Analysis.* Just as there is no one way to value all businesses, no one chapter will ever give you every detail on how to value all businesses. However, if you recall from my example in Chapter 1 about our bicycle shop, the ultimate considerations were based on a few variables: operating history, future cash flow generation, competitive threats, and the price of the business.

Any sensible business valuation hinges on a few critical points. For instance, when looking at oil companies, two variables dominate the analysis: the company's production level and the price of oil *over the long run.* These two variables alone represent the critical valuation metrics of oil companies. While no two businesses can ever be valued in identical fashion, when it comes to valuing any business, a large portion of the valuation will hinge on a small handful of variables.

Does this suggest that investors should ignore the little details? Absolutely not. Serious investment requires a keen knowledge of all the information. One of the wonderful aspects of investing is that you are constantly learning something new each day. One business's negligible data could be another's relevant information. Back to our oil analogy, in addition to the oil price and production level, you would also pay attention to production costs. This is helpful as you begin comparing different oil companies. When the price of oil is artificially high, it would appear that all oil companies are extremely profitable, thus making management look very competent to shareholders. Excessively high profits based on the price of oil are beyond the control of management. What management can control, however, are production costs. And when oil prices decline, oil companies with the right blend of rising production levels and stable production costs will benefit while the undisciplined companies hurt. The point of all this is to expand on the quote of Paul Clitheroe at the beginning of this chapter: Business valuation is not that hard if you train yourself to look at the important things over and over.

When the topic of business valuation is discussed in investing circles, lots of words are thrown around, such as intrinsic value, margin of safety, free cash flow, discount rate, and so on. These are all very important concepts that are at the core of valuing a business. Before getting started in valuing any business, it's important to have a true understanding of these terms and concepts.

Value Investing 101: Margin of Safety

Warren Buffett calls margin of safety the "the three most important words in all of investing,"[1] and Benjamin Graham gave rise to the term in *The Intelligent Investor,* where he devoted an entire chapter to expanding on its importance as the central concept in any investment operation. The concept of a margin of safety is the supreme foundation of *any business valuation.* The margin of safety eliminates catastrophic investment risks. When many investors are first thinking about what gains an investment offers, the investor focused on a margin of safety first thinks about the likelihood of permanent loss an investment offers.

The idea of a margin of safety stems from the reality that no investor, not even Buffett, can determine the exact intrinsic value of any business. Because a company's intrinsic value is derived from aninvestor's calculated set of assumptions, intrinsic value is merely an approximation. Sure, an investor as skilled as Buffett probably would have a *better* approximation of intrinsic value than most, but then again he's been investing a lot longer than most of us. Nonetheless, his assessment of intrinsic value is still an approximation. When you invest with a margin of safety, you're investing in such a way that your success is not dependent on exact accuracy future forecasts.

This is why the margin-of-safety concept is of paramount importance to the valuation process. It gives the investor a degree of protection from the market's uncertainties. There is no formula that determines how wide a margin of safety you need. Obviously the wider the better, and many value investors like a 50 percent margin of safety to feel really comfortable with making an investment. And anything less than 25 percent is not significant. Remember, the point of a margin of safety is to account for the fact that you are making estimates about the future results of the business and any temporary uncertainties in the marketplace. Ultimately, the business will dictate the degree of a margin of safety. A 30 percent margin of safety in Wal-Mart is likely better than a 50 percent margin of safety in the Cheesecake Factory because you can estimate with a higher degree of certainty the future cash flows of a large, stable business that dominates its industry like Wal-Mart versus a discretionary restaurant like the Cheesecake Factory that competes with thousands of restaurants each day. The margin of safety is like an investor's insurance policy. The wider the coverage of that policy, the more protection you have. Investing with a margin of safety does not eliminate investment loss. Investing with a margin of safety, however, does reduce the likelihood of losing significant sums of money in any particular investment.

Investing with a margin of safety of your choice means that your first goal when looking to invest is to focus on return *of*—not *on*—capital. Once you've determined a floor price based on a fundamental valuation approach, then investing at or below that floor price ensures that your return of capital is not at a high risk of loss.

The most common type of margin of safety occurs when a company's tangible assets far exceed its market value. Graham was famous for seeking out net-net values, or securities selling for less than two-thirds of current assets, less all liabilities. That's the ultimate margin of safety. In a situation like this, if the company were to liquidate, the odds are very good that the equity investors would get their capital back. But as more investors have entered the game, these special situations have become exceedingly more difficult to find.

Many investors have a hard time grasping the concept of a margin of safety because it requires them to truly separate the value of the business from the price of the stock. By way of example, suppose XYZ Corp. was determined to have an intrinsic value of $50 a share and the current stock price was $30 a share, implying a very comfortable 40 percent margin of safety. Suppose over the next month the share price declines 33 percent and now trades at $20 a share. In many cases, the declining stock price would scare investors away although the margin of safety has just gotten wider. Suppose, however, that the stock price declined to $20 and the intrinsic value declined $10 to $40. Both have declined, but your margin of safety is still very wide. While declining stock prices seem to imply greater risk to many investors, a declining stock price accompanied by a stable intrinsic value *actually gives investors less risk because the margin of safety is higher.*

So, the question on many investors' minds is: How and when will the stock price reach intrinsic value?

The concept of a margin of safety will be more meaningful and understandable after the discussion on intrinsic value, which is the next concept to be covered. Keep in mind that a margin of safety is affected by the intrinsic value of the business. When the intrinsic value changes, so does your margin of safety, and you'll need to determine whether to keep holding the investment or dispose of it.

Any further attempt at investing intelligently becomes useless and potentially disastrous if you do not incorporate the concept of a margin of safety. Intrinsic values, discounted cash flow assumptions, and other fundamental tools are ineffective if you forget the concept of a margin of safety. Everything you will read in this book centers around this fundamental concept; never forgot it in any single investment consideration.

Value Investing 201: Intrinsic Value

To have a satisfactory margin of safety, you first must determine a company's intrinsic value, because a margin of safety occurs only when a business can be acquired at a significant discount to its intrinsic value. The wider the gap, the stronger the margin of safety. Warren Buffett likes to invest with a 50 percent margin of safety. Mason Hawkins at Longleaf Partners says his group looks for businesses trading at 60 percent or less of intrinsic value. The key focus is to look for opportunities with the widest degrees of margin of safety.

Intrinsic value is a term that is often cited by value investors. It's a very important concept because all investment decisions should be based on the current market value of the business—the number of shares outstanding multiplied by the current stock price—relative to the true intrinsic value of the business.

What Is Intrinsic Value?

Every business has an intrinsic value. According to John Burr Williams in his 1938 publication *The Theory of Investment Value*, intrinsic value is determined by the cash inflows and outflows—discounted at an appropriate interest rate—that can be expected to occur during the remaining life of the business. The reliance on cash flows instead of profits is critical in determining intrinsic value. At the end of the day, it's all about the cash that the business generates. Cash is real and tangible and cannot be manipulated as profits can. For example, a company can easily increase its sales and hence its profits by extending very generous credit terms to its customers. When you use your Macy's charge card to make a purchase at Macy's, the sale has been made and is recorded. But until you pay your bill, the cash has not been received. The profits look good because of the increased sales, but the cash flow shows the real financial picture.

The definition of intrinsic value is painfully simple. Let's consider an illustration.

Imagine that at the end of this year, your local movie-rental store is up for sale, and the owner is offering it at $500,000 today. Further, let's assume that the movie store can be sold for $400,000 after 10 years. The store generates free cash flow—money that can be pulled out of the business—of $100,000 a year for the next 10 years. Meanwhile, you have an alternative low-risk investment opportunity that would yield an annualized 10 percent return on that same $500,000. Tables 6.1 and 6.2 display the results of discounted cash flow analysis of both investment options. Should you buy the movie store, or take the virtually assured 10 percent return? Take a look.

Obviously, the intrinsic value of the $500,000 invested at 10 percent and discounted at 10 percent is exactly $500,000. The movie-store investment provides a better investment opportunity, provided that your annual cash flow and sale price are virtually assured.

Table 6.1 Discounted Cash Flows of 10 Percent Low-Risk Investment

Year	Free Cash Flow	Present Value of Cash Flows
2008	$50,000	$45,454
2009	$50,000	$41,322
2010	$50,000	$37,566
2011	$50,000	$34,151
2012	$50,000	$31,046
2013	$50,000	$28,224
2014	$50,000	$25,658
2015	$50,000	$23,325
2016	$50,000	$21,205
2017	$50,000	$19,277
2018	Return of $500,000 Investment	$192,772
Total		$500,000

Table 6.2 Discounted Cash Flows of 10 Percent Movie Store

Year	Free Cash Flow	Present Value of Cash Flows
2008	$100,000	$90,909
2009	$100,000	$82,645
2010	$100,000	$75,131
2011	$100,000	$68,301
2012	$100,000	$62,092
2013	$100,000	$56,447
2014	$100,000	$51,315
2015	$100,000	$46,650
2016	$100,000	$42,410
2017	$100,000	$38,554
2018	Sale Price of $400,000	$154,217
Total		$768,674

For the most part, however, cash flows are never guaranteed, and that's why the intrinsic value figure is only an approximate value, not an exact amount. Yet it does provide the most *accurate* approximation of a business's true worth. The better your understanding of a business, the better your calculation of intrinsic value will be. And the more data and reasoning you have, the more accurate your intrinsic value becomes.

Comparing the two investment opportunities, you see that the movie store is worth over 50 percent more at the end of the 10-year period. Thus, it may *seem* that there exists a 50 percent margin of safety in making the movie-store investment when compared to the low-risk investment. Such a level of safety is valuable because it protects you, the investor, from uncertainties that may arise over the course of the next 10 years. A new movie store could open up and take away a little (or a lot of business), which would affect the cash flows. In reality, several other factors must be considered before determining that such a wide margin of safety exists in the movie store versus the low-risk investment.

This example was deliberately simplified to illustrate how intrinsic values are calculated and how to determine the margin of safety. The price, or $500,000, is where it all begins. Had the movie store been selling for $700,000, you can see from the numbers that you have very little room for error in your analysis. Also, annual cash flows were kept stagnant, which is not what happens in most businesses. And as you can see, the most significant variable in an intrinsic value analysis is the discount rate applied to the cash flows.

A Primer on the Discount Rate

Most of us are familiar with the concept of the time value of money. Simply put, a dollar today is worth more than a dollar in the future. It's easy to see why. If someone offered you $1,000 today or $1,000 three years from now, you'll take the money now and put it in an interest-bearing account, and it will be worth more three years from now.

When valuing the cash flows that a business will generate years from now, you need to discount them back to the present to see what they are worth today. When calculating intrinsic value, you want to compare the intrinsic value today with the market value today.

There's a never-ending discussion about the appropriate discount rate to use when calculating intrinsic values. Many investors and the examples in this book use 10 percent as a default discount rate. Ten percent is often cited as a good multiple because of the historical market return of 8 to 10 percent a year. And the historical market return is a function of historical corporate profit growth rates, which average in the high single digits when you combine stable slow growth businesses with younger, more rapidly growing businesses.

However, the most important consideration when thinking about applying a discount rate is the reliability of the cash flows over a period of years. More reliable cash flows can be assigned lower discount rates because the lower the discount rate, the higher the present value of the cash flows. This makes sense when you consider the safest investments on the planet, U.S. Treasuries, which are bonds that are backed by the full faith and credit of the United States government. When investors speak of U.S. Treasuries, they are often referring to the 10-year note, which yielded 3.75 percent in June 2009. Like our 10-year low-risk investment chart, if you buy a $1,000 10-year Treasury note that pays 3.75 percent a year, you are guaranteed two things: that you will earn 3.75 percent per year ($37.50) and get your $1,000 back after 10 years. U.S. Treasury notes are similar to certificates of deposit at banks, except that your money is backed by the government.

Since you know that your cash flows and principal is guaranteed, U.S. Treasury notes serve as an initial starting point for figuring out the appropriate discount rate. Corporate cash flows are not as safe and secure as U.S. Treasury cash flows, so any discount rate used to determine the intrinsic value of a business should be higher than 3.75 percent. The issue then becomes what rate is appropriate: 5 percent, 10 percent, 15 percent, or something else?

This is when investing becomes part art and part science. If you use too low a discount rate, then lots of not-so-great businesses will look cheap relative to the intrinsic value. Use too high a discount rate and every business looks overpriced. While many brilliant investors advocate using 10 percent as a discount rate, in no way should it be the default rate at all times. You have to account for the riskiness of the cash flows. A start-up company could easily be valued at a 25 percent discount rate while a business like Coca-Cola could be valued using something less than 10 percent. You can be comfortable knowing that the world will continue to drink Coke, and you have decades of cash flow generation to back you up. But if you're trying to value a new restaurant chain, you have to account for the lack of operating history, future competitive threats, and so on. I wish there were a scientific formula for applying discount rates, but if there were, investing wouldn't be investing.

The other companion to the discount rate is the growth rate in the cash flows. By now you might conclude that a 10 percent discount rate for the movie-store example was too low a figure. The example was used to illustrate the significance of intrinsic value and the margin of safety. Based on the competitive landscape for movie rentals, however, 10 percent was not an appropriate discount rate, especially if we are assigning a 10 percent discount to the low-risk investment. A much higher discount rate would need to be applied in order to get a more conservative intrinsic value for the movie store.

Ideally if you are investing in a business, you are doing so because you are confident that, over time, the business will be earning more profits and thus generating higher levels of cash flow. But again, projecting cash flow growth rates is also an estimate and an estimate can easily be different from the actual future results.

There's a good reason why guys like Buffett stick to simple, easy-to-understand businesses. Determining the cash flows of a business such as Wrigley or Coca-Cola several years out will likely prove to be more accurate than figuring out how much cash Advanced Micro Devices will produce.

Value Investing 301: Seek Businesses with a Wide Moat

Since calculating an intrinsic value involves predicting future cash flows, you need to have some reasonable confidence in the future earnings growth of a business. For earnings to grow, a company needs to increase revenue and at least maintain costs. And for the most part, increased earnings *should* lead to increased cash flows in the long run. Don't spend a lot of time looking at one-time quarterly charges and the like when you're looking for increased cash flows. Instead, you might want to look at annual cash flow statements for signs of a good, healthy increase in the rate of cash flow growth.

Businesses that have competitive advantages or wide moats around them usually throw off tons of cash, and they allow you to predict future cash flows with a higher degree of certainty. Once you find an attractive business that you understand, you need to determine whether the business has staying power or is under constant threat from new entrants. An investment approach that focuses on investing in wide-moat businesses and avoiding the no-moat businesses will produce satisfactory long-term results.

The definition of a great business with a wide moat is one that has at least some of these characteristics:

- Recurring revenue streams
- Ability to produce at low costs
- A monopoly or oligopoly type of market positioning

- A strong franchise or brand that gives the company insulation from most of the competition
- Ability to raise prices ahead of inflation

Let's look at some examples of businesses that have one or more of these characteristics.

"The Security I Like Best"

Insurance companies take in a lot of premiums up front and pay out claims at a later date. Find an insurance business that masters the art of taking in the *most* and paying out the *least*, and you have yourself a wonderful business. Warren Buffett knew that when he found GEICO, one of the nation's largest auto insurers. He wrote an article about the company, titled "The Security I Like Best," when he was 21—long before he bought it. Even then, Buffett saw that GEICO had a recurring revenue stream that would never go away as long as humans use cars.

By insuring drivers all over the country, GEICO naturally shields itself from the risk of being geographically concentrated. It also has a history of insuring the *best* drivers, so its claims payout is low. That means GEICO can lower its premium, which it does. And that gives the company a good, wide moat.

Monopolistic Tendencies

Companies that dominate their industry tend to do quite well over the long run. American Express is a wonderful example of a business operating in a monopolistic type of industry. For decades, credit cards and travelers' checks were synonymous with AmEx, and if you look at the company today, you can still find tons of cash generation, despite the current restrictive credit environment.

Home Depot and Lowe's are other great examples of businesses that own their industry. Without exception, Home Depot, Lowe's, and American Express have rewarded people who have invested in them for the long term. Odds are next to nil that a new mega-store home improvement retailing chain will open up. It would take way too much time and capital.

The Real Value of Competitive Advantages

Value investors often speak of efforts to seek out wonderful businesses run by capable, competent management with a durable competitive or economic advantage. But what does a "competitive advantage" really mean for a company?

A true competitive advantage exists in only a few forms. The simplest type occurs when a government grants licenses to a few companies and excludes everyone else. Cable companies, electric utilities, and telephone companies are the most common. But these companies don't enjoy the same incumbent competitive advantages they did 50 years ago.

Other competitive advantages exist when a company is the low-cost producer (such as USG in wallboard), holds a patent (which is good for a finite period of time), or possesses another attribute that turns potential competitors away. However, to truly understand the value of competitive advantage, it's best to follow Charlie Munger's advice and "invert" the process: understand where competitive advantages don't exist.

Commodity-type businesses rarely have sustainable competitive advantages. Ultimately, they must share the market space with many competitors until the economic profit is zero or, in other words, the cost of capital is equal to the required rate of return that investors demand on their money.

To illustrate my point: A hypothetical company, Soft Pillow Inc., makes pillows. Soft Pillow has been quite successful and has earned $10 million each year for the past three years. Its investors are willing to accept a 10 percent return on their investment. This gives

Soft Pillow an earnings value of $100 million (earnings value = 1/ cost of capital of 10 percent).

Soft Pillow has $50 million in assets, which includes both tangible and intangible assets. A potential competitor will look at this company and realize that for an investment of $50 million, it, too, can command an earnings value of $100 million. And if the market assigns Soft Pillow a value of $120 million, the gap is wider, which is even more of an inducement for competitors.

So what happens next? A new company will put up $50 million and start making similar pillows, so now Soft Pillow earns only $7 million. It now has an earnings value of $70 million. A second competitor will be induced by the opportunity to invest $50 million in a company that has an earnings value of $70 million. The process continues until earnings for Soft Pillow reach $5 million, at which point there is no excess profit to be made. Soft Pillow, a good company, resolves to earn only its cost of capital and no more. Sure, commodity companies could tinker with their products to differentiate them, but so will everyone else in the long run. In the end, you're back where you started.

The Franchise Value

The last example illustrates how having no competitive advantage will slowly erode a business's profits. Franchise-type businesses, however, are extremely valuable. Simply defined, a franchise exists where a company benefits from barriers to entry that keep potential competitors away. A strong franchise virtually insures that if competitors enter, they will operate at a severe disadvantage. In 1987, Warren Buffett and Charlie Munger invested $1 billion from Berkshire Hathaway's cash pile into Coca-Cola Company. At the time, this investment represented more than 20 percent of Berkshire's book value! You won't find a more dominant franchise than Coca-Cola. If someone offered you $1 billion to go out and build a new soft-drink company to compete with Coke, you couldn't do it no matter how brilliant you are. Although the Coke franchise is unique in the world, plenty of examples exist. Johnson & Johnson, Wrigley's, and Gillette are names that easily come to mind.

You need look no further than these companies to see the awesome value of a franchise. Coca-Cola benefits from the advantage of having high switching costs. As you drink more Cokes, you begin to develop a habit that's hard to break. Or as Buffett remarks, who is willing to save a nickel on chewing gum, a product that you put in your mouth? I can't think of anyone who will give up Coke for another brand to save a dime per can. If you're traveling in a foreign country, I'd be willing to bet that you grab a Coke, not the local brand. Coke has an amazing moat that will likely stay strong for a very long time.

Same goes for Gillette razors. Buffett loved the idea that each morning millions of men woke up to use a product they would have to replace on a regular basis. How many people would sacrifice the safety of their face or legs to go with a cheaper, inferior razor?

When you can find a company with a truly remarkable, durable competitive advantage at an attractive price, you can follow Buffett's mantra about holding stocks forever. As you can surmise from the names listed, it's not easy to build up a franchise. Many of the most dominant businesses have been around for decades and have spent billions over many years developing themselves. But the efforts and expenditures can pay off immensely. Franchise businesses consistently earn rates of return way above their cost of capital, and they do so without serious threat from outsiders.

While the best returns may have already come and gone for businesses such as Coke and Home Depot, capitalism never fails to produce a new crop of companies in industries that could become the next investment of the same caliber. Great investments like this aren't easy to find. But they are out there, and a little diligence (and good search strategy) can lead you to them.

Value Investing 401: Calculating a True Intrinsic Value

By now it is clear why the concept of margin of safety, the reliance on intrinsic value to make investing decisions, and the value of great businesses with wide economic moats is central to the value investing approach. Once you've taken those steps and found a business that looks attractive, you next need to determine the intrinsic value of that business, to find out whether an undervalued investment opportunity exists. In Chapter 10, some case studies illustrate both the qualitative and quantitative connection in valuing a business. But for now, let's calculate the intrinsic value of a real life publicly traded company using actual financial statement numbers. Keep in mind that this example is provided merely to illustrate how you would go about using the actual numbers from a company's actual operating results.

As a refresher, intrinsic value is determined by the cash inflows and outflows—discounted at an appropriate interest rate—that can be expected to occur during the remaining life of the business.

This definition is painfully simple, but it works. Let's apply it to a couple of businesses so you can see for yourself.

Intrinsic Value Analysis: ENSCO Corp

Ensco is one of the world's premier global offshore oil and gas drilling contractors. It charters out its fleet of offshore oil drilling rigs to various oil companies all over the world. For those unfamiliar with the oil industry, oil rigs or oil platforms are the large structures that oil companies use to drill wells into the ocean bed, extract oil, and ship the oil back to shore. Table 6.3 is a condensed cash flow statement taken from Google Finance.

In looking at Table 6.3, the number needed is the free cash flow figure, which we have to calculate. Free cash flow simply defined is equal the cash flow from operating activities (CFFO) less capital

Table 6.3 Ensco Corp. Cash Flow Statement

USD (except for per share items)	12 Months Ending 2007-12-31	12 Months Ending 2006-12-31	12 Months Ending 2005-12-31	12 Months Ending 2004-12-31
Net income/starting line	992.00	769.70	284.90	93.00
Depreciation/depletion	184.30	175.00	153.40	133.00
Amortization	–	–	–	–
Deferred taxes	0.40	15.90	6.90	18.90
Non-cash items	38.50	24.40	23.20	35.50
Changes in working capital	26.80	-37.50	-110.10	-24.80
Cash from operating activities	1,242.00	947.50	358.30	255.60
Capital expenditures	-519.90	-528.60	-477.10	-304.50
Other investing cash flow items, total	7.70	26.60	135.40	-8.40
Cash from investing activities	-512.20	-502.00	-341.70	-312.90
Financing cash flow items	2.50	2.60	-8.10	1.50
Total cash dividends paid	-14.80	-15.30	-15.20	-15.10
Issuance (retirement) of stock, net	-485.80	-118.20	67.20	7.80
Issuance (retirement) of debt, net	-167.20	-17.10	-58.30	-23.00
Cash from financing activities	-665.30	-148.00	-14.40	-28.80
Foreign exchange effects	-0.80	-0.20	-0.70	-0.90
Net change in cash	63.70	297.30	1.50	-87.00
Cash interest paid, supplemental	4.60	15.30	29.70	33.40
Cash taxes paid, supplemental	214.30	206.30	143.10	18.00

Source: Google Finance (finance.google.com).

Table 6.4   Ensco Free Cash Flow ($ millions)

Year	CFFO	Cap Ex	Free Cash Flow
2004	$256	$304	–$48
2005	$358	$477	–$119
2006	$948	$528	$420
2007	$1242	$520	$722

expenditures. Table 6.4 shows the four-year period, 2004 to 2007, free cash flow.

A couple of observations should grab your attention. First, Ensco is becoming more and more profitable. Cash flow from operations has grown at a phenomenal rate, not surprising for a smaller player in the oil services industry. Second, although capital expenditures are increasing as the company grows and expands its fleet, they are more than offset by cash generated from operations leading to growing levels of free cash flow. Finally, the free cash flow growth rate of nearly 70 percent in 2007 is not at all indicative of future cash flow growth rates. The rate of growth will surely be much less.

As you might imagine, the demand for Ensco's services is very much affected by the price of oil. The year 2007 was a great one for oil prices, but as we saw in 2008, the economy spiraled into a nasty recession and the price of oil fell over 50 percent. However, because many major oil companies plan their drilling projects based on multiyear horizons, drilling demand won't completely die. Further, oil rigs typically are leased out on multiyear contracts, which provide some stability during weaker environments. These are some of the things that you should be aware of when forecasting future cash flows.

At the end of 2008, Ensco's CFFO was $1.2 billion and capital expenditures were $772 million, or free cash flow of $428 million. Ensco is currently in the middle of expansion plan as it seeks to acquire ultra-deepwater drilling rigs over the next few years.

Table 6.5   Ensco Discounted FCF Analysis

Year	Free Cash Flow	Present Value at 12%
2009	$450	$401
2010	$500	$399
2011	$575	$409
2012	$660	$419
2013	$760	$431
Total		$2,059

Table 6.5 shows a discounted cash flow analysis for Ensco over the next five years. To be conservative, these assumptions will be made:

- 2009 remains a slow year for the economy, so free cash flow remains stagnant at $450 million.
- Free cash flow picks back up in 2010 as cap ex declines and oil industry improves and more ultra-deepwater rigs come on board.
- 2010 free cash flow of $500 million, or an 11 percent growth rate.
- 15 percent free cash flow growth over the next three years.
- 12 percent discount rate to account for oil industry volatility.

I purposely chose a five-year analysis in this case to keep the example simple and concise. A lot can happen in 10 years, and assuming cash flow growth for 10 consecutive years can come back to haunt you. Notice also how the free cash flow figure in 2013 is almost equal 2007, a conservative assumption considering the demand for ultra-deepwater drilling rigs is expected to increase over time. Unless this business commits a major blunder, it should easily surpass 2007 levels by then, but let's stick to the listed assumptions.

The final piece is to determine the terminal value of the business, or what it would be worth to a buyer. Based on the numbers and growth rates given, a multiple of 12 times 2013 free cash flow would be appropriate. The company has the ability to grow free cash flow by 10 to 20 percent because of its relatively small size and the future increased need for oil drilling in more remote (and thus more profitable) areas. This would create a terminal value of $5.2 billion discounted back to the present. The terminal value of $5.2 billion plus the $2 billion of cash flow yields to a total value of $7.2 billion. In 2008, Ensco had 142 million shares outstanding.

Dividing the $7.2 billion by the 142 million shares outstanding produces a stock price of approximately $51 a share. So, according to the analysis, Ensco's intrinsic value is $51 a share. If the company performs better than the given assumptions, intrinsic value will be higher, and vice versa. In June of 2009, shares were trading at $35, having rallied sharply as oil prices rebounded from their precipitous decline in 2008. Having rallied over 50 percent since March 2009, Ensco shares aren't the undervalued bargain they were, based on the above analysis.

However, the initial analysis is a big step in the right direction and shows that Ensco could still be a great investment if the company delivers results stronger than those used in the above analysis. Nonetheless, investors will probably do well over time buying businesses at a 50 percent discount to intrinsic value.

Even more so, you need to know the business inside and out in order to estimate cash flow growth with a high degree of confidence. The ability to assess the quality and competence of management thus becomes critical. Knowing how management spends company dollars tells you a lot about how much cash the company will produce years down the road. In short, do your due diligence . . . and when you are done, do it *again*.

Calculating intrinsic value is simple and straightforward. It's having accurate data that's the difficult part. That's why Benjamin Graham remarked: "You are neither right nor wrong because the crowd disagrees with you. You are right because your data and reasoning are right." That's also why Warren Buffett, the best investor on the planet, spends a lot of time focusing on businesses with durable competitive advantages, such as the brand value that Coca-Cola offers, or the monopoly-like industry that American Express operates in. They are dominant businesses with consistent long-term earnings power, which adds a layer of certainty when forecasting future cash flows.

The Value of Management

No matter how much due diligence on a business is performed, all investing requires a leap of faith. Most of that faith is placed in the ability of corporate managers to utilize the assets of the business to maximize shareholder value in an honest and ethical manner. While the ability and competence of management is crucial and should be considered when making any investment, investors should carefully read and understand these quotes from Warren Buffett:

> Our conclusion is that, with a few exceptions, when management with a reputation for brilliance tackles a business with a reputation for poor fundamental economics, it is the reputation of the business that remains intact.

> You should invest in a business that even a fool can run, because someday a fool will.[2]

Management is important, but a good company is even more important. You will often hear value investors speak volumes on the superb management overseeing the companies that they have invested in, but if you look deeper, I'd imagine you will find that many of these investments are already excellent businesses. Great management at a great business is a home run. If you get both, you will be rewarded many times over if you stick with the investment.

Putting a great chief executive officer (CEO) in a great company is like icing on the cake. Such was the case when Roberto Goizueta took the top job at the Coca-Cola Company in 1981. During his time, the Coca-Cola brand became the best-known trademark in the world. Some of Coke's most famous ad campaigns, such as "Always Coca-Cola" and "You Can't Beat the Feeling," were launched under Goizueta's leadership. During the 16 years in which Goizueta ran Coke, the total return on Coke stock was more than 7,100 percent.[3] A $10,000 investment in Coca-Cola when Goizueta took the top job in 1981 was worth $710,000, including reinvested dividends, in 1997. By all measures, the 1980s and 1990s were destined to be great decades for the Coca-Cola Company. It benefited from the untapped global demand for its product along with a historical bull market in the United States. Nonetheless, no one doubts Goizueta's magic touch on the fortunes of Coke.

While management can make a vital difference, the value of quality management should be subordinate to the quality of the business. One of the finest companies in the world, Johnson & Johnson, illustrates the value of the business before the management approach. For over 100 years, Johnson & Johnson has grown its sales and profit by over 10 percent per annum. Clearly, the company has had more than one management team making acquisitions, creating expansion plans, and developing new products. Some of those management teams were more able and competent than others, yet Johnson & Johnson continued to show progress. To this day, Johnson & Johnson is one of the few companies that has unlimited growth potential with respect to the products it sells. This fact will remain true regardless of who steers the ship.

Understand, however, that this doesn't imply that any run-of-the-mill executive should steer the ship of the company. Incompetent and unethical behavior can damage a company's reputation. If the business is weak, this damage can be deadly. But if the business is loaded with strong fundamental economics, ultimately it will prevail.

Understanding all of this information helps put the management factor in perspective so you can analyze and discuss the key considerations in assessing the quality of management in a business. The next list is by no means exhaustive but it offers the most compelling considerations in "valuing" the management. In no order of importance, when investigating management, investors ought to give serious consideration to:

- Management ownership of stock
- Compensation structure of top management
- Qualifications and experience
- Operating results report card

Eating Their Own Cooking

Not many people would visit a restaurant if they discovered that the head chef was dining elsewhere. The same standard should be applied to our corporate "chefs." Nothing is more indicative of complete alignment of interest with shareholders than meaningful ownership of company stock. The proper way to determine whether ownership is meaningful is based on percentage of net worth represented by the underlying stock as well as the consideration paid for the stock.

Looking at percentage of net worth represented by stock ownership versus percentage of company owned is more meaningful especially when large companies are involved. If an executive is earning $10 million a year running a $100 billion company, owning 0.1 percent ($100 million) of the company can be very meaningful if it represents a significant portion of his or her net worth. Focusing on percentage of net worth represented by stock ownership allows for an apples-to-apples comparison when comparing management at large companies to those from smaller ones. The exception to this rule is if the CEO is a founder or other individual tightly associated with the business. For instance, Michael

Dell, founder of Dell Computer, a multibillion-dollar company ($23 billion as of December 2008) owns over 10 percent of the outstanding stock, according to a 2008 Dell Proxy Filing. Warren Buffett, who took over Berkshire Hathaway in the 1970s, owns over 30 percent of the stock.[4] In both instances, substantial portions of net worth and company ownership are involved.

How the stock is owned is also worth an investigative look. The reason has to do with stock options, or rights given to company insiders to purchase stock at a predetermined price. Debate abounds regarding use of stock options. Some defend stock options as a motivating incentive that aligns management's interest with shareholders (increasing the stock price). Others see options as a blank-check way for companies to reward management at the expense of shareholders (diluting the existing shares). Regardless of your viewpoint, what is factually accurate is that options have an asymmetric payoff structure for those who receive them. An executive who receives options benefits tremendously if the company prospers as the stock options become more valuable. If the company performs poorly, the executive is not any worse off because the options expire worthless. It's a classic case of heads you win big, tails you lose nothing.

If the majority of stock owned by insiders is in the form of options that were granted that represent little or no cost to the grantee, don't ascribe to them the same weight as you would to outright ownership of the stock. It's much more impressive and confirming of their dedication to the success of the company to see managers make outright market purchases of stock just like any other shareholder.

Understanding all of these considerations, look for management that eats their own cooking.

Executive Compensation

The debate regarding executive compensation is one without conclusion. There will always be those who view it as too generous and others who feel it's reflective of the responsibilities of the job. For purposes of this discussion, we evaluate executive compensation merely to discern the motives and intentions of management. At one end of the spectrum you have Warren Buffett, who continues to earn the same $100,000 annual salary he has been getting for decades without any bonuses or stock options. On the other end, you have Steve Jobs of Apple Computer, who took home over $646 million in 2007, the vast majority of which came in the form of vested stock options.[5] You won't see shareholders in Apple Computer complaining, however. In 2007, shares in Apple appreciated by over 120 percent, according to the Value Line Investment Survey.

For purposes of assessing the quality of management, executive compensation should be evaluated on a case-by-case basis. There is no magic formula or percentage to aid investors in this task. A businesslike frame of mind is the most valuable tool in tackling the appropriateness of executive compensation for each company. For instance, is it appropriate for the CEO of a $30 million dollar company to earn $1 million in a year during which the company's operating performance has deteriorated? Nearly everyone would answer in the negative. Conversely, Apple shareholders will have no problem with Steve Jobs earning over $600 million in cash and stock in a single year in which he doubled shareholder investments.

With the exception of extreme outlier scenarios, the appropriateness of executive compensation for any business will differ from investor to investor. The key for the value-oriented investor is to consider the compensation in the context of the overall value created in the business.

Qualifications and Experience

There is no need to dwell on the obvious. In most cases, a company's board of directors will ensure that an adequately qualified candidate is running the company. But it doesn't hurt to spend a little time getting to know the skills of the man or woman responsible for the company.

Often a simple reading of the annual proxy filing will give you a good idea. If the current CEO was once CEO of another company that did exceptionally well under his or her tenure, all the better. The main reason to investigate here is to catch any red flags that may surface. For instance if a pharmaceutical company has a CEO who used to work in the fashion industry, you might want to dig a little deeper. Most times, any concern arises from recent management changes. If a CEO has been in charge for many years, there's usually a good reason for that.

Operating Results Report Card

The heading refers to how the company has performed under current management. Obviously it's not fair to judge newly appointed management, so this discussion is limited to management that has been in charge for at least four years, enough time for the market to react to the true fundamentals of the business.

In valuing management, many investors mistakenly focus on the performance of the stock price as the proxy for quality management. In the long run, if the fundamental operating metrics of a company have improved, management usually will pass the stock price performance test. Ben Graham explained this as being due to the fact that markets are voting machines in the short run but weighing machines in the long run.

While stock price performance ultimately matters, it's important for investors to rate management more on the things they can control. For instance, when evaluating oil companies, if the underlying price of a barrel of oil is increasing, most oil companies' stock prices will rise in response. In such instances, managements across the entire industry will appear to have done an excellent operating job when, in fact, the price of oil, an uncontrollable item, was responsible for the increased value. Management has no control over the price of oil, but it does have control over exploration costs, an excellent barometer of long-term value creation or destruction. In the short run, focusing on stock price performance can hide management's true operating skill.

In evaluating the quality of management, focus on the variables that management can control. Concentrate on the operational efficiency of the business: in other words, how the money is being spent. In trade terms, this commonly is referred to as capital allocation. Discover a great capital allocator and you will have discovered a great manager. Good capital allocation can be judged by two controllable variables within a business: book value per share and return on invested capital.

The Net Value of a Business

Book value is the net worth of a business. It's equal to a company's assets minus all its liabilities. Great managers focus on increasing book value each and every year. There's nothing more obvious than the value created from increasing the per share book value of a business. If a company's per share book value is higher than it was the previous year, then value was created. It's that simple. Naturally, long-term annual growth in per share book value is more indicative of superior operating performance. Management has no control over the value of the stock price; it does have complete control over the assets of the business and hence the change in book value each and every year. Since Warren Buffett began writing the Berkshire Hathaway letter to shareholders, he begins each one in this way:

> Our gain in net worth in 2007 was . . . which increased the per share book value of both our Class A and Class B stock by 11%. Over the last 43 years (that is, since present management took over) book value has grown . . . [at] a rate of 21.1% compounded annually.

By starting each annual letter this way, Buffett is defining the ultimate yardstick that should be used to grade management:

the performance of book value per share. Book value per share is affected by changes in three categories: a change in assets, a change in liabilities, or a change in the number of shares outstanding. All three factors are at the complete discretion of management. While stock price performance and book value performance might not behave similarly in the short run, a long-term pattern of increasing book value ultimately will be followed by a similar performance from the stock price.

Great Managers Focus on Return on Invested Capital

Value creation is simple to understand in the context of a business. If the business is investing its capital in projects that generate rates of return that exceed the cost of that capital, value is being created. It's no good if a company is earning 8 percent on its invested capital if the cost of capital is 10 percent.

A common definition for return on invested capital (ROIC) is the net after-tax operating profit divided by invested capital. Operating income, or operating revenue minus operating expense, is the purest form of judging a business's results. Operating income strips out nonrecurring items and interest costs, which (excluding those of financial service firms) don't have much to do with the actual business itself. The formula for the return is:

$$(1 - \text{tax rate}) \times (\text{earning before interest and taxes})$$

Invested capital (IC), as you would imagine, measures how much capital a company has invested in its business. Although there are many different ways of measuring IC, a generally sound way of calculating is:

$$(\text{total assets} - \text{cash}) - (\text{noninterest-bearing current liabilities})$$

Basically, this equation says that the capital invested is the sum of all the assets, and subtracts out the assets that haven't yet been invested (cash and cash equivalents). Noninterest-bearing current liabilities are also subtracted out because they represent "interest-free" loans. For example, if you own a shoe store and a supplier extends you credit to buy and sell its shoes, no capital was dispensed to get the use of the assets (the shoes), so this doesn't go into the IC equation. What we're left with is the total invested capital. Many different investors have subtle differences in the way they calculate ROIC, but the general idea of what you are after is the same: the return a business generates relative to the capital deployed to get that return. When the return on capital is greater than the cost of capital—usually measured as the weighted average cost of capital—the company is creating value; when it is less than the cost of capital, value is destroyed.

Capital comes in two forms, debt and equity. Calculating the cost of debt is relatively simple, as it is comprised of the rate of interest paid on the debt. The cost of equity is a bit more complicated, as equity typically does not pay a return to its investors. In specific cases—such as real estate investment trusts and energy master limited partnerships—the high dividend yield can represent an accurate cost of equity, but in general, calculating the cost of equity is not as clear-cut as calculating the cost of debt. Modern finance theory uses the capital asset pricing model (CAPM) to determine the cost of equity. Under the assumptions of CAPM, inputs such a stock's beta (or volatility) are used to determine the cost of equity capital. Because value investors often disregard beta as an inappropriate measure of risk, the CAPM model is flawed. The cost of equity should merely reflect the sum of the risk free rate of return (refer back to the discussion on discount rate earlier in the chapter) and an equity risk premium. Similar to the discount rate, the equity risk premium will vary depending on the company in question. Wal-Mart's cost of equity, and hence its equity risk premium, will be a lot less than the cost of equity for Ford Motor Company. Given the market confidence in the greater stability of Wal-Mart's operating revenues compared to that of Ford, investors will demand a lower

Table 6.6 American Eagle Outfitters (NYSE: AEO)

Metric	Value ($ millions)
Earnings before interest and taxes	$297
Total assets	$1,963
Cash	$473
Accounts payable	$327
Tax rate	37%

Source: Yahoo! Finance.

equity risk premium from Wal-Mart leading to a lower cost of equity for Wal-Mart.

Let's examine a simple ROIC calculation for American Eagle Outfitters, a specialty retailer. Table 6.6 looks at the numbers for the fiscal year 2008.

ROIC = Return/Invested Capital
Return = $(1-0.37) \times (297) = \$187$
Invested Capital = $(1,963-473) - (327) = \$1,163$
ROIC = $\$187/\$1,163 = 16\%$

American Eagle's 2007 ROIC was a very respectable 16 percent. In 2008, the company had no debt, so its cost of debt was zero. As for the cost of equity, with the risk-free rate around 3 to 4 percent, assigning an equity risk premium of 10 percent still suggests that American Eagle is indeed delivering value in the atmosphere of one of the worst retail environments in decades. One year is certainly not indicative of long-term value creation, but in years past American Eagle generated equally impressive returns on invested capital. While impressive, American Eagle's ROIC is down from the 28 percent it earned in 2007. If the retail environment remains choked by the cautious U.S. consumer, such impressive figures may be a thing of the past, at least over the next few years.

When a company has no debt, the return on equity (ROE) can be just as meaningful as ROIC. In the next section, we see how an understanding of this concept helped create one of the world's most successful companies.

Understanding Return on Equity: Microsoft Corporation

While profits are essential, understanding how they fit into the value creation process is critical. This is where return on equity comes into play.

An initial yet meaningful way of looking at return on equity is similar to a coupon on a bond. A bond that earns a higher coupon yield than the prevailing rate of interest will trade at a premium, or above its par issued price. A bond that is issued paying 10 percent a year will be worth more in the future if future rates on interest have declined. The reason is simple economics: No investors will pay the same price for an 8 percent bond if they can buy a 10 percent bond for the same price. So the price of the existing 10 percent bonds will increase until the new market price represents an approximate 8 percent effective yield. If the bond had a face value of $1,000 and initially paid $100 a year, its new price would be $1,250 because at an annual payment of $100, the return is 8 percent. Similar to a bond in a fundamental sense, businesses with sustained high returns on equity usually are followed by appreciating stock prices, but not for the same specific reasons as bonds. In the real world, of course, investors in stocks don't just buy and hold. In the long run, the rate of return of a stock should equal its return on equity.

Consider Microsoft. Microsoft continues to deliver unbelievable returns on equity of over 40 percent and has done so for decades. Yet for years, Microsoft shares have not followed suit. The times are different. In the beginning, Microsoft had lots of space in the software market to deploy its capital. So when Microsoft was generating an ROE of, say, 40 percent, it was able to continue investing that excess capital and generate a similar rate of return. What this means is that Microsoft could take $1 million, invest it in its operations, and earn $400,000. Microsoft could then take the excess capital and still earn that same 40 percent. It was able to do this with billions of dollars, years before the Internet boom.

It is no surprise, then, that Microsoft stock rocketed for many years after its initial public offering and why early investors, Bill Gates, and company employees got so fantastically rich off the stock. The company was compounding existing and excess capital at a phenomenal clip. Anytime you can do this for a sustained amount of time, the intrinsic value of a business mushrooms and eventually so will the stock price.

Microsoft still generates returns on equity of over 40 percent, yet the stock price sits still. Microsoft is so huge and has so much cash that now it is able to generate those returns only on the capital needed to run the business. It can no longer take the excess capital and redeploy it at such a high rate of return. This is why it paid a huge dividend a few years back. It made more sense to pay out some of that excess capital to shareholders than to reinvest back in the business.

Anytime you locate a company that offers the talent and the ability to redeploy its existing and excess capital at above-market rates of return for any sustainable period of time, odds are the stock price will follow suit. An ability to earn excess returns on equity signals that the company offers certain competitive advantages not easily reproduced by its competitors.

In the 1980s, Warren Buffett bet over 20 percent of Berkshire's book value on the Coca-Cola Company. Buffett noticed, among other things, that Coke was earning excellent returns on its equity and deployed the excess capital into other infant markets. Berkshire Hathaway itself is a huge capital deployment vehicle. It takes the float from its insurance company and any excess cash from its operating subsidiaries and invests the excess capital very successfully. Berkshire has risen an amazing 7,000-fold since Buffett took control of the company in 1965.

Profits and earnings growth are vital. But what businesses are able to do to with those profits sets apart great businesses from good ones.

In 1978, Warren Buffett wrote an article for *Fortune* magazine titled "How Inflation Swindles the Equity Investor." In it, he noted that there are only five ways to improve return on equity:

1. Higher turnover, that is, sales
2. Cheaper leverage
3. More leverage
4. Lower taxes
5. Wider margins on sales

Companies have the least control over tax levels, although management certainly can use creative accounting to alter the tax rate temporarily. Investors would do better focusing on the other four ways, as improved sales, prudent use of leverage, or cost-cutting initiatives can indicate excellent businesses.

All else equal, sales increase should create an increase in profits. Of course, you should carefully examine the quality of sales. As sales increase, the accounts receivable level should naturally follow suit. However, if receivables are demonstrating a trend of growing much faster than sales future, troubles may lie ahead when it's time to collect. Additionally, inventory management is important. The application of last in, first out or first in, first out inventory valuation methods will affect the profit statement differently during inflationary or deflationary periods.

When used prudently and wisely, leverage can increase returns on equity. Similarly, if a business can lower its cost of debt, the corresponding effect is a higher return on equity. Today we are seeing exactly how the mismanagement of leverage has affected those businesses participating in the credit markets. The painful lesson is similar to buying stocks on margin. If you are leveraged 5 to 1, a 10 percent return on the leveraged portfolio equals a return on equity of 50 percent. The same corresponding loss occurs with negative returns. Unfortunately, most businesses fail to use leverage appropriately and opportunistically and employ leverage at alarming multiples to equity. The results, as we can clearly see, have been disastrous.

Wider margins are created in one of two ways: increasing prices or decreasing costs. Very few companies can raise prices at will without incurring competition or meaningful declines in volume. Again, this is why Buffett bet so big on Coke. For decades, Coke has been steadily increasing the price of its famous syrup with no meaningful loss in market share as a result.

Profits count, but it's what you can do with those profits over time that really matters.

Key Takeaways

- Business valuation is a blend of art and science. Models are never completely accurate. Compensate for this by always demanding a satisfactory margin of safety.
- Knowing the intrinsic value of a business allows you to apply the margin of safety. Understand that intrinsic value is an approximation and not a precise figure.
- Seek out businesses with durable competitive advantages. They are the ones with the greatest ability to continue earning record profits, which increases the intrinsic value over time.
- Understand that the quality of the business comes before the quality of management. Fundamentally poor businesses are likely to stay that way regardless of the ability of management.
- When examining management, seek managers who eat their own cooking and are significantly invested alongside their shareholders.
- Judge management on the increase in the book value of the company, over which it has complete control, not on stock performance, which is controlled by the market.
- Invest in businesses that demonstrate consistent ability to increase book value and returns on capital. Sooner or later, the stock price will catch up with improved fundamental performance.

Have the Discipline to Say No

THE FOURTH ELEMENT

The intelligent investor is likely to need considerable willpower to keep from following the crowd.

—Benjamin Graham

Arming yourself with a sound investment philosophy and search strategy puts you on the path to selecting businesses suitable for investment. Once a business is valued, the most difficult determinants of whether to invest or not come into play. Unlike valuation, which primarily relies on quantitative measures, investors now must rely on qualitative factors:

- Having the discipline to say no
- Being patient
- Having the courage to make a significant investment at a maximum point of pessimism

These factors are exceedingly important because the probability of suffering investment loss is significantly higher due to the emotional underpinnings of these factors. Consider the next fictitious example.

A particular security is selling in the market for $25 a share. The strong fundamental qualities of this security are well known, and as a result, the stock has typically traded at a fair to overvaluation. At the current price of $25 a share, the stock is indeed slightly above fair value. Eager to buy, an investor is on constant watch for any dip in stock price, but the dip never comes. Instead, over the next few weeks the stock seems only to go up in price and is now at $35. Not wanting to miss out on the continued rise, the investor rushes to buy in. In the next few weeks, the stock is back at $25 and the investor, an able and bright fellow, feels like the dumbest man on the planet. His downfall had nothing to do with intelligence. Instead, it had everything to do with emotions dictating the investment decision. Whether the security will trade above his purchase price a year from now is irrelevant. Even if that happens, it's just as foolish to dismiss the investment as an intelligent one because the investment process was manipulated by emotional decision making. Next to taking a loss, nothing is more painful than the aforementioned chain of events. Learning to say no until the price is right is of paramount importance.

Most investors are smart; few, however, are disciplined enough to say no and move on or, more important, be patient. This chapter illustrates and explains the benefits and consequences of an undisciplined investment approach versus an investment approach characterized by discipline. Very few activities in life can be practiced successfully without some degree of discipline. Being disciplined requires you to think independently and ignore crowd psychology. Discipline requires investors to be confident in their research and analysis and be prepared to receive criticism from all angles. Yet disciplined investors clearly realize that investment success comes from sticking to their methods and not participating in crowd folly.

In Investing, Discipline is Everything

Rarely do you find a field where the level of intelligence is not directly proportional to long-term success. Investing in the stock market is one such area. After a certain level of competency with respect to fundamental mathematics and reading comprehension, your success as an investor is no longer predominantly dependent on how much smarter you are than the rest of the field. Instead, discipline and temperament take over as the defining contributors to long-term success. After a certain IQ level, an increased IQ does not guarantee added investment success.

Referring to our fictitious example, the ultimate failure (or success) of the investment decision was not based on intelligence but on emotion. The investor could not allow himself to "miss" the continued rise in the price of stock. Disregarding any fundamentals whatsoever, he made the assumption that because the shares had continued to go up for weeks, they would continue to do so. What is important here is not the investment performance but rather *the process employed to make the investment.*

In many ways, investing is very similar to baseball. One particular similarity stands out. A batter who bats .300 during his career will in all likelihood reach the Hall of Fame. Such is not the case if your batting average is .250. The difference between a .250 batter and a .300 batter is 50 more hits for every 1,000 at bats. Think about this for a moment. The difference between making it to the Hall of Fame rests on achieving 5 extra hits during every 100 times at bat. An additional 5 percent success rate is the key to immortality in baseball. Achieving long-term successful investment results runs in a very similar way. A successful market-beating investment track record is not reliant on having an abnormally high success rate. It is possible to be right 30 to 40 percent of time in your investment picks and still deliver hall of fame type results. The key is to make sure that the winners grossly overcompensate for the other 60 to 70 percent of unsuccessful decisions. The only way this is possible is through unwavering discipline in your investment approach.

Discipline is what separates sensible market loss from foolish market loss. If you are disciplined and your approach to investment is sound and businesslike, your winners will more than compensate for your losers. The undisciplined investor is the one who racks up losses similar to the fictitious example given earlier. Succumbing to investment losses in this manner can mean the difference between an above-average and a below-average investment track record.

In cases like this, be disciplined enough to walk away and search elsewhere. Always remember that any business is undervalued at one price, fairly valued at another, and overvalued at yet another. The intelligent investor's goal is to buy at the undervalued price, avoid at the fairly valued price, and sell at the overvalued price. Only by maintaining a very disciplined approach can this strategy be carried out effectively.

Discipline Affects the Price Paid, Which Determines the Value You Get

As is often repeated in value investing, price is what you pay and value is what you get. Once you have identified a potential investment, and your data and reasoning lead you to conclude that you have a great business run by able and honest management, you still have to be willing to hold off *if the price is not right.* Amazon. com is a wonderful business that has forever changed the way we order books, but when it was trading for $75 a share, investors were paying more than 100 times earnings. Amazon still may have some fantastic growth potential, but at that price, you are earning less than 1 percent return on your money and hoping that not even the slightest hiccup occurs.

Price is the key determinant of value in investing. In investing— and in business in general—your profits are made when the asset is bought; you just don't realize at the time. The price paid will determine the discount from intrinsic value received. The price paid will determine the margin of safety an investment carries. If the stock pays a dividend, the price paid determines the dividend yield, as a lower stock price increases the dividend yield. Emotional habits can be quite expensive over time. In investing, the starting point of every investment is significant. An additional 2 to 3 percentage points per annum earned on an equity portfolio over a 20-year investment horizon add an additional 45 to 73 percent to the nest egg at the end of the 20-year period. A little means a lot.

The concept of price paid and value received in investing deserves a greater degree of significance than many other concepts because it is so easily misunderstood. Unlike the concept of margin of safety, which is relatively straightforward, the concept of price versus value can be misinterpreted easily. All too often, a disproportionate amount of attention is focused on the price aspect and not the value aspect. Comparing two similar businesses, many investors automatically presume the one with the lower stock price to be the one offering the greater value. Such blanket assumptions require investors to exert even more effort when comparing price paid to value received; otherwise, they fear that they might make expensive errors.

When Ben Graham was teaching his investing course at Columbia University in the 1950s, he used a brilliant form of instruction to illustrate relationship between price and value. He often took two consecutive securities from the stock tables and analyzed the fundamentals. This method proved to be an effective tool for illustrating the price/value relationship. Of significant importance is the inaccurate notion that a lower absolute price automatically equates to a better value.

Let's borrow a page from Graham's instruction method and consider two companies in the energy sector, shown in Table 7.1.

As of this writing, ConocoPhillips was trading for $52 a share and traded as high as $95 a share in 2008, while Cabot Oil and Gas traded for $26 a share and $72 a share at its peak in 2008. Eager investors may look at Cabot's price relative to its all-time high and determine that the possible resurgence to the previous high price

Table 7.1 **Finding Value**

	ConocoPhillips	Cabot Oil and Gas
P/E ratio	4.3	12.7
P/B ratio	0.83	1.64
Return on equity	21.29%	15.4%
Market value ($B)	$78	$2.76
Free cash flow (3-year avg.)	$8 billion	–$80 million
Free cash flow yield (3-year avg.)	~10%	n/a

The numbers reflect December 2008 figures.

Source: Yahoo! Finance and Securities and Exchange filings.

offers the greater value. Yet based on some very sound metrics of profitability noted in the table, ConocoPhillips appears to offer the greater value *at the current given price*. The value is not only evident in potential price appreciation; of more importance to value investors, value is evident in *the form of capital preservation*. Over the past three years, ConocoPhillips has delivered a free cash flow return of greater than 10 percent based on today's current price level while Cabot's increasing capital expenditures have exceeded cash flow from operations. Cabot is a fine oil company, but when examining the price paid versus value received, *at current prices,* ConocoPhillips seems to offer investors the better bang for their buck. Also missing from Table 7.1 is the dividend yield: Currently ConocoPhillips pays investors an outstanding 3.7 percent annual dividend while Cabot pays 0.40 percent. Clearly investors have further benefited from free cash flow generated by Conoco over the years.

The greatest error to which investors fall prey is relating the price level of a security with the anticipated future value to be received. The common mode of thought is this: A security trading at $2 a share can easily get to $4 whereas a company like ConocoPhillips will have a far harder time getting to $104 from $52.

In one sense, this may indeed be very true. It will require far more capital and investor interest to add the $70 billion in market value that would be needed to double the share price of ConocoPhillips; far less capital would be needed to move shares from $2 to $4. The danger in thinking this way is that the approach is no longer of that of investing but of speculation.

We have all heard investors who rationalize that when a stock price gets so low, it surely *cannot* go any lower. Thinking about a stock in this manner is misguided and usually leads to financial pain. Stock prices should always be thought about in relation to intrinsic value and degree of discount offered from intrinsic value. After all, until a stock price has reached zero, it *always* can go lower. It is crucial to realize the element of uncertainty in investing. The market hates uncertainty; in most cases, the low price due to uncertainty is justified. In some cases, though, the uncertainty leads to a price level that offers tremendous value. The goal of the intelligent investor is to exert diligent effort in understanding and valuing the specific situation. If that is not possible, the investor should abandon the security until he or she has a better view of things.

The notion of price to value with respect to discipline cannot be overemphasized, especially when we are talking about money and Wall Street. Wall Street has turned the investment profession into one dominated by egos motivated by who can accumulate the most in the shortest amount of time regardless of the soundness of the approach. If you are not participating in the moneymaking operation of the time, you've lost your touch. The mortgage and credit fiasco that imploded in the fall of 2008 with the fall of Bear Stearns and the bankruptcy of Lehman Brothers illustrates exactly what can happen when a disciplined approach takes a backseat to emotion and envy.

Eager to exploit the abundance of credit and rising property values, financial institutions raced each other to extend the most credit. Whether it was a storied Wall Street institution or a newly opened mom and pop with a shingle reading "Mortgages Available Here," the money to be made by lending, selling the loans, and lending some more was too easy to pass up. There was no need to hold back and be disciplined; houses were the safest asset next to Treasuries, the financial pros told us, because house prices would always go up over time and there would always be buyers. Hundreds of billions of dollars were invested based on complex models that all relied on one simple assumption: The price of a house could never decline. Never was the question asked "But what if...?" Despite the fact that these financial institutions were home to some of the most brilliant financial experts in our industry, their lack of discipline (and their large dose of arrogance) prevented them from asking the most elementary of rational questions. You can't expect an investment banker to drive a BMW when the mortgage broker is driving a Ferrari. The regrettable outcome is that the consequences are usually borne by many more than just those who were caught reaching for the cookie jar one time too many.

Be Prepared to Look Stupid

The economic crisis that began in late 2007 turned into one of the worst recessions since the Great Depression. Trillions of dollars of stock market value were wiped out in little over a year's time, and many investors suffered life-altering financial consequences. As the recession continued to affect businesses and the economy, many investors' distaste for equities grew. What is certain is that something will come along again and capture the heart of Wall Street. It happened with tulips in the seventeenth century,[1] with Internet stocks in the late 1990s, and with the housing and credit markets in the second half of the 2000s. In the meantime, value investors should be comforted and excited by the fact that the market is providing bargains and, in some cases, investment opportunities of a lifetime for those willing to be patient.

While discipline alone will not completely insulate you from the painful consequences of blind greed, it will have a significant impact on your success as a long-term investor. Most important, discipline can be the difference between surviving and getting wiped out. Time is an investor's best friend. If you are able to ride out the worst storms with your armor relatively intact, that means you are around to participate in some of the market's better buying opportunities. While Warren Buffett's investment acumen is without question, it's his disciplined approach to his craft that truly sets him apart from the rest. Buffett's discipline is so unwavering that even as he became best friends with Bill Gates and often was advised by Gates to invest in Microsoft, Buffett still refused to do so except for a token 100 shares just so he could receive the annual reports. Even after years of learning about the tech industry from Bill Gates himself, Buffett remained disciplined and said no. Buffett easily could have invested $100 million without any meaningful consequence to Berkshire Hathaway. He would have been able to do so after being told about the future of industry, where it was going, who the dominant players would be—which included Microsoft—but he still he refused to invest in any significant way. While many might argue that Buffett's discipline has cost him numerous lucrative investment opportunities—Microsoft and Wal-Mart some 20 years ago might have been the biggest—the real value is found when you invert the argument.

Buffett's discipline has enabled him to avoid potentially larger losses than any of his missed opportunities might have created. Having the discipline to walk away from an investment in spite of a favorable consensus view reveals a nonemotional, independent frame of mind, one of the most prized qualities in all of investing. And best of all, this quality doesn't require you to have a high IQ but only a disciplined approach.

Ultimately, the key to Buffett's disciplined approach has been his strict adherence to staying within his circle of competence. The term "circle of competence" is widely known but not necessarily truly understood. It goes beyond simply understanding a business. Since befriending Bill Gates over 15 years ago, Buffett probably has read every single Microsoft annual report. I think he understands the business better than many technology investors. But Buffett doesn't simply define his circle as understanding the operations of a business. He wants to know the entire industry, the competitive forces, the regulatory environment, and anything that might be of significance. Armed with this information, Buffett then can handicap his investment odds and determine if they meet his requirements. The technology sector doesn't meet Warren Buffett's requirements.

All investment activity involves some risk. In exchange for that risk, the market offers investors an opportunity to earn rates in excess of the U.S. Treasury's risk-free rate. Otherwise, stock markets would be of little value. Discipline prevents investors from assuming risks that they don't need to take on to earn excess returns. Having the discipline to remain inside your circle of competence enables investors to do two very important things.

1. Disciplined investors rarely ever abandon an investment at the first sign of trouble.
2. Disciplined investors rarely ever chase an investment that is the fad of the day.

Not falling prey to these two actions may be the most valuable skill that any investor can hope to possess. When it's all said and done, you succeed in investing by selling a security for more than you paid for it. By not jumping at the first sign of trouble or chasing rising stock prices, you stand a better chance of investment success.

Regardless of the company, it takes conviction to invest against the general market consensus. By zigging when the market zags, you are sticking your neck on the line. You are setting yourself up for criticism from the investing establishment. When Warren

The Whole Foods Company: An Exercise in Patience

It's easy to see why maintaining the discipline to stay inside your circle of competence significantly aids investment success. Investors who have taken the time and effort to completely understand a particular business and the characteristics of its operating environment will focus more attention on the performance of the business and not the performance of the underlying stock price.

Consider Whole Foods or any other business that you are familiar with. I've shopped there for years and have visited many stores for lunch when I'm traveling so I've gotten to see the quality and passion the company has for its products and services. Until recently, Wall Street seemed to hold similar admiration for the company. With the economy firmly in a recession in 2008, however, Mr. Market hates the uncertainty that surrounds a business that sells premium priced foods. For the first time since going public, Whole Foods is trading very close to book value.

I consider the company well within my circle of competence. So far I've maintained the discipline to say no because I felt the market had always afforded Whole Foods a premium valuation based on its unique long-term growth prospects. So while growth may contract for the next year or so, the price now creates an opportunity for great value and satisfactory returns over a multiyear horizon. What does all of this mean? If I invest in Whole Foods today, and next month the stock is down 40 percent, I wouldn't think twice about selling (except for an abnormal occurrence, such as fraud, etc.). If anything, I would be thinking about whether to add to the investment. Without getting into unnecessary detail for purposes of this chapter, my reasoning is straightforward. First, I am buying a business at book value that I'm confident will be worth substantially more than book to any private buyer. During the end of 2008, the enterprise value of Whole Foods (market value plus the net debt) was about $2.2 billion. What does this enterprise value get you? How about 275 stores located in some of the most desirable locations in the country that generate over $8 billion in annual sales. Not only that, Whole Foods has spent millions of dollars marketing itself as the number-one purveyor of foods and products to consumers oriented to the healthy lifestyle. In the

(Continued)

(Continued)
United States, the Whole Foods brand is synonymous with natural and organic foods. Ask any rational businessperson if they could replicate all of that for $2.2 billion and the answer you will get is no. Even Wal-Mart, which has added some organic foods in its superstores, hasn't had any meaningful effect on Whole Foods.

Whole Foods is in a class by itself. Even knowing this, investors need to have the discipline to say no when the company is valued at 2 times annual sales and 40 times earnings. On top of all this, the company will very likely be earning more profits several years from now than it did before the economic recession took hold. Investors who understand the important characteristics about a business and invest at a bargain price will not abandon the company after a few quarters that don't meet Wall Street expectations. They won't sell a cheap business at a cheaper price. When the consensus is cheery, however, disciplined investors refrain from paying an expensive price. Remembering that the price you pay reflects the value obtained and knowing when to say no will eliminate a lot of unforced mistakes.

Buffett was shunning technology while the used car salesmen were doubling their money in months investing in Internet stocks, it was said that Buffett was stupid and out of touch with the new era of investing.

If your goal is to invest in undervalued businesses, prepare to look stupid in the short run. Often some of the best investment opportunities can be found in unloved areas. The market punishes stocks without abandon if it doesn't like what it sees ahead. Just as stock prices can overshoot when the mood is euphoric, stock prices can easily get below intrinsic value when the mood is dour. Wall Street has a vested interest in promoting the popular investments of the day, and what is popular is expensive. You won't find battered-down stocks being talked about at cocktail parties. Instead, the "smart" money is always talking about the crowd pleasers, without regard to any fundamentals. As 2008 came to an end, the markets were down over 40 percent, one of the worst annual performances on record. With scores of equities priced at valuations that will likely reward investors in future years, stocks are now perceived to be riskier than ever. Some things never change. Disciplined investors should rejoice during these times of emotional misbehavior.

Don't Split Hairs

As with all characteristics of investing, maintaining a disciplined approach is part art and part science. It is of paramount importance to separate a disciplined investment approach from a rigid investment approach. The greatest common fallacy that many investors fall prey to is attempting to invest at the absolute bottom. Investors feel highly intelligent when they believe they have timed the bottom of the price of a stock. Just as failing to maintain discipline can lead to avoidable losses, attempting to invest at the absolute bottom can eliminate potentially powerful investment gains. It's futile to invest in this way. It's great if you do catch the bottom, but remember if you do that it's more luck than investment skill. Nevertheless, as foolish as it is, many investors always look to catch bottoms. As long as Wall Street looks at the market through glasses oriented to the short term, people always will attempt to time the markets perfectly.

Consider the next two investment situations, which illustrate the general uselessness of bottom fishing in the overall investment landscape.

Investor A buys shares in ABC Corp., confident that the company is undervalued. She invests in the business and, shortly afterward, the stock drops by as much as 50 percent. For well over a year, the stock price remains dormant. All the while, the investor sees share prices rising at other businesses she's familiar with. Investor A reassesses

Table 7.2   Timing Isn't Everything

ABC Corp. Share Price = $50	Year 1 Stock Price = $25	Year 2 Stock Price = $50	Year 3 Stock Price = $80	3-Year Annualized Return
Investor A performance	–50%	100%	60%	17%
Investor B performance	0%	100%	0%	26%

the situation and determines that she still has an attractive investment with superior fundamentals. As a result, she ignores the noise.

Investor B, who also favors ABC Corp., begins buying shares a year later at about half of Investor A's cost basis. Over the next couple of years, Mr. Market catches up with ABC, and the stock doubles in year 2 and rises by another 60 percent in year 3. Thrilled with his 100 percent return, Investor B cashes out. Investor A continues to hold on. Table 7.2 shows the investment results for both investors.

Which investor would you rather be? Naturally it would be great to be Investor B, and there is nothing wrong with *buying a cheap business for much cheaper*. That part is without dispute. With hindsight, it seems that Investor B looks smarter, while Investor A just got unlucky buying at the wrong price or the wrong time. Unfortunately, the immediate preference of Investor B over A is putting the cart before the horse. Indeed, over a substantial period of time—say, at least 10 years—Investor B's 9 percent outperformance over Investor A is extremely significant and could be used to qualify the two investors. Even so, if Investor A's biggest flaw is arriving to the party before B but her analysis still turns out to be correct, a 17 percent annual rate of return will get you nothing but praise. Both investors could be smart and savvy, or they both could be victims of lucky timing, one more favorable over the other. But that's not the correct way to look at the situation. Instead, the situation should be viewed from a totally different perspective: that both investors' results reinforce the idea that successful value investing always emphasizes the process first and the outcome second. The value-seeking investor doesn't time stock prices but instead prices stocks.

Successful investing is about one thing: buying good businesses for less than they are worth. The movement of the stock price is only a tool to aid investors in doing this, nothing more.

Unveiling Investor A: Warren Buffett

Back to our tale in the last section: What if I told you that Investor A was, at one point, Warren Buffett? Indeed, in 1973, Buffett began buying shares in the Washington Post for Berkshire Hathaway. Based on a historical stock chart in *The Warren Buffett Way* by Robert Hagstrom,[2] shares in the *Post* declined after Buffett's purchase, and it took more than a year for the company's stock price to surpass Buffett's purchase price.

Regardless, Buffett is just an example of the bigger picture for investors. All too often, the terms "luck" and "skill" are tossed around the investment field inaccurately. The truth is that investment skill will always lead to certain moments of luck, but in the long term, luck simply cannot last long enough to produce a consistent, profitable result.

The Investor Bs of the world are often considered to be more skillful than the Investor As. That's a misguided view. In this case, both classes of investors have skill. The point to understand is that *very few investors will ever buy at the bottom.* Investor B, while a skillful, prudent investor, merely got lucky by purchasing a security at the bottom. Investor B realizes this and understands that in the future, he will miss the bottom more often than not. In both instances, he is investing based on intrinsic value assessments, not on market volatility.

Investor A also realizes that she is no less skillful an investor because Mr. Market has suddenly decided that the business is "worth" half of what she paid. In fact, Investor A welcomes the decline because it offers an even better bargain investment. Again, she makes the investment solely on the basis of intrinsic value, not Mr. Market's value.

Just as having the discipline to say no is crucial, it is equally important to know when not to split hairs. If a business is truly a good investment, it makes no difference whether you invest at $32 or $33 or $34 a share. Your qualifications as an investor aren't weaker if you deliver 15 percent returns while the other guy earns 18 percent. If you're looking to buy a private company with strong earnings and growth power and your offer is $500 million, you're not going to walk away from it at $520 million if you're reasonably confident that the business will be earning more profits several years into the future. You should apply a similar mind-set when buying partial ownership stakes in public companies via the stock market. Attempting to bottom fish often produces the opposite result and ultimately leads to investors paying a higher price for the stock than they would otherwise have. As an investor decides for to wait for a $32 stock to reach $30 before buying, one of two mistakes may occur. The first is that the target price to invest starts to move. Once the stock reaches $30, the investor now decides to wait until $29. As this train of thought continues, the approach no longer is about investment but about market timing. In some cases, investors can get lucky, but in taking on this unnecessary element of luck, they may miss out on a bargain investment. Or worse—and the source of the second mistake—the investor ends up paying more for the stock, and the future returns are no longer satisfactory. Being a disciplined investor cuts both ways. Table 7.3 illustrates the folly of stock price anchoring. The table shows the one-year return based on an initial share based on an ending price, P. Anchoring is a common mistake of many investors. The concept relates to investors fixating on the price to pay for a share of stock. Price does matter but only in relation to the assessed intrinsic value of a company. Because value investors often seek investments

Table 7.3 Folly of Anchoring On a Price

Initial Share Price	Return (P = $60)	Return (P = $50)	Return (P = $30)
$32	88%	56%	–6%
$33	82%	52%	–9%
$34	72%	47%	–12%

selling at significant discounts to intrinsic value, anchoring on a set price often causes more harm than good as it leads to many missed opportunities.

Indeed, prices do matter. A 12 percent loss is much more severe than a 6 percent loss. But comparing the expected gains if the security appreciates with the potential losses confirms that if an investment is made in a quality company with a comfortable margin of safety, price anchoring can do more harm than good. One final note: The percentage difference between paying $32 or $34 (6.2 percent) a share versus paying $9 or $11 (22.2 percent) can be very significant in determining overall investment returns. While all investments should be made with respect to price paid versus intrinsic value received, price differentials are meaningful with smaller numbers.

Investors all too often make investing much more difficult than it really is by spending far too much time trying to time every single detail. When Buffett says that investing is simple but not easy, he means that many investors pay far too much attention to variables and factors that don't affect the overall future value of the business as much as they think they do.

Underpinning the aforementioned assertions, of course, is the assumption that investors have diligently researched the security and are investing with a comfortable margin of safety. If you determine that the intrinsic value of a stock is $45 a share, there is no benefit gained by waiting to invest at $20 a share versus $22 or even $24 with respect to the potential opportunity loss that may arise if the stock price doesn't reach your target. It's silly to forgo a potential 82 percent return for the possibility of earning a 100 percent return at the risk of missing out on the opportunity to invest at an already attractive price. Attempting to bottom fish makes investing much more difficult—and potentially more damaging—than it should be.

It's crucial to understand that these discussions are intended to provide a framework for how investors should be thinking about stocks if their goal is to truly invest. The purpose of making investments is to allocate capital today that gradually will appreciate at an acceptable rate of return over a period of years. In order for investing to prove beneficial, investors must invest at sensible prices and do so for a period of years, the longer the better. The year 2008 was horrific for stock market investors and easily the worst year for the current generation of investors. Reading this book and thinking about 2008 will make it seem that the philosophies espoused about investing are outdated or no longer valid. In thinking in this way, you are training your mind to think in exactly the manner that is most detrimental to investment success: You are equating short-term market votes with long-term fundamentals of the businesses. No one will dispute that markets today have it more right than they did 50 years ago, but if you stick to your principles and invest based on sound value-oriented business fundamentals, the markets will pay you for it over time.

Consider Table 7.4, which clearly illustrates the market's short-term viewpoint against the long-term fundamentals for the following group of randomly chosen businesses.

As you can see, if you had invested in any of the businesses in the table in 2000, three years later you were likely sitting on losses. The market experienced a severe correction in 2000, after the euphoria that engulfed the Internet came to a crashing halt. Regardless of the industry, most investments made in 2000 declined substantially in the following years. The table clearly illustrates

Table 7.4 Short-Term Vote versus Long-Term Fundamentals

Company	Business	2000 Price	2001 Price	2003 Price	2007 Price
Apple Computer	Computers	$7–$38	$7–$13	$6–$12	$82–$200
Vulcan Materials	Aggregates	$36–$50	$37–$55	$29–$49	$77–$129
Tesoro	Oil refining	$4–$6	$5–$8	$2–$7	$32–$66
Transocean	Oil-drilling rigs	$30–$65	$23–$57	$18–26	$73–$150

Note: Prices reflecting lows and highs for the year are rounded to nearest dollar for illustrative purposes.

Data source: Value Line.

the difference of the market's short-term voting machine reaction compared with the market's assessment of the long-term quality of the business fundamentals. Depending on the price paid, investors were sitting on losses with Apple for three years before earning a return. If you bought at the high price in 2000, the 2001 recession cut your investment by up to 80 percent. You can see what happened when the market votes were outweighed by fundamentals beginning in 2004 and beyond. The table chart could easily include over 100 stocks with a similar pattern. And they would all be excellent businesses capable of earning more and more profits over the years.

Back in 2001, I began buying the refiners Tesoro and Valero, paying four and five times earnings respectively. I got in around $8 for Tesoro. In 2002, the stock hit a low of 60 cents as earnings went from $1.05 a share in 2001 to a loss of $0.97 in 2002. In 2003, the stock was still languishing, trading between $1 and $7 during the year. Within a year, I was down over 80 percent on this investment and still down two years later. The stock was performing poorly, but the company's fundamentals were sound and the balance sheet was strong. In 2005, I sold at around $30. Two years later, the stock was trading at $65. I held the shares for four years, the first two of which I was down on my investment. In the end, my gains were in excess of 300 percent.

This stroll down memory lane is not meant to defend the notion that it is always best to sit and wait out your investments. Every market correction and economic recession is different in terms of duration and ultimate severity. But where the market hasn't failed investors is in restoring fair valuations to those businesses that are capable of earning more and more profit. No single business can ever expect to generate continuous increasing profitability. What matters is how the business will look several years down the road. If that particular business will be earning more profits and generating greater levels of cash flow, the market price will catch up to its fundamental performance.

It's very difficult for investors to sit on 50 percent-plus losses and not be tempted to sell out. If you're managing money for others, it's nearly impossible to hold such losses and not do anything. The principal reason many investment funds fail is because many investment managers feel pressured to deliver short-term results to their clients. In many cases, this pressure stems from the fact that many investors are taught to focus on short-term returns. Money managers with the greatest yearly return are rewarded with an influx of new capital, and managers with an underperforming year can find themselves out of a job. While the ultimate success or failure of an investment manager will depend on his track record, the majority of individuals are taught to think of outcome first and process second. This backward approach to evaluating investment results is just as foolish as suggesting that Buffett had "lost his touch" because he failed to participate in the Internet boom. Many investors are quick to discount discipline and are eager to participate in whatever is popular. The consequence of such thinking is a lose-lose proposition for both manager and investor.

Discipline Is Simple but Rarely Easy

A disciplined approach may be simple enough to follow, but it is not an easy thing to do. It's simple because you don't need to have a high IQ or super-analytical skills to be a disciplined investor, but it's not easy because you are battling against your emotions and Mr. Market.

When it comes to bull markets, no one wants to be off the boat when it's riding a rising tide. Emotions have a way of being one-sided when the mood is jubilant. People often forget about the long-term goals of investing when everyone seems to be profiting in the short term. Writing in 1776, Adam Smith defined what he called "the trade of speculation." According to Smith:

> The speculative merchant exercises no one regular, established, or well-known brand of business. He is a corn merchant this year, and a wine merchant the next, and a sugar, tobacco, or tea merchant the year after. He enters into every trade when he foresees that it is likely to be more than commonly profitable, and he quits it when he foresees that its profits are likely to return to the level of other trades. His profits and losses, therefore, can bear no regular proportion to those of any one established and well-known branch of business. A bold adventurer may sometimes acquire a considerable fortune by two or three successful speculations; but is just as likely to lose one by two or three unsuccessful ones.[3]

Smith concludes that sudden fortunes and sudden losses were the *equally likely* results. His definition of speculation agrees very closely with that of an "investor" who exercises no discipline in security selection. Investing should always be about capital preservation first and capital appreciation second. Having the discipline to say no is a key part of successfully adhering to that approach. Value investors are not bold adventurers; that is, not with respect to investment approach.

Key Takeaways

- In investing, and in life, having the discipline to say no can mean the difference between success and failure.
- Price is what you pay, and value is what you get. The price paid for an investment will determine the value gained.
- Being disciplined usually means avoiding what's popular on Wall Street.
- Be prepared to look stupid in the short run when you are saying no while everyone else is saying yes.
- Having discipline cuts both ways: Don't split hairs trying to bottom fish a stock price. Focus on pricing the business, not timing the stock. An undervalued business with a wide margin of safety will be a good investment whether it's bought at a share price of $20 or $17.
- In the short run, market prices reflect investor sentiment; in the long run, market prices weigh on the fundamentals of a business.
- Invest for capital preservation first and capital appreciation second.
- Maintaining a disciplined approach and not being emotional are not easy in investing, but the qualifications needed to do so are simple.

CHAPTER 8

Practicing the Art of Patience

THE FIFTH ELEMENT

All men's miseries derive from not being able to sit in a quiet room alone.

—Blaise Pascal

The financial media does a great job of sensationalizing the day trader who made 100 times his salary in one year or the hedge fund manager who timed the mortgage crisis just right and earned $3 billion in one year. For every one of these outliers, though, there are thousands of others who have failed terribly. Many investors tend to forget that slow and steady will always win the race. Investors who embark on a strategy of trying to reap riches quickly often face a similar outcome: continued loss of permanent capital.

Value investing, by its very nature, is about the gradual appreciation of capital. At times, value investors certainly will be rewarded with quick profits, but such bounty should be viewed as an added bonus to a disciplined approach. Value investing is a comprehensive investment philosophy that emphasizes the need to perform intense fundamental analysis, pursue long-term investment results, minimize risk, and, above all, resist herd mentality. The true value investor understands that patience is an asset, not a hindrance. A slight revision to Pascal's quote might apply to our investment managers today: "All investment managers' miseries derive from not being able to sit quietly in a room alone."

Too many investors approach the stock market as a speculative endeavor, often because share prices go up regardless of underlying valuation. Investing, however, rests on the foundation that securities are purchased at a discount to estimates of intrinsic value, thereby implying that the basis for investment gain will result from purchase price nearing intrinsic value. Unlike speculators who strive to achieve rapid gain, value investors strive to limit capital loss. As such, true value investors will gladly wait for as long as it takes to make investments that satisfy those investment philosophies. Along with discipline and risk aversion, the fifth element essential to the value investing approach is patience.

There are tremendous benefits to being patient in investing. The most obvious reason is that less activity reduces transaction costs and helps defer taxes. Moreover, in investing, you are afforded the luxury of waiting until opportunity arises. There are no time limits, 18 holes, or strikes that restrict the opportunity find the investment ace. This luxury is crucial in the markets because the prevalence of networks like CNBC and Internet trading all serve to turn investing into a minute-by-minute activity. The ability to buy and sell securities in a split second has led to havoc for many investors. Patient investors welcome the buy-and-hold approach, knowing that the ultimate determinants of when to "buy" and for how long to "hold" is predicated on a market value being below intrinsic value.

Underpinning all of the above, the powerful advantages of patience will only be fully appreciated when a basic understanding of stock valuation is understood.

Stocks derive their valuations from the cash flows they will produce in the future. Simply stated, stocks are worth the present value of the future cash flows they will provide to their owners. A business can do one of two things with its cash flow: either reinvest the cash back into the business or pay it out in the form of dividends. Unlike bonds, equities don't expire. In financial terms, this longevity implies that stocks have a very long duration. As a result, the vast majority of cash flows that will accrue to a holder of common stock will occur far out into the future. And if a business is growing those earnings over time, then the substantial gains that are to be had from holding equities will also occur further out in the future.

The greatest advantage, of course, comes to the patient investor who can purchase common stocks of quality businesses at a substantial discount of the present value of those future cash flows, often referred to as intrinsic value. This fundamental aspect of stock valuation is why true value investors are comfortable investing in undervalued stocks, regardless of whether or not the purchases are made at the absolute bottom. Even more so, value investors are comfortable holding bargain securities during temporary periods of distress.

Additionally, it's this above premise that renders dividends so extremely important in certain investment considerations. Over time, dividends can begin to account for more and more of the value derived from holding equities. Naturally, investors should always emphasize the security of the dividend over the rate of the dividend.

To really appreciate the value of knowing when to sit still, look no further than the Johnson & Johnson Company (J&J), arguably one of the finest companies ever. Sales at Johnson & Johnson have grown at over 10 percent a year for over 100 years, and that was after the company had been established for 23 years. For decades J&J has paid and increased dividends annually almost without interruption. Back in 1944 when the company went public, one share of J&J cost $37.50. That one single share today, with dividends reinvested, would be worth $900,000—a stunning annualized return of 17.1 percent. Without those dividends, that one share would be equal to 2,500 shares today or about $142,000 as a result of stock splits. And that one share would be producing $4,500 in annual dividends today.[1]

Many investors are quick to ignore the enormous value that a dividend yield can add to the overall results of a particular investment; this ignorance comes with an expensive price tag.

Swimming against the Current

The modern financial world does everything it can to exacerbate the short-term orientation of many investors. The perilous consequence of these activities is promoting the mistaken belief that investing is easy, when in truth investing demands rigor, intensity, and painstaking work. For example, CNBC today uses a digital clock format to constantly update investors with the changes in the market indexes. This clock goes so far as to measure time in hundredths of a second; the numbers flash by so fast that you can't see them. What rational purpose does this mechanism purport to offer the serious investor? Absolutely nothing. Such tactics serve only to mesmerize the viewer's attention with levels of adrenaline that are deadly to a sound investment philosophy. To the crowd, patience is madness; to the value investor, patience is wisdom.

Further waging the fight against a steady and patient investment approach is the industry's view of cash. The investment industry trains us to think of cash as a deteriorating asset. If you are sitting on cash, then you obviously do not know what you are doing. To the patient long-term investor, the value of cash is indirectly proportional to the availability of bargain securities. As bargain securities flourish, holding cash is as imprudent as investing in overvalued securities. When bargain securities are scarce, sitting on cash is the most intelligent investment decision. As is often the case with cash, when you don't have it is when you need it most.

The patient investor is very comfortable waiting, ready to make an opportunistic investment when the time is right. Cash allows the investor (a) to avoid selling what is cheap in order to buy another cheap asset and (b) the opportunity to take advantage of any special situations. As we end 2008 with many security prices approaching 1973 valuations, the population of those hiding in cash is as great as ever. This is evidenced by investors' willingness to accept a yield of .05 percent on 3-month Treasury bills and 2.4 percent on 10-year Treasury notes. In comparison, some of the strongest and most profitable U.S. companies are serving dividend yields north of 4 percent and selling at very attractive valuations. With the pool of investment bargains greater than it's been in decades, the vast majority of "market investors" prefer cash. Contrast this with the euphoria of the Internet boom, when cash was viewed as the dumb man's asset against equities trading at 40 times earnings.

As the saying goes, the more things change, the more they stay the same.

The Benefits of Waiting for a Good Pitch

Warren Buffett has often compared investing to baseball. Like a batter, investors are simply waiting for Mr. Market to serve up a fat pitch to knock it out of the park. But investors have one very distinct advantage over baseball batters: There are no called strikes. Investors have the luxury of waiting as long as they want before making a swing. Waiting can be of immense value to investors *if they are disciplined and patient enough to use it to their advantage.* It's far more profitable to wait for the fat pitch and then invest big. Investors can wait and wait until Mr. Market throws them the perfect pitch before they decide to invest big.

Unfortunately, many investors invest as if they truly were under the three strikes and you're out rule. This leads investors to feel the need to be buying and selling something all the time. No matter how you examine it, more activity in the stock market generally leads to poorer results. If it's not the investments that do you in, the increased frictional costs—namely brokerage fees and increased administrative costs—will add up.

There are many advantages to making a few sound, sizable investments and just sitting back and waiting:

- You pay fewer brokers' commissions.
- You'll hear a lot less nonsense from everybody and anybody eager to give you sales pitches.
- And if your investments work, the government will let you keep more of your profits every year as they compound over and over again.

A simple mathematical example illustrates that last point. If you buy something that compounds at 15 percent per annum for 30 years, and you pay a 35 percent tax at the end of those 30 years, after taxes you keep about 13.3 percent of that compound rate. In contrast, if you bought the same investment and had to pay 35 percent in taxes each year on the 15 percent you earned, your net return would be about 9.75 percent per year compounded. By doing nothing, you earned a spread of more than 3 percent. How significant is 3 percent? Mutual fund legend John Bogle discovered that 85 percent of mutual funds lag the Standard & Poor's (S&P) 500 Index after all fees and expenses. Bogle also found that only .5 percent of all mutual funds beat the indices by more than 3 percent. How many disciplines pay such an unbelievable premium to sit still?

It's easy to speak of the benefits of patience and long-term investing; but as is characteristic of many investing philosophies, it's easier said than done when it comes to patience. Most investors have become trained to have their minds think dependently, not independently, when it comes to the stock market. They operate under the assumption that the market realizes their existence when in fact the market exists at the mercy of the investor. The stock market is nothing more than a voting machine on the price of securities. Each day security prices are determined by the available supply of buyers and sellers in the market. Value investors understand this important distinction and thus view the stock market only for what it is: a forum to acquire ownership interests in undervalued companies or dispose of those securities at fairly valued prices. Aside from these two purposes, value investors are content to sit still and wait until the market serves up prices conducive to their liking. When there are no bargains, patience is bliss to value investors.

The stock markets, especially the U.S. markets, have arguably been one of the most successful wealth-creating machines on the planet, besting returns of all other asset classes over the long haul. Unfortunately, the unmatched wealth creation created by the stock market over the decades also leads to crippling wealth destruction. Investors fail to see the markets for what they truly are—creators of long-term wealth—and instead conclude that simply being invested in the stock market, regardless of the general level of valuation, automatically creates wealth. This thinking is a tragic mistake, and it's the source of much investor anger toward stocks. When the mood is jubilant, folks are glad to put money in stocks, often at overvalued prices. When the market is filled with euphoria and stocks are expensive, the financial world tells you what a wonderful place the market is for your hard-earned money. Many investors are made to feel stupid from all angles by not participating. Some will get lucky and happen to get in and out having made great sums of money. Those outlier success stories are the ones you will read on the front page of the paper. For the majority, the end result is substantial loss of capital and a permanent detachment from stocks. When you participate in the market as a gambler and not an investor, why should you expect results any different from what you would expect at a roulette wheel?

The independent-minded value investor, however, observes this euphoria and sits still while the market is consumed with speculative activity and overvalued securities. Value investors realize that sometimes doing nothing is the best thing you can do. The possibility of earning quick returns is of no concern when it comes alongside a heightened risk of permanent capital loss. Instead, value investors will wait patiently and continue to analyze securities, learning as much as they can in anticipation of a better buying opportunity. Armed with more capital and information, the value investor is in the ultimate sweet spot when bargains do begin to crop up. Patience is a painstaking process in investing because you never know how long the wait will be. But the future opportunity to make significant investments at bargain prices *alongside a minimal probability of permanent capital loss* rewards patient investors magnificently. The philosophies of value investing—deep fundamental analysis, limiting risk, and margin of safety—are by nature designed for unfavorable (or bear) market environments. During bull markets, the value investing approach is deemed unnecessary. If bull markets were constant, the need for the value investing framework would not be required.

Many might be surprised to find out that Warren Buffett's investment strategy often has consisted of long periods of doing nothing, or what Buffett likes to call "sitting on my butt." The next excerpts from an article by value investor Mohnish Pabrai illustrates Buffett's periods of inactivity and shows why many more people would benefit more (and lose less) by simply sitting on their butts. It's an insightful examination of the benefits derived from simply sitting still.

"Buffett Succeeds at Nothing"

Why should portfolio managers sit and do nothing? And why would that be good for them? Well, let's start with the story of D.E. Shaw & Co. Founded in 1988, Shaw was staffed by some of the brightest mathematicians, computer scientists, and bond trading experts on the planet. Jeff Bezos worked at Shaw before embarking on his Amazon.com journey. These folks found that there was a lot of money to be made with risk-free arbitrage in the bond markets with some highly sophisticated bond arbitrage trading algorithms.

Shaw was able to capitalize on minuscule short-term inefficiencies in the bond markets with highly leveraged capital. The annualized returns were nothing short of spectacular—and all of it risk-free! The bright folks at Shaw put their trading on autopilot, with minimal human tweaking required. They came to work and mostly played pool or video games or just goofed off. Shaw's profit per employee was astronomical, and everyone was happy with this Utopian arrangement.

Eventually, the nerds got fidgety—they wanted to do something. They felt that they had only scratched the surface and, if they only dug deeper, there would be more gold to be mined. And so they fiddled with the system to try to juice returns.

What followed was a similar path taken by Long-Term Capital Management (LTCM), a fund once considered so big and so smart on Wall Street that it simply could not fail . . . .

Compared to nearly any other discipline, I find that fund management is, in many respects, a bizarre field—where hard work and intellect don't necessarily lead to satisfactory results. As Warren Buffett succinctly put it during the 1998 Berkshire Hathaway annual meeting: "We don't get paid for activity, just for being right. As to how long we'll wait, we'll wait indefinitely!"

Buffett and his business partner Charlie Munger are easily among the smartest folks I've come across. But, as we've seen with Shaw and LTCM, a high IQ may not lead to stellar investing results. After all, LTCM's founders had among them Nobel Prize–winning economists. In the long run, it didn't do them much good. In fact, they outsmarted themselves. In a 1999 interview with *BusinessWeek*, Buffett stated:

> Success in investing doesn't correlate with IQ—once you're above the level of 25. Once you have ordinary intelligence, what you need is the temperament to control the urges that get other people into trouble in investing.

Events at Shaw and LTCM show that high-IQ folks have a hard time sitting around contemplating their navels. The problem is that

(Continued)

(Continued)

once you engage in these intellectually stimulating problems, you're almost guaranteed to find what you think are the correct answers and act upon them—usually leading to bad results for investors.

Having observed Buffett and Munger closely over the years, and gotten into their psyche through their speeches and writings, it is clear to me that, like the folks at Shaw and LTCM, both men need enormous doses of intellectual stimulation as part of their daily diet. How do they satisfy this intellectual hunger without the accompanying actions that get investors into trouble?

Consider the following:

While Buffett plays bridge (typically 10–20 hours per week), Munger spends his time mostly on expanding his worldly wisdom and constantly improving his latticework of mental models. He is a voracious reader of intellectually engaging books on a variety of subjects, ranging from the various Ice Ages to *The Wealth and Poverty of Nations*. He spends considerable time in applying perspectives gained from one field of study into other disciplines—especially capital allocation.

At the Wesco annual meeting this year, Munger acknowledged that the first few hundred million dollars at Berkshire came from "running a Geiger counter over everything," but the subsequent tens of billions have come from simply "waiting for the no-brainers" or, as Buffett puts it, "waiting for the phone to ring."

Buffett still has a tendency to run his Geiger counter over lots of stuff. It's just too enticing intellectually not to. How does he avoid getting into trouble? I believe there are three reasons:

1. Running the Geiger counter can work very well if one knows *when* to run it. Reflect on the following two quotes:

    In 1970, showing his dismay at elevated stock prices, Buffett said: "I feel like a sex-starved man on a deserted island."

    In 1974, expressing his glee at the low levels to which the market had fallen, he said: "I feel like a sex-starved man in a harem filled with beautiful women!"

    By 1970, he had terminated his partnership and made virtually no public market investments until 1974. The P/E (price-earnings) ratio for the S&P 500 dropped from 20 to 7 in those four years. By 1974, he had acknowledged selling "stocks he'd bought recently at 3 times earnings to buy stocks selling at 2 times earnings."

Then, from 1984–1987, Buffett did not buy a single new equity position for the Berkshire portfolio. Berkshire Hathaway was sitting on a mountain of cash, and still he did nothing. In the latter half of 1987, Berkshire used that cash pile to buy over a billion dollars' worth of Coca-Cola over 5 percent of the company. He invested 25 percent of Berkshire Hathaway's book value in a single company that they did not control!

What were Buffett and Munger doing from 1970–1973 and 1984–1987? Both men realize that successful investing requires the patience and discipline to make big bets during the relatively infrequent intervals when the markets are undervalued, and to do "something else" during the long periods when markets are fully priced or overpriced. I'm willing to bet that Buffett was playing far more bridge in 1972 than he was in 1974.

2. The Geiger counter approach works better in smaller, under-followed companies and a host of special situations. Given their typical smaller size, investing in these companies would do nothing for Berkshire Hathaway today. So Buffett usually makes these investments for his personal portfolio. A good example is his recent investment in mortgage REIT (real estate investment trust) Laser Mortgage Management (LMM), where there was a decent spread between the liquidation value and quoted stock price. These LMM-type investments are significant for Buffett's personal portfolio and, more importantly, soak up intellectual horsepower that might lead to not-so-good results at Berkshire Hathaway.

Being versatile, he moves his Geiger counter away from the equity markets to other bastions of inefficiency whenever the public markets get overheated. These include high-yield bonds (Berkshire bought over $1 billion worth of Finova bonds at deep discounts in 2001), REITs (bought First Industrial Realty in 2000 for his own portfolio at a time when REIT yields were spectacular), or his recent investing adventures in silver.

(Continued)

(Continued)

3. The Munger/Buffett relationship is an unusual one. Both men are fiercely independent thinkers, and both prefer working alone. When Buffett has an investment idea, after it makes it through his filter, he usually runs it past Munger. Munger then applies his broad lattice-work of mental models to find faults with Buffett's ideas, and shoots most of them down. It is the rare idea that makes it past Buffett, and it has to be a total brain tease to make it past both of them.

The Buffett/Munger approach of multi-year periods of inactivity contrasts starkly with the frenzied activity that takes place daily at the major exchanges.[2]

Ignorance Can Be Bliss

Our daily lives are comprised of a series of decisions. What we do with those decisions and the choices we make shape the life we lead. As a toddler, your parents forced you to do things you hated, like eating your vegetables. The vegetables taste bad, but your parents love you and know that you must eat your vegetables to get your vitamins. At the same time, your parents will refrain from giving you candy and soda, even though they know how much you would enjoy the joy gained from the sugary sensation. They know that sometimes the things that seem good for you actually aren't and those things that seem bad for you can actually be beneficial.

Investors would be well advised to take this dose of wisdom along with them during their investing careers. What are often perceived as stock market advantages can turn out to be the root cause of many investment mistakes for those individuals who fail to realize it. The market's dangers are firmly rooted in human nature—specifically, our ability to feel the pain of loss more acutely than the pleasure of gain. Too many bad losses can rob us of our investing discipline. Eager to recoup losses in the shortest amount of time, many investors begin to accelerate the investment making process, often at the expense of sound analytical judgment. When we make bad decisions, we have no one to blame but ourselves.

The ease and speed with which investors can trade stocks, and the barrage of market data now available to us, certainly don't help. The ability to get in and out of investments at the click of a button feeds the speculative urges of market participants. Many of the market's beneficial attributes often can be the source of the most detriment to the investor. Let's examine some of those attributes now.

Ups and Downs of Market Liquidity

The same liquidity that provides many of the stock market's advantages can also produce the most severe consequences. I'd argue that less liquid investments are better for investors' well-being, providing fewer opportunities for them to make impulsive and costly buy or sell decisions. Liquidity is a very important function of our equity markets. Faced with unexpected financial needs, the ability to easily turn your securities into cash is a comforting option. Then again, given the unpredictable short-term volatility of stocks, a fair assumption is made that prior to investing in stocks, you have allocated away some funds for emergency purposes in the bank. This assumption further eliminates the need to engage in short-term oriented speculative activities in order to make money. One of the basic tenets of prudent capital allocation is that money allocated for the participation in equity investments should have a multiyear horizon, ideally at least 10 years. Yet many investors plunge into the stock market with unrealistic, if not foolish, expectations of overnight wealth creation.

The technology mania of the late 1990s solidified this false belief that stocks could make you rich overnight. For a lucky few, they did become rich overnight. Tragically, investors saw this market as the new era of investing. You couldn't afford not to be in the stock market, not when the auto mechanic was earning triple-digit returns on the side. Value investing has nothing to do with such anomalies. When stock prices are overvalued, as was clearly the case during the height of the Internet boom of the 1990s, the rational decision is to be on the sidelines analyzing the securities. Value investing is an investment framework that focuses on the process, not the outcome. With the right process, the outcome usually will be satisfactory investment returns.

Market liquidity has its place, however. Aside from enabling investors to access capital in times of need, liquid markets can serve investors by letting them sell that which is cheap to buy something cheaper. Realize that this is just the value investing process at work: scouring the market for the best available bargains. But when you are selling a 50-cent dollar to buy a 30-cent dollar, you are utilizing the markets for what they are: arenas to acquire ownership stakes in businesses at the cheapest possible price. Once you make an investment, the stock price will change daily based on the whims of investors on any given day. If your analysis was sound, then any short-term decline in price is merely price volatility. Before rushing to sell a stock that's declined 25 percent weeks after a purchase, ask this question: What has happened to the long-term fundamentals of the businesses over the past two weeks to make the entire business worth 25 percent less? For good businesses acquired at sensible prices, the answer is nothing at all. Occasionally, you may come to discover that you neglected some important information that, when incorporated back into your analysis, leads you to reduce your estimate of intrinsic value. In such instances, you will have to determine the appropriate course of action. Selling out is tempting, and the liquid markets make it easy to do so. But by doing so, you turn volatility into a permanent loss of capital.

For an effective comparison, consider today's real estate market. In 2007 and 2008, home values were declining across the board, reaching double-digit percentages in California and Florida. But whether they realize it or not, homeowners actually *benefit* from houses' inability to be sold as quickly as stocks, given that the same measures of safety and prudence have been applied as if one were making an investment in stocks. If the home was (a) bought at a sensible price, (b) purchased with a long-term ownership orientation and not a short-term speculative purpose, and (c) paid for using money for that stated purpose, then homeowners won't be subject to accepting Mr. Market's offered prices. Unlike stocks, homeowners aren't seeing quoted prices flash by the minute across their computer or television screens. But even if they did, no rational homeowner would rush to sell a home because the "quoted" price was 10 percent less in the afternoon than it was in the morning. With stocks, a quick call to your broker or click of a mouse is all it takes to unload your shares. Selling homes requires more time. But if houses were bought and sold as quickly as shares of stock, most homeowners and real estate investors would likely sell at the first sign of trouble—and thus sell too low.

Indeed, there are meaningful differences between home ownership versus stock ownership. Even if your home is worth less, it still provides you shelter whereas a declining stock price only serves to reduce the value of your portfolio. Nonetheless, the general thought process behind the buying and selling of either asset is of great value when thinking about stocks. The litmus test question, again, is to ask yourself whether the true worth of the underlying business has equivalently changed by the same amount as the stock has in the six and a half hours that make up each trading day.

Unfortunately, investors have their work cut out for them in utilizing their patience to the greatest advantage. Nothing in the field of investment today serves to promote a patient approach. Mutual fund managers are only as good as their most recent year's investment performance. Brokers don't get paid to tell you to do nothing; they earn a living by promoting activity. Analysts pump out information on the performance of a company based on the next quarter or two of operating results. From all angles, investors are given data in meaningless forms. The financial media breaks down the performance of stocks by the hour, as if investment results were determined at the end of the day. If the market were open only a few times a year, I believe many more investors would enjoy far better performance.

Avoid Meaningless Data

Today's investors are bombarded with split-second information from all directions. Whether it is the flashing numbers and charts on CNBC or Bloomberg or market opinions from the hundreds of financial media Web sites, investors have more information than they need. While such plentiful information might seem like an advantage, it can often do more harm than good. Seeing a stock decline 20 percent in a single day is very unsettling to most investors and often prompts them to reach for the "sell" button.

Stock prices are important on only two occasions: (1) when you are presented an opportunity to buy a good business at a cheap price, and (2) when you can sell a once-undervalued business at or above fair value. Any other time, they're meaningless. Sure, if you're investing for future major expenditures, such as a child's college tuition, knowing the value of your portfolio at a certain time is quite helpful. Still, if you buy at the right price and base your asset allocation on your specific needs, daily price changes don't mean much.

The Benefits of a Buy-and-Hold Approach

The stock market exists to let investors buy stakes in businesses, and business owners know that temporary setbacks are inevitable. You don't see them rushing to sell their business to the highest bidder, and neither should you. The market should serve your investment decisions, not guide them.

Many investors knowledgeable in market history will correctly argue that a simple buy-and-hold strategy is not as sound as all of its proponents make it out to be. The most-often cited defense of this assertion is the performance of the Dow Jones Industrial Average from 1964 to 1981.

Dow Jones Industrial Average

December 31, 1964   874.12

December 31, 1981   875.00

After the market's dismal performance in 2008, we now have another period where the markets "destroyed" value for the long-term investor.

Standard and Poor's 500 Index

December 31, 1997   970.43

December 31, 2008   903.25

The goal of the value investor is simple: to buy those securities trading at an undervalued price, sell securities trading at a fairly valued price, and avoid those securities trading at overvalued prices. These actions are done without regard to the general level of the markets. Obviously, market levels do play a role in this approach by determining the abundance of securities that would fall into each category. Nonetheless, bargains can be found when the market is fully valued, often in places where no attention is being paid. When the market was in love with technology and the Internet some 10 years ago, investors could have found wonderful value in the steel industry. Nucor, a U.S. steel producer that employs the more efficient mini-mills, is one example. A $10,000 investment in Nucor at the beginning of 1998 would have been worth approximately $200,000 at the end of 2008, for a compounded annual rate of return of approximately 35 percent over the past decade. The same investment in health insurer UnitedHealth Group in 1998 would have been worth over $150,000 at the end of 2008, producing a 31 percent annual rate of return. Even Wal-Mart experienced a three-fold rise in its share price over the period from 1998 to 2008, during which time the broad market declined in absolute terms. All three of these companies were sizable enough to be known by a wide investor base; they were covered by analysts and were considered best in class in their respective industries.

The advantages of a buy-and-hold investment approach has been deeply ingrained over the past several decades as a sound approach for investment. The advantages of reduced transaction costs and deferral of taxation are widely known. And the impressive power that compounding can have on small incremental sums of capital is also understood. But investors often mistake buy and hold to mean buying any equity at any price and just waiting. The value gained from any investment rests on the discount from intrinsic value that is obtained when the investment is acquired, which in turn is determined by the price paid for the investment. So the two elements of buy and hold are defined by these two parameters. Investors should seek to buy those securities with market prices that are below intrinsic value and accompanied by a satisfactory margin of safety. Then the security should be held until the conditions of undervaluation and satisfactory margin of safety no longer hold up.

Money is made at the time an asset is bought; it's just not realized at the time. When an asset is sold, the ultimate price paid will determine the corresponding gain or loss recorded. If a security is to be bought when the price is comfortably below intrinsic value, then it should be sold when the price closely approximates intrinsic value. Because intrinsic value is, by definition, a moving target, then the buy-and-hold approach is at the mercy of the intrinsic value of the business. Thus, when hearing the value investor promote buy and hold, understand the implicitly assumed underlying assumptions with regard to intrinsic value and price paid. There are two general ways in which a security can qualify as being undervalued with respect to intrinsic value:

1. Market price is comfortably below intrinsic value, or in certain cases net asset value.
2. Growing intrinsic value provides undervaluation.

We explore both of these ways in the next section.

DryShips: Hidden Value in the Assets?

An interesting example of an undervalued security can at times occur when the price of company X is trading below intrinsic value. For example, at the end of 2008, shares of DryShips (DRYS), a dry bulk shipping company, hit a low of $3 a share, having once traded as high as $115 per share. The severe economic recession that engulfed 2008 sent shipping rates down over 90 percent, which had a greater effect on DryShips due to its greater exposure to spot market shipping rates. Nonetheless, DRYS had average earnings of over $5 a share over the past several years, so if future earnings were even a fraction of this, the current price suggested a potential undervalued investment opportunity. Still, in spite of the unprecedented market correction and anticipated prolonged market recession, further analysis was needed to determine if DryShips was still cheap *assuming several years of deeply depressed shipping rates.* Table 8.1 is an initial balance sheet analysis based on the most recent figures.

It would appear that the implied book value of $49 a share against a share price of $3 a share reflects a grossly undervalued asset based on liquidation value alone, saying nothing of future earnings power. However, the more conservative, and necessary, balance sheet analysis would require investors to value each individual item in the balance sheet and make the necessary adjustments to reflect the current market conditions. In this case, the analysis is shown in Table 8.2.

Table 8.1   Stated Liquidation Value of DryShips

Balance Sheet Entry	Value
Assets	$5.2 billion
Liabilities	$3.1 billion
Shareholders' equity	$2.1 billion
Shares outstanding	43 million
Book value per share	$49

Source: SEC 10-Q Filing for quarter ending September 2008.

Table 8.2   Conservative Liquidation Value of DryShips

Balance Sheet Entry	Stated Value	Conservative Value
Assets		
Current assets	$456 million	$425 million
Fixed assets	$3.9 billion	$2.9 billion
Other noncurrent assets	$811 million	$120 million
Total Assets	**$5.2 billion**	**$3.4 billion**
Liabilities		
Current liabilities	$637 million	$637 million
Noncurrent liabilities	$2.4 billion	$2.4 billion
Total Liabilities	**$3.1 billion**	**$3.1 billion**
Shareholders' equity	$2.1 billion	$300 million
Shares outstanding	43 million	43 million
Book value per share	**$49**	**$7**

Source: SEC 10-Q Filing for quarter ending September 2008.

To provide maximum protection for the investor, very conservative adjustments were made to the asset side of the balance sheet. Current assets, of which $311 million were represented by cash, were essentially left alone. On the fixed asset side, conservative and prudent judgments had to be made with regard to possible market values for the ships and the drilling rigs.

- Vessels, on the balance sheet at $2.1 billion, were discounted by 50 percent because the supply of ships had greatly exceeded the current demand. Recent ship sales of similar vessels were at 30 percent to 50 percent less.
- The drilling rigs, at $1.4 billion, were discounted 10 percent. The long-term market for ultra-deepwater business, while temporarily affected by the reduced price of oil, was still sound. Long-term demand exceeded supply, and these rigs took years to build, which suggested that cash-rich oil companies would easily pay full price today to secure the rigs for future expansion.
- Goodwill, which represented $700 million of other noncurrent assets, was completely written down to zero. This goodwill represented the excess price over net asset value of prior acquisitions and should not be counted on in a buyers' market.
- Liabilities are not affected since creditors are first in line to be paid should a business be forced to liquidate.

These adjustments totaled approximately $1.8 billion, for an equity value of $330 million. At 43 million shares, this equates to conservative liquidation value of $7.70 a share. *At the then-current share price of $3 a share,* DryShips passes one test—the liquidation value of the company under extremely stressful conditions—of investment suitability.

Growing Intrinsic Value Provides Undervaluation

It might come as a shock to some that value investors love growth. While the investment world likes to separate investors as value oriented or growth oriented, value and growth are one and the same. Growth is a major determinant of value creation. The only difference is that value investors have a limit as to how much they will pay for growth. The greatest investment that a value investor can find often is referred to as a growth at a reasonable price (GARP) business. The logic is simple: If you buy a security today and that business continues to earn greater profitability and free cash flow, the intrinsic value also will grow. And as that intrinsic value grows, the investment becomes more and more undervalued from the price paid.

Ben Graham, the man commonly known as the architect of value investing, focused on finding businesses selling at less than the net liquidating value of their assets. Back during Graham's time, the proverbial "50-cent dollar" was more abundant, as the stock markets had fewer participants and the information flow was not as rapid as it is today. I think most investors will agree that today's markets are much more efficient when compared to the markets that Ben Graham and even Warren Buffett (during his early years) were involved in many decades ago.

But Mr. Market is not perfect, and the markets occasionally will confuse true value with market value. During the Internet boom, for example, market valuations far exceeded intrinsic valuations for many companies. Similarly, after the bear markets of the early 1970s, plenty of stocks were selling for cheap and discounting any future earnings growth. By definition, investing is simply the acting of seeking value by attempting to buy something for less than it is worth. You find such investments in one of two forms. The first, discussed earlier, are those businesses that would sell for more than the stated market price in a private transaction. The second, and more preferred form, is buying cheap growth.

Believe it or not, most "value investors" prefer the latter over the former. Value is created as a company continues to grow its business and, consequently, its profits. The best investment is one that promises steady growth and is selling at a discount to that growth. For instance, a likely GARP investment would be a business that trades for, say, 10 times earnings and grows its profits by 15 percent or more a year, along with similar returns on equity.

It cannot be stressed enough that discovering a business with future growth prospects selling at a reasonable price is only the first step in the investment process. Never, ever invest simply because such conditions exist. But if you do find them, you can go on to determine whether the business can sustain this growth for a period of years and whether this growth will require high levels of capital expenditures. As the company grows, so will intrinsic value and, ultimately, so will the market value. Johnson & Johnson is a wonderful example of this second type of business. A look at the most recent report of the Value Line Investment Survey shows that since 1992, Johnson & Johnson has grown profits by over 10 percent per annum.[3] Further, the dividends declared per share have also increased every single year since then. Book value per share has demonstrated a similar growth in value over the same time. However, what the Value Line report doesn't show is that Johnson & Johnson has grown both sales and earnings by greater than 10 percent for over 100 years. This type of tested stability coupled with the strong future prospects for the company justify a reduced margin of safety and still satisfy the conditions of an undervalued investment. As intrinsic value continues to grow each year, the original purchase price grows to offer a greater discount to intrinsic value. This is indeed evidenced by the Value Line report. Shares in Johnson & Johnson could have been acquired at an average of $30 each in 1997 with earnings of $1.21 per share.[4] At the end of 2008, the share price was near $60 with earnings of approximately $5.50 after a two-for-one stock split in 2001. Thus, the investor in 1997 was today earning $5.50 a share on a split adjusted purchase price of $15. On top of this, a dividend payment of $1.80 was received in 2008.

Buffett's renowned investment track record is a result of a handful of truly terrific investments that fit the mold of GARP-style

Table 8.3 **Benefits of Sitting on Your Assets**

Company	Stock Price on 1/02/1980	Stock Price on 12/31/2008	Total Return
Coca-Cola	$1.40	$45.27	3,134%
American Express	$1.91	$18.55	871%
Washington Post	$20.25	$390.25	1,827%
S&P 500 Index	105.76	903.25	754%

Note: 1980 prices are split adjusted.

Data source: www.bigcharts.marketwatch.com.

businesses. The obvious ones that come to mind are Coca-Cola, American Express, the Washington Post, and GEICO. Remember that we are investing in growth at a reasonable price, not growth at *any* price. This distinction is of paramount importance, and understanding it can prevent serious loss to the investor. GARP businesses, when you find them, are very simple investments. You buy them and sit still. See Table 8.3.

Even when sitting still, however, the investors' work is not complete. On the contrary, once an investment is made, the work becomes more painstaking. Determining that a security is undervalued and suitable for purchase is one thing; ensuring that the business remains an attractive investment is quite another. At a minimum, investors should check on the status of the investment quarterly along with the required regulatory filings issued by the business to the Securities and Exchange Commission. The purpose of these regular checkups is to be on the lookout for any significant signs that the overall fundamental condition of the business is deteriorating. Making such a determination is both part art and science. Generally, quarterly performance should be of no significant concern if the investment made truly satisfied the conditions of an undervalued one with a satisfactory margin of safety. Of course, careful detail and analysis should be given to the annual report, which lays out the results of the year and the future prospects of the company. In addition, investors should be well aware of the industry and competitive forces that might affect the investment. Doing all of this analysis will significantly increase the likelihood that the investment is disposed of when it reaches intrinsic value, which should result in a gain if the security was purchased at significantly below the intrinsic value. If not, then again, investors face a good possibility that the investment will be sold at a minimal loss.

Conservative Tests of Safety a Must

Most readers of this book (including the author) are not old enough to recall the pain of the Great Depression, and some may not even remember the bear market of the early 1970s. Unfortunately, many were exposed to the severe market decline in 2008 as a result of decades of excessive borrowing in the United States.[5] The year 2008 managed to eclipse the 1973 bear in terms of total loss for a year: 38.5 percent for the S&P 500 index. Not since 1931, at the height of the Great Depression, has a market lost so much in a single year.[6]

The severe economic recession that took hold in 2008 highlights the need for conservative tests for safety when analyzing investments. Going a step further, 2008 illustrated the need for investors to analyze companies under the severest of operating conditions. No longer was it satisfactory to assess future intrinsic values based on earning results of the past several years. In time, many companies likely will be earning record profits as severe economic conditions force out weaker, less efficient competitors. The market collapse of 2008 simply reinforces the absolute requirement for a margin of safety that can pass the test during prolonged periods of economic contraction. In the case of DryShips, it was absolutely necessary to reevaluate the carrying costs of the assets in light of reduced valuations for the vessels. Simply assigning the stated book value of $49 a share was not satisfactory in order to assign a conservative book value for the company. In the case of Johnson & Johnson, over 100 years of profitability during various economic conditions was in itself a satisfactory condition that the company was still a suitable investment.[7]

Key Takeaways

- Investment in stocks should be made with a long-term orientation. In the short run, market prices are affected by the votes of the market participants. In the long run, stock prices will catch up with the fundamentals of the business.
- Along with reduced trading mistakes, a patient investment approach minimizes transaction costs.
- The level of cash in a portfolio should be affected by the availability of bargain investments.
- Some of the market's greatest benefits—liquidity and establishment of prices—can also be a source of great loss to investors who fall prey to the unnecessary noise they often create.
- General undervalued investments arise from two situations: market prices below private sale value or buying growth businesses at reasonable prices. Both situations allow for an investment to be made at prices sufficiently below intrinsic value.

CHAPTER 9

Invest Significantly at the Maximum Point of Pessimism

THE SIXTH ELEMENT

Investors should remember that excitement and expenses are their enemies. And if they insist on trying to time their participation in equities, they should try to be fearful when others are greedy and greedy when others are fearful.

—Warren Buffett, Berkshire Hathaway
2004 Annual Report

Bull markets are born on pessimism, grow on skepticism, mature on optimism, and die on euphoria. The time of maximum pessimism is the best time to buy, and the time of maximum optimism is the best time to sell.

—Sir John Templeton, 1994

To succeed in investing over the long run, you must be prepared to look stupid in the short run.

—Mason Hawkins

We now come to arguably one of the most defining charac-teristics of a successful investment philosophy. As to be expected, buying during periods of pessimism is also one of the most difficult things to do because it requires the investor to go against the crowd psychology. It requires the investor to do the opposite of what the majority is doing. It requires the investor to go at it alone. Doing these things goes against most other conventional aspects of society and human nature. Our minds and our lives are geared toward accepting the overall consensus. Our president is elected by a majority vote; victory in sports is determined by the collaboration of the team; and important decisions are made after consultation and agreements of the members involved. In these instances and many others, there is tremendous value in going with the group, or crowd. However, when it comes to investment, there are going to be moments when an investor is out on his own and his handling of the pressures that come with being the solo man out will be crucial.

Before proceeding to detail the benefits of purchasing securities during moments of maximum pessimism, it's instructive to aggregate the requirements that have been outlined so far for a value-oriented intelligent investment philosophy.

Putting It All Together

The ability to make a significant investment in a security at time of distress and uncertainty is very a tough thing to do because it requires a high degree of mental fortitude. However, the difficulty in this decision is significantly reduced when you have established the fundamental framework to successful value investing that has been outlined in the last five chapters of this book.

First and foremost, you must develop a sound investment philosophy. This book wholeheartedly favors the philosophy established over 70 years ago by Ben Graham and his colleague David Dodd at Columbia University. It simply states that investments are made when thorough research, capital preservation, and satisfactory returns are anchors upon which the investment decision rests. Decades later, the teachings and philosophies of Graham and Dodd, promoted by the success of Warren Buffett and several others, came to be known as value investing. Today, value investing is simply the process of buying assets for significantly less than what they are worth. The process of investing in bargain securities provides the margin of safety. The margin of safety provides room for error, imprecise estimates, bad luck, and shelter from the surprises or shocks of the economy and stock market. More important, value investing *emphasizes the process first and the outcome second.*

According to value investor Seth Klarman, who has been producing market-beating returns for nearly three decades, the requisites for value investing may be beyond one's control: "While it might seem that anyone can be a value investor, the essential characteristics of this type of investor—patience, discipline, and risk aversion—may well be genetically determined."[1]

What Klarman is suggesting is that when you first learn of the value investing approach, it either takes hold of you or it doesn't. You're either disciplined and patient or you're not. You either view the stock market as a long-term wealth-creating mechanism or you don't. Many can learn and recite the value rhetoric with the greatest of ease. Tell people that your investment approach entails buying 50-cent dollars and investing with a high margin of safety . . . and presto, you're a value investor. Unfortunately, merely saying something doesn't actually mean you are doing it. However, I will add that if you really are committed to investing intelligently, the first course of action is to have a true understanding of the value investing philosophy.

Second, you must have a good search strategy. There are tens of thousands of publicly traded securities all over the world at investors' disposal. Knowing where and how to look are of crucial importance in order for investors to maximize their time. Ultimately, the more securities you look at, the greater your opportunity for finding a bargain investment. Understand that, ultimately, if you desire to pursue security investing as a profession, there is no short cut with regard to a search strategy. Even when the general level of equity prices are elevated, serious value investors are diligently researching companies and constantly learning so that they can more knowledgeable when the next opportunity of bargain hunting arises.

Today, investors have the added advantage of being able to search Securities and Exchange Commission documents via the Internet and see what other well-regarded investors are buying and selling. An effective search strategy that includes regularly checking up on the quarterly portfolio holdings of more experienced investors can be an excellent source of ideas. Investing is a painstaking process and will reward those willing to pursue it with a degree of intensity.

After your search strategy has produced worthwhile ideas, then comes the process of learning about the company and its operations, assessing the quality and competency of management, and valuing the business. Obviously, this is the crucial step in the process because investors cannot go any further without determining what the business in worth. Remember that business valuation is part art and part science and that all values are estimates. By definition, valuation process incorporates future operating results extrapolated from the past performance of the business. Because the business world and the stock market are both vulnerable to a host of shocks, the valuation is always an estimate of intrinsic value; thus the need for a margin of safety—investing only in those securities that are selling for substantially less than intrinsic value. The ultimate value of a business rests on how much future cash flow it can produce. The intrinsic value of business is the sum of those future cash flows discounted back to the present at an appropriate discount rate combined with an appropriate terminal value. Of course, a business also may be valued based on liquidation value or its value to a private buyer, but these scenarios should be relied on only when compelling analytical data justifies the likelihood of either type of event occurring.

The first three steps of the value investing framework rely principally on analysis and research. While business valuation does incorporate an element of art, most of the valuation process is based on facts and statistical data. The remainder of the value investing framework—discipline to say no, patience, and investing at maximum points of pessimism—becomes much more difficult to apply because it relies not on intelligence or IQ level but more on temperament and emotion.

The discipline to say no goes beyond application to individual securities. When presented with a security that is trading for substantially less than intrinsic value, the decision then rests on determining if the business meets the standards of quality and soundness that will allow for (a) intrinsic value to increase over time and (b) existence of future catalysts that will cause the stock price to reach intrinsic value. Vastly more important is staying away from the market euphoria that often leads to inflated prices. One of the core tenets of value investing is that whatever area of the market the masses find attractive is the area with little or no value at all. For example, the 38-percent market decline in the Standard & Poor's 500 Index in 2008, the worst performance since 1931, led to a massive exodus to the safety of U.S. Treasury securities. The desire for the safety of cash was so high that the 3-month Treasury note was, at one point, actually yielding 0 percent. The 30-year Treasury was yielding only 2.53 percent, the lowest level in decades.[2] Frightened investors were willing to accept a negative real rate of return in exchange for the safety of principal. Yet with the United States government fully dedicated to flooding the markets with newly printed dollars in order to resuscitate the economy, it seems very likely that U.S. Treasuries are not the place to be at the present moment. Having the discipline to say no and go against the popular sentiment of the day requires investors to separate themselves from the masses. It is not easy to make such a decision, especially in the short run when it seems that the lone man out is wrong. Yet, as is often the case in value investing, sometime it's necessary to look stupid in the short run in order to succeed in the long run.

Remaining patient also demands an independent frame of mind. As Klarman says, you're either patient or you're not. The market can't teach you patience. Reading books won't instill patience in investors, no matter how much they agree with the lessons laid out. Patience is essential to value investors because often they are investing in securities that are currently out of favor in the marketplace; often it takes many months before the market has a change of heart. Value investors feel no remorse as they patiently wait for the market price of their investments to catch up with the intrinsic value of the business. Their patience is rewarded by their knowledge that they are involved as stakeholders in a business, not a moving stock price, and that, in time, they will be compensated with satisfactory capital gain.

One can understand Klarman's assertion that the essential characteristics of value either immediately take hold in the mind of the investor or are never truly applied. In order to make an investment at the maximum point of pessimism, the essential characteristics of value investing have to be seared in your mind. And it's an all-or-nothing proposition. Working backward proves this point. Before investing in a security currently out of favor with Mr. Market, investors have to know that they are patient because it is highly likely that the investment will take some time to reach intrinsic value. At the same time, investors also must know when to say no, which also means knowing when to say yes. The value of the business is what enables investors to go from being disciplined and patient to actually investing. Before you value a business, you first have to seek it out. And before seeking out potential bargain investments, you must establish a sound investment philosophy. There are no shortcuts to take or areas that can be neglected. There's no halfway to value investing; it's either there or it isn't.

Pessimism Leads to Value

A value-oriented investment approach in the style of Graham and Buffett is not designed for bull markets.[3] If our stock market were always bullish, there would be no need for a value investing approach. Unfortunately, markets can't go up forever, so value investing—the act of purchasing assets or securities for less than what they are worth—focuses on markets characterized by declining prices and valuations. During bull markets, a lot of people are mistaken for investment geniuses when in fact it's the rising tide that's moving them up in the world. Bear markets, however, distinguish the intelligent investor from the fly-by-night speculator.

In his 1961 letter to partners, a 31-year-old investor in Omaha named Warren Buffett said that they should be judging him during times of turmoil and not times of jubilance. "I would consider a year in which we declined 15% and the [Dow Jones Industrial] Average 30%, to be much superior to a year when both we and the Average advanced 20%." Very early on in his career, Buffett was aware that performing well during market turmoil was the key to long-term success as an investor. During the 13 years that Buffett ran his partnership, not only did his performance destroy the Dow Jones Average during both bull and bear markets, but he also never had a down year. While other investors have come along and produced records that outshine Buffett's, Buffett's preservation of capital has allowed him to compound money at a staggering rate.

It should come as no surprise that the most fertile hunting ground for picking up good companies cheap is during the height of bear markets, when fear and uncertainty run rampant. Fear is an emotion. When investors are making decisions based on emotion, such decisions are very likely to be irrational. Numerous psychological studies have demonstrated that humans feel the pain of loss much more acutely than the pleasure of gain. Merely sitting on losses, even ones that have not yet been realized, is too painful for many. The instant reaction when it comes to stocks is simply to sell off the loser so the "loss" is no longer visible. Successful investors understand this erratic behavior and seek to exploit it. Back in 1973, after nearly two decades of stock price appreciation, the markets fell hard. Most people fled the equity markets, thus missing out on one of the century's best buying opportunities. A similar situation occurred from late 2002 into 2003, after the tech bubble: Dirty laundry was washed out and securities were cheap again, but everyone was afraid—even though the gap between value and price was wider than it had been in a decade. Investors who are overcome by emotion always disregard market fundamentals, buying when they should be selling and vice versa.

A brilliant illustration of this madness-of-crowds syndrome occurred in 1987 as U.S. equities underwent an enormous surge in share prices between January and August only to collapse by 22.6 percent on October 19. Echoing the comments by William Ruane and Richard Cuniff that were given in Chapter 4, it's pure folly to believe that the value of American businesses were worth 44 percent more in eight months or 23 percent less in a single day.

The comments by Ruane and Cuniff are very insightful for both their simplicity and their convincing logic. The comment clearly illustrates their businesslike approach to investing. Great businesses spend many years—in some cases, decades—growing and becoming more profitable. If this is the case, are investors behaving rationally when they value a business 23 percent less in a single day when it can take years for a business to be worth 23 percent more? It was this type of thinking that sent value investors buying on October 20, 1987. One of the worst days in the stock market just happened to be one of the best buying opportunities in the stock market.

Value investors thrive when markets are consumed with fear. A fearful market environment leads to an inefficient market. When markets are inefficient, the discrepancy between market value and true value is as wide as ever. Instead of finding 50- or 60-cent dollars, you begin to see 20- or 30-cent dollars. And therein lies the real value brought about during periods of market pessimism: Owning stocks actually becomes a less risky proposition. Very few people find comfort in distressed markets, and owning stocks is seen as being more speculative. This viewpoint only confirms the backwardness with which many investors continue to pursue investing. The question that has yet to be answered is "How is it that buying a dollar's worth of assets for 75 cents is comforting, yet when that same dollar of assets is now selling for 35 cents, the investment is regarded as carrying more risk?" The answer, of course, is that it is not. Unfortunately, when investors rush for the exits during bear markets only to return upon the arrival of good news, they have chosen to forgo the 35-cent purchase and wait to buy when the price hits 75.

Avoid That Which Is Most Valuable

Regarded as arguably the greatest stock picker of the twentieth century, Sir John Templeton, brilliantly remarked, "The four most dangerous words in investing are 'This time it's different.'"[4] Euphoric markets always seem to have a way of fooling many investors into thinking stock prices will always go up. Such nonsensical beliefs are the number-one reason why many investors make poor investment choices that lead to permanent losses of capital.

Templeton is widely known for making investments during periods of extreme pessimism. In 1939, after World War II broke out in Europe, the 26-year old Templeton borrowed $10,000 and he used that money to buy 100 shares each in 104 companies that were selling at $1 a share or less on the New Stock Exchange, including 34 that were in bankruptcy.[5] In the end, Templeton reaped large profits on 100 of the companies while the remaining 4 turned out to be worthless. Fifteen years later, in 1954, Templeton launched the Templeton Growth Fund. From 1954 to 1992, the flagship fund delivered a 14.5 percent annual rate of return; a $10,000 invest-ment, assuming all dividends were reinvested, would have been worth $2 million. All great investors always have had the courage to make significant investments in a business during maximum points of pessimism. Warren Buffett did just that with American Express in the 1960s when the company was suffering from the salad oil scandal, a major corporate scandal in 1963 that involved American Express extending millions in loans to Allied Crude Vegetable Oil backed by Allied's salad oil inventory. When it was discovered that the collateral was containers of water and not oil, American Express shares declined over 50 percent as a result.

With many investing luminaries exhibiting similar traits in their investing activities, it's worthwhile to go deeper into their approach to see why it pays to invest during the direst of situations. Examining these activities by understanding the opposite approach—invest-ing in businesses at the maximum point of optimism—offers great value. Since the market punishes the stock prices of those busi-nesses to which it assigns maximum pessimism, then it would make sense that the most highly valued business in the world are the ones that the market views with maximum optimism.

Table 9.1, taken from an article written by Mohnish Pabrai, "The Danger in Buying the Biggest," offers great insight as to why it is often harmful to investment returns to invest in the most valuable businesses.

Pabrai examined this list and determined that if you had started with $10,000 invested in the most valuable businesses in 1987, when *Fortune* released its list, and every subsequent year reinvested the funds in what was at the time the most valuable business, in 2002, you'd have an annualized gain of 3.3 percent. During the same period, the Standard & Poor's (S&P) index delivered about a 10 percent annualized return.

You can clearly see from the results that buying the darlings of Wall Street is not as intelligent as it might initially appear.

Table 9.1   Most Valuable Businesses (in Billions)

Year	Company	Market Cap	Revenue	Net Income
1987	IBM	$89	$51	$4.8
1988	IBM	$68	$59	$5.8
1989	IBM	$70	$63	$5.2
1990	IBM	$61	$69	$6.0
1991	IBM	$75	$65	$2.1
1992	Exxon	$69	$103	$4.8
1993	Exxon	$78	$100	$5.3
1994	GE	$90	$60	$5.9
1995	GE	$92	$70	$6.6
1996	GE	$126	$79	$7.3
1997	GE	$120	$91	$8.2
1998	GE	$260	$100	$10.7
1999	Microsoft	$419	$20	$7.6
2000	Microsoft	$492	$23	$9.4
2001	GE	$407	$126	$14.1
2002	GE	$401	$131	$16.6

Source: Published by www.TheStreet.com by Mohnish Pabrai and included in the book
Mosaic: Perspectives on Investing by Mohnish Pabrai.

Rephrasing Buffett, odds are very high that you are paying full value or a premium price to invest in the popular issues of the day. It would seem crystal clear to us all that anytime an asset is bought in an environment characterized by many buyers, the price paid will not be as attractive as when the same asset is bought in the presence of few buyers. The economic laws of supply and demand apply to the markets. When demand is high for securities—during bull markets—prices increase to satisfy that demand. Conversely, when there is very little demand for equities—the consequence of bear markets—prices decline.

Auction houses are proof positive of this theory. By attracting more bidders, auction houses are attempting to extract the best possible price they can. Many distressed assets are sold via auction in an attempt to maximize the price attained for the asset. Realizing this, value investors understand that the best possible time to buy securities is when very few buyers are present. The absence of demand creates a very high probability of purchasing assets for substantially less than replacement cost or intrinsic value. By investing in a business during the rosiest of times, investors almost guarantee that the price paid will be at a premium to the underlying intrinsic value, thus creating an investment without any meaningful margin of safety. As a result, investors place their capital at greater risk for loss should the business suffer a slight mishap. During bull markets, this investment approach will surely be confused with an intelligent approach, as a rising tide lifts all boats. Then again, if all we had were bull markets, a value investing approach would not be needed, since all the attributes of investing—exercising due diligence, investing with a margin of safety, looking for companies with excellent economics and honest and able management—are for the purpose of weathering the bear market storms and emerging with your capital intact.

As renowned investor Shelby Davis astutely observed: "A down market lets you buy more shares in great companies at favorable prices. If you know what you're doing, you'll make most of your money from these periods, you just won't realize it until much later."[6] Bear markets are characterized by widespread disdain toward equities, causing many buyers to exit the markets at the first sign of trouble. This disdain is fueled by endless negative newspaper headlines and television programs that further fuel investors' disregard for equities. Forgetting that media outlets are talking about the current state of affairs while the markets focus on the future state of affairs, investors abandon equities at the height of bad news, thereby selling low and buying high. As the saying goes, what has risen shall fall, and what has fallen shall soon rise again. Surely not every stock that deteriorates will again rise—it's up to you to provide the thorough analysis and determine whether a superior investment opportunity exists.

It's not easy going at it alone and buying securities when everyone is selling and companies are experiencing setbacks. Investing during times when the market mood is at its worst requires investors to be comfortable with the fact that prices could go lower still. Many investors have a misguided fascination with trying to buy at the bottom and sell at the top. That idea rests on the belief that investors can time markets perfectly, suggesting that the quoted price of the stock is the central object of focus. Value-oriented investors, however, rely on the stock price only in as much as it serves to determine whether the business is undervalued. And as is often the case, value investors usually buy before the bottom is reached and sell before the absolute top. But what counts is what happens in between: buying low even though the price may go lower and then selling high even though the price may go higher. In the end, the result is a gain on investment. Also, armed with the knowledge that the security is undervalued, investors have the added benefit of buying more as the price declines and thus getting an even greater bargain. The result of the value approach is ultimately a win-win for value investors. They buy cheap regardless of whether the purchase is being made at the bottom. Should the price decline further still, value investors see this as an even better opportunity to buy more for less.

The late Benjamin Graham and David Dodd summed up their investment philosophy brilliantly in a passage from their seminal work *Security Analysis*. During Graham's day, the concept of value investing was oxymoronic in the sense that if you weren't investing with the goal of buying assets for less than they're worth, then you were speculating. The term "value investing" was not even used 60 years ago during Graham's time, but what Graham and

Dodd defined as the key to successful investing applies to any self-described investment approach:

> It is our view that stock-market timing cannot be done, with general success, unless the time to buy is related to an attractive price level, as measured by analytical standards. Similarly, the investor must take his cue to sell primarily not from so-called technical market signals but from an advance in the price level beyond a point justified by objective standards of value. It may be that within these paramount limits there are refinements of stock-market technique that can make for better timing and more satisfactory over-all results. Yet we cannot avoid the conclusion that the most generally accepted principle of timing—that purchases should be made only after an *upswing* has definitely announced itself—is basically opposed to the essential nature of investment. *Traditionally the investor has been the man with patience and the courage of his convictions who would buy when the harried or disheartened speculator was selling.* If the investor is now to hold back until the market itself encourages him, how will he distinguish himself from the speculator, and wherein will he deserve any better than the ordinary speculator's fate? [Emphasis added.][7]

Remain Flexible in the Approach

Value can be found in various different ways in various businesses. One business might be undervalued in relation to the free cash flow it generates. Another business, like the DryShips example earlier, might be undervalued based on a very conservative appraisal of the value of its assets. Another business might be undervalued because its future growth potential suggests that the intrinsic value will continue to increase over time (Johnson & Johnson). Yet another business might be undervalued because it would be worth a lot more to a strategic buyer.

It is very easy for investors to take the lessons and philosophies of value investors and conclude that the approach is rigid in its nature. Four common myths include:

1. Value investors *only* invest in bear markets.
2. *Only* low price to earnings (P/E) ratio stocks qualify as bargain investments.
3. High-growth businesses *cannot* be value investments.
4. Value investors *never* sell stocks short.

These myths are discussed in the next sections.

Myth: Value Investors Only Invest in Bear Markets

Value investors love bear markets only inasmuch as they provide more fertile hunting for bargain securities. Value investors invest in any type of market as long as the ability to buy an asset for less than its intrinsic worth exists with a comfortable margin of safety. Bear markets offer greater opportunity to find such investments, but not the only opportunity.

Myth: Only Low P/E Stocks Qualify as Bargains

Value investing is, by its very nature, a very flexible approach. That's not to say that the four aforementioned "myths" don't appeal to value investors because in fact they do. Many value investors love to search for low P/E stocks, but while a business trading at three times earnings merits a very close look, it certainly doesn't mean the business is a screaming bargain. If the business is able to continue increasing profitability, then the opportunity becomes very intriguing. Otherwise, the P/E of 3 this year can easily become a P/E of 25 next year. What matters most in investing is the future performance of the company over a reasonable period of time. In fact, many bargain investments arise from opportunities in which the business has suffered a temporary net loss, thus leaving it with no P/E multiple.

The market often punishes the stock prices of these businesses to the point that they may qualify as the best bargain opportunities.

When discussing P/E ratio in the context of whether the figure is too high, fair, or too low, the discussion becomes very arbitrary. While many investors might agree on the fact that paying 75 times earnings for any business is grossly high, what qualifies as an appropriate P/E multiple for the value investor is far from specific. The P/E multiple is important but not so much on its own and more so with regard to the overall fundamental strength of the business. A company like Berkshire Hathaway that trades for 17 times earnings in 2009 cannot be considered expensive on a P/E basis, once the quality and operating performance of the company over the past 40 years are taken into account. Similarly, electronics giant Best Buy cannot automatically be assumed to be cheap trading at a P/E of 10 in 2009 in relation to a P/E of 14 for the S&P's 500 Index. The goal of the value investor is to determine whether low valuations are a temporary or a permanent issue. If temporary, then the work begins in determining if the current price justifies making the investment.

Myth: High-Growth Businesses Cannot Be Value Investments

Again, the mistake of this assumption is that there exists a different set of analytical assumptions and investment underpinnings that is used to classify a business as a value or growth security. In fact, both aspects of a business are no more than two sides of the same coin: growth creates value. Indeed, the best investments that value investors can hope to make are in those securities that hold the greatest promise for long-term future growth in revenues and profits. What distinguishes value investors, however, is that they have a price limit that they will pay for this future growth. The concept of "price is what you pay, but value is what you get" is at the cornerstone of a value investing approach.

However, there is one distinction between value and growth that can lead to opportunity. Companies perceived as "growth" stocks are often assigned higher valuation multiples by Mr. Market. If the "growth" of such a company slows down, the valuation multiples will likely decline as well. This action could lead the growth stock to become a value stock. The opportunity to the value investor is that if the business can earn greater profits in the future, growth chasers will buy it again leading to a higher multiple and higher share price.

Myth: Value Investors Don't Short Stocks

Similarly, many value investors shun shorting stocks. Going short a stock is essentially the process of buying low and selling high, but in reverse. (Being long means owning a stock; being short means selling a stock one does not own.) Instead of first buying the stock, an investor will go short, or sell the stock first. This is done by borrowing the shares from the broker. The goal is that the stock price will decline and the investor is able to buy back the shares at a cheaper price; the shares are then returned to the brokerage firm, with the investor keeping the difference. When going short a position, an investor is betting that the share price will depreciate in value, not appreciate in value. The strongest argument against shorting is an economic one. When you go short, your upside returns are limited to 100 percent because a stock can only go to zero. If you go short a $20 stock and the price hits zero, you've made a 100 percent return on your money. If you go short a $100 stock, it's the same return if the shares approach zero. However, your downside is unlimited because, theoretically, a stock can go up in price infinitely. That same stock that was shorted at $20 can go up to $30, $40, $60, and on and on. At $60, the loss is 200 percent. The basic reason against shorting is that it's a bet made with a capped upside but unlimited downside. In more technical terms, there is an asymmetry in the risk/reward ratio between being short or long in the stock market. The asymmetry reveals itself in this way: Losing on a long position reduces an investor's risk exposure while losing on the short position increases the risk exposure because it means that the stock price is going up. However, at times, short selling certain stocks can be a very value-oriented investment.

In the early 1970s, a group of large investor favorites known as the Nifty 50 were widely regarded as "one-decision" buy-and-hold stocks. Regardless of how high the stock prices rose, investors came to believe that the predictable rapid earnings growth of the Nifty 50 was sufficient to justify their purchase at any price and produce market-beating results. During this time of unyielding optimism, the average P/E of the Nifty 50 stocks was 37 versus a market multiple of 18. It was clear that the valuations afforded to this select group of stocks were dependent on continuous growth at a rapid rate, which becomes more and more impossible as the numbers become larger. Indeed, it would appear that the margin of safety existed in going short a basket of Nifty 50 stocks as there wasn't any margin of safety at a P/E of 37. The severe market downturn of 1972 to 1974 brought devastation to Nifty 50 stock valuations and taught investors that price does matter and that people can pay too much for even the soundest of companies.

This lesson didn't last long; the technology mania ushered in a reincarnation of the Nifty 50 episode. This time, the Nifty 50 was replaced by the NASDAQ 100 Index. Whereas the Nifty 50 episode consisted of the best-of-best businesses with long records of operating history—including Polaroid, McDonald's, and Johnson & Johnson—the NASDAQ 100 included new start-ups with little or no operating history to speak of. Clearly, investors had forgotten the lessons learned in the early 1970s because the valuations afforded to this new group were extraordinary. At the height of the tech bubble in 2000, many fly-by-night businesses were trading at astronomical valuations without any fundamentals to back them up. In February

2000, the NASDAQ 100 P/E reached 134.7, four to five times the P/E ratios of companies in the Dow Jones Industrial Average or the S&P's 500 Index. The NASDAQ Composite Index reached a P/E ratio of 245![8] Again there was no value or margin of safety by buying these equities at these ridiculous valuations, and being on the short side would not have been deemed a speculative activity.

It would be unfair and ignorant to leave out one very crucial aspect of participating in short sales: the consequences of time. Investors who short a stock are borrowing those shares from their brokerage house and making the investment on a margin account (on borrowed funds). This means that unlike long investments that do not require the use of margin (although many investors choose to do so), a short position that goes against you can require you to deposit additional capital or sell other securities in your portfolio to raise the necessary capital. In other words, investors who are correct in their analysis of shorting a stock can still lose money on the trade if the stock continues to go up before finally coming down to more realistic valuations. This was the case for many investors in 1999 who correctly concluded that the NASDAQ Composite Index was grossly overvalued at a P/E of 100. Unfortunately, before the valuations headed south to more realistic levels, the P/E ratio climbed to over 245, effectively wiping out some investors who were overexposed on the short side. In hypothetical terms, an investor can correctly short a stock trading at $100, but months later, the shares can easily be trading for $200, at which point a capital infusion may be required. Without the additional capital, the investor must sell and is forced to take a loss. Yet several months later, the shares could be trading at $20. The bet was correct but if an investor enters the position early and the shares continue to rise, the result could be a painful loss. The asymmetry of shorting is that you can be more patient being long and wrong than being short and wrong. This asymmetry serves to discourage the short selling of stocks. Many of the myths cited run together, further indicating that value is found in many ways.

Four things that are true about value investors is that:

1. They only invest in business they understand.
2. They get excited when equity prices are declining.
3. They first think about the probability of capital loss before thinking about the capital gain.
4. They tend to find great bargains in unloved areas of the market.

These characteristics signify a complete resonance with the principles of value investing. Unlike the four myths, these four characteristics are not flexible. Just as keeping your head down is essential to a consistent and effective golf swing, so are these four characteristics.

All or Nothing

If an investor does not truly understand the business under consideration, the approach is speculative regardless of the bargain offered. Not knowing the strengths and weaknesses of the business, the industry the business operates in, or how to effectively value the business will eliminate any possibility of intelligently and analytically buying the business at an undervalued price and selling it later at a higher price.

Lower prices excite value investors because they understand that when general equity prices are declining, many great businesses will also suffer unwarranted price declines. The abundance of low equity prices provides the foundation for future great returns.

Risk aversion is the name of the game for value investors. Preserving investment capital is the cornerstone of an absolute return investment approach. Unlike relative return investing, where investment performance tracks the broad market index, absolute-return-oriented investors focus on the skill and ability of the investment manager to outperform the market. A focus on capital preservation, the number-one goal for value investors, recognizes the fact that value investing focuses on bear markets and how to best weather the storm.

What the market hates, value investors often love. When the market is down on a particular business, sector, or industry, the demand from buyers is at an all-time low, leading to greatly depressed security prices.

Key Takeaways

- Buying securities during periods of pessimism is the most difficult task in investing; appropriately, it the greatest determinant of investment success.
- Before investors can be truly successful at investing during periods of maximum pessimism, they need to be wired with the characteristics of the value approach: patience, discipline, and risk aversion.
- The key characteristics of the value approach rely more on investors' temperament than on their level of intelligence.
- Pessimism leads to lower security prices, which offer investors the likelihood of finding more bargain investments and thus the greater chance for future capital gain.
- Euphoria in the stock market can be a great indicator that security prices are at premium valuations.
- The most valuable businesses often have stock prices that offer little or no value.
- Value investing has defined characteristics, but the approach can be very flexible with respect to where value is found.

10

More Than One Way to Find Value

CASE STUDIES SHOWING
THE APPROACH AT WORK

*The individual investor should act consistently as an investor and
not as a speculator. This means that he should be able to justify
every purchase he makes and each price he pays by impersonal
objective reasoning that satisfies him that he is getting more than
his money's worth for his purchase.*

—Benjamin Graham

So far, the goal of this book has been to alert investors to the
ways in which a value-oriented investment mind approaches investing. Tell people that your investment approach entails buying
50-cent dollars and investing with a high margin of safety and,
presto, you're a value investor. But *saying* something isn't the same
as *doing* it. It's time to *do* now.

This chapter presents three case studies that illustrate how to
approach investing in an intelligent, businesslike fashion. They
are examples of why a value-oriented investment approach makes
sense. Each case study presents a different way to determine that
the company under investigation is indeed a bargain investment
opportunity at the time.

Case Study #1: Sunrise Senior Living. Back in 2002, this provider of managed care for the elderly was showing strength in an industry that appeared to be weakening. The company's business strategy was twofold: (1) by developing and selling premium assisted living properties, Sunrise was making profit on real estate sales and (2) managing assisted living properties, thus using its expertise to provide a recurring revenue stream. A closer look at both of these aspects of the business revealed great value.

Case Study #2: Ternium Steel. As one of the most profitable steel companies in the world, Ternium was generating enormous levels of free cash flow. But because the company had operations in Venezuela, Mr. Market overreacted and discounted the share price above and beyond what the company would be worth without any business in Venezuela.

Case Study #3: Mueller Water Company Arbitrage. Mueller Water Company is a manufacturer and supplier of water infrastructure products. However, this was an arbitrage investment that was seeking to exploit a wide inefficiency in value between Class A and B shares of Mueller and had nothing to do with the actual operations of the business.

Keep in mind that some of these case studies took place in the past and reflect the environment and opportunity at that time; these businesses may be quite different today with respect to size, soundness, and management from how they were when the analysis actually took place. What can be said unequivocally about the three case studies is that they are, or were, actual investments that were made by the author at various points in time.

In the investment management business, eating one's own cooking should be the standard, not the exception. Investment managers who have their own capital invested alongside that of their clients is a powerful sign of alignment of interests. Likewise, I believe an author who is recommending an investment approach should use examples in which he participated.

A Reminder: Process First, Outcome Second

The effectiveness of any fundamental analysis hinges on the quality of the analysis. As such, value investing emphasizes the process first and the outcome second. Indeed, the outcome ultimately matters: If you continue to do thorough analysis on potential investments and all outcomes lead to poor results, then there is a flaw of some sort in the analysis. The point of focusing first on the process is that it ensures that the work is done in the most rational manner. Value investors are first concerned with whether the particular business is trading at a discount to its intrinsic value, not with the possibility of future gain. The purpose of putting the process before the outcome is to seek safety first and capital appreciation second. During up markets, it seems that many businesses can be bought at fair or overvalued prices and still continue to deliver investment gains. Of course, this outcome is due solely to the general nature of the market and has nothing to do with the underlying fundamentals of the business. Then again, the value approach would be unnecessary if markets continuously went up.

Because markets fluctuate and an investor's primary focus should rest on capital preservation, focus has to rest on the process. Tiger Woods doesn't go out and hit 500 golf balls on the driving range. He goes out and hits 500 golf balls with a specific target and ball flight in mind for each shot. Tiger's concentration is not on practicing but on practicing as perfectly as he can. This too is the goal of value investors: to ensure their data and reasoning behind their research and analysis is satisfactory and to use that analysis to determine whether the investment should be made.

Readers will maximize the benefits of the case studies by approaching them in this "process first, outcome second" manner. This distinction cannot be emphasized enough as Sunrise Senior Living in particular would no longer pass the rigorous test of investment suitability. Each analysis is annotated to tie it to an earlier chapter. While the aim of the case studies is to be as simple as possible (the best valuations tend to be those easiest to understand), they delve into detail when necessary in order to offer value to both beginners and advanced students of value investing.

Case Study #1: Finding Value in an Unloved Industry Sunrise Senior Living (SRZ)

In late 2002 and 2003, shares of Sunrise Senior Living were trading in the high 20s and low 30s. Many competitors in the assisted living industry were disappearing due to poor balance sheets and high costs of capital. Unlike the others, Sunrise appeared to be well run and in the hands of good management. Not surprisingly, Mr. Market was disappointed with the entire industry, and Sunrise Senior Living was being punished as well.

One day when I was driving back home from the airport, I spotted a Sunrise facility in Atlanta, Georgia, and decided to take a look. I was impressed with the quality of the facility and the people in it. Once you stepped inside, you had no idea you were in an assisted living facility. It felt more like a mansion. I began to take a much closer look at the company to see if any value was to be found.

Note

This case study is based on an investment that occurred in 2002 and 2003. As with all case studies in value investing, the goal is to illustrate by concrete facts and examples the value approach at work and how it relates to the philosophies set forth in this book. Unless exactly specified, the investment qualifications of the past are not necessarily indicative of investment suitability now. All data used was accurate at time of analysis.

Company Background

Sunrise Senior Living offers senior living care services including assisted living, independent living, and specialized living services. At the end of 2002, SRZ owned or operated over 200 living centers in the United States, Canada, and the United Kingdom. Sunrise was founded in 1981 by the husband-and-wife team of Paul and Theresa Klaassen. Together they owned more than 10 percent of company. They both lived in the first community they opened in 1981.

Unlike its competitors, Sunrise's properties didn't take the form of traditional assisted living communities. My visit to the Atlanta property confirmed what the company was saying in the annual report. Rather, their communities look like Victorian houses, high-rises, and elegant mansions. In addition, the landscaping supporting the properties was immaculate. Management's pride in the uniqueness of the properties was evident in the attention and detail that went into each property development.

As I began to perform the research and analysis on Sunrise, some important facts came to light:

- Sunrise tended to cluster its facilities in the top 20 largest metropolitan areas in the country with 6 to 25 properties per cluster. This makes it more efficient to manage, staff, and grow the entire area. Sunrise has been selling or closing stray properties outside these clusters.
- Since 1998, development of new assisted living facilities dropped off dramatically due to the poor health and over-extended financials of most players. During this dismal time, Sunrise was growing at a steady clip and was adding 20 communities in 2002 and more in 2003.
- Assisted living costs were approximately $90 to $150 per day. The economics of assisted living expenses at the time were such that over 99 percent was private pay and not reliant on insurance. And payments typically were made by family members, usually a child of the assisted living resident. This compared

very favorably with typical home care cost, which ranged from $60 to $400 per day, or nursing homes, which typically cost $100 to $400 a day.

- The Sunrise facilities have three types of residents: Assisted Living, Higher Acuity Assisted Living, and Alzheimer's/Dementia Care. As residents move through these stages, the daily rate rises. Their typical homes can accommodate all three.
- The average age of the SRZ resident is between 80 and 84 years. This demographic is growing three times as fast as the rest of the population.
- There existed two very high barriers to entry: capital and time (it took about 4 years beginning with site selection before properties became cash flow even), management expertise, regulatory approval, and economies of scale.

Sunrise was arguably the best in the industry with regard to site selection. The company carefully studied income and age demographics and developed properties accordingly. As an example, the facility I visited is located in an area known as Buckhead, a very upper-scale part of Atlanta with a concentration of high-income residents. It's next door to a lot of high-rise residences, a mall, restaurants, and a pharmacy. If you missed the Sunrise sign on the building, you might mistake the building for a high-end apartment complex.

At the time, Sunrise was the only company in the industry that developed assisted living properties. The company developed its properties by forming joint ventures with Sunrise retaining a minority portion. After development, Sunrise would manage the property and earn a 6 to 8 percent management fee.

As you can see, the initial attraction to Sunrise was triggered by the market's dislike for the entire industry because of the poor capital structure facing many assisted living companies. As a result, the market had reduced the valuation of the entire industry, albeit for a good reason. But Sunrise was a different company at the time, and the overall market pessimism for the industry created an opportunity to acquire it at an attractive price.

Investment Analysis

Sunrise essentially had two sources of revenue:

1. The sale of mature properties, in which case Sunrise would retain the right to manage the properties for a fee
2. Long-term management of Sunrise properties and others using its expertise

At the time, the economics of the Sunrise "develop, build, and sale" model went something like this: It cost Sunrise about $11 million to build a facility plus start-up costs of $700,000, so the total cost was $11.7 million. Sunrise would use a combination of debt and equity to fund each property development. Each facility was being funded with about $2.5 million in equity with the remaining $9 million or so coming from debt.

Once developed, Sunrise would sell the properties for about $16 million, yielding a pretax profit of $4.3 million, or about 170 percent return on investment.

$$ROI = \$4.7/\$2.5 = 1.7 \, or \, 170\%$$

As part of the sale, Sunrise typically would retain a 20 percent residual interest so it was getting about $12.3 million after the sale. With the pretax profit of $4.3 million, Sunrise was able to internally finance the build-out of four properties for each two sold. The economics of this model creates tremendous value. The company would invest $2.3 million, sell the property for $16 million, and have enough left over to repeat this process twice. At the time, Sunrise was still a company with tremendous growth potential, and this model was able to use leverage to create tremendous value.

Because Sunrise was building properties and incurring start-up costs, net income was artificially low initially. Even more so, income would always be lumpy depending on the volume of construction that was going on at the time. Mr. Market doesn't favor irregular streams of income because he is unable to get comfortable with the future earnings of the business. When the construction slowed down, net income would rise significantly. In the meantime, Sunrise was building about 20 to 30 units each year and selling the same amount, so net income was around $60 million. With approximately 20 million shares outstanding, earnings per share were $3. The buyers of the properties were blue-chip companies, so it was safe to assume that they would not lose appetite. Buyers included General Electric and Prudential.

While the sale-leaseback gains historically have driven earnings, over the long term Sunrise was going to generate most of its earnings from management contracts. This segment's earnings per share (EPS) was growing at over a 25 percent annual rate and was due to:

- Development of new properties
- The emerging "Sunrise At Home" care services
- Management contracts on third-party-owned assisted living facilities
- Annual price increases per resident

The EPS of the management services was:
2000 $0.59
2001 $0.79

Expectations were $1 and $1.29 for 2002 and 2003. Residents were staying an average of 2.5 years, and growth was coming in at 29 percent per year, so it was safe to assume that 20 percent was achievable over the next four to five years.

Valuation

Assigning a multiple of 15 to 20 to the $1.29 2003 EPS gives a price range of about $19 to $25 per share. This a fair multiple range, as it would have been below the EPS growth rate and implying a price to earnings/growth (PEG) ratio of less than 1.

A very common rule of thumb metric in business valuation is that businesses that are selling for earnings multiples that are less than the rate of growth of earnings often can create more value, all else being equal. It's a logical assumption: Paying 12 times earnings for a company that is growing profits at 20 percent a year is much more attractive than paying 10 times earnings for a company that is growing 5 percent a year. Such was my thinking when determining an estimate for the stock price based on future earnings expectations.

Further, it was clear that the balance sheet value of the real estate was undervalued. Going back and looking at the company's past real estate verified this assumption.

Table 10.1 looks at the historical real estate transactions. In 2002, Sunrise had about $800 million in property on its balance sheet. The entire $800 million was related to the real estate properties. Given

Table 10.1 Sunrise Senior Living Historical Real Estate Transactions ($ millions)

Date	Sales Price	Book Value	Premium to Book
December 2000	$130	$75	80%
August 2001	$86	$67	43%
May 2002	$200	$140	62%
August 2002	$48	$29	72%
September 2002	$200	$140	42%
Average Sales Price over Book Value			53%

Source: Company financial reports.

the past sales transactions, it was obvious that the properties were being understated on the balance sheet by an average of 50 percent, or approximately $400 million, based on the real estate sales in the past. Based on the shares outstanding, real book value was understated by about $15 a share. Tangible book value was about $20 while real book value was actually close to $35.

Adding the real book value with the management division value of $19 to $25 yielded an intrinsic value of anywhere from $54 to $60 per share.

Free Cash Flow Valuation

The above analysis is one effective way to properly value the business. Looking at the value of the company by determining the future free cash flow generation yielded these results.

For many years, Sunrise was exceeding the earnings estimates of analysts. So if you took the $2.55 in earnings per share that it was expecting for 2003 and added back depreciation—depreciation which wasn't really occurring since Sunrise's depreciable assets were real estate, which appreciates over time—of $30 million, or $1.25 per share, you've got an operating cash flow figure of about $3.80 per share.

The company's annual capital expenditures were about $6 million or so, or approximately $0.25 to $0.30 a share. Deducting that from the operating cash flow produced free cash flow of approximately $3.50 a share. Given the quality of this business and its future growth rate, a multiple of 14 to 15 times earnings was fair. Assigning such a multiple led to an intrinsic value of about $49 to $52.50 per share. As you can you see, on both fronts, intrinsic value was way above the current price range of $25 to $30 per share. (See Table 10.2.)

Coupled with management's announced stock buyback commitment, Sunrise was a clear value and provided a strong margin of safety as well. Figure 10.1 shows a stock price for Sunrise. After 2002, Mr. Market seemed to catch up with value creation happening there.

Table 10.2   Sunrise Intrinsic Value Ranges

Stock Price	Intrinsic Value	Margin of Safety (%)
$25	$54 to $60	> 50%
$30	$49 to $53	≥ 40%

Figure 10.1   Sunrise Senior Living Stock Price Chart

Case Study #2: Money Machine South of the Border
Ternium Steel

This analysis took place in the middle of 2007. Up until the fourth quarter of 2008, the fundamentals of the business were slowly being reflected in the stock price. Then in late 2008, an unprecedented number of investment funds were forced to liquidate positions due to the freezing up of the credit markets. Many funds employed leverage to juice returns. When faced with margin calls coupled with declining assets prices, liquidation was the only alternative. These events exacerbated the slowdown in the economy and as a consequence, commodity prices, including steel, took a free fall. Ternium's share price was not spared. This case study took place when the shares were trading in the $25 to $30 range. The shares subsequently climbed to $45 over the next year and continued to outperform the broad market until the markets completely froze and commodity prices tanked. As of early 2009, the shares were trading for $10.

While certainly not impossible, it's doubtful that the shares will reach or exceed the price reached in the second half of 2008 anytime soon. Although Ternium still remains one of the world's most profitable steel companies, no business can escape a decline in market value when the price of your principal product falls precipitously. As with any sound investment analysis, the primary focus should first be the process of valuation. A sound process ultimately will lead to a desirable outcome. Ternium certainly appears to be a company that will survive the severe economic recession that began in late 2007/early 2008. It has a quality management team, lean cost structure, and a product that will once again experience more and more demand. This case study should first and foremost serve as one potential way to develop a sound investment process.

Company Background

Ternium Steel is one of the leading steel companies in Latin America with principal operations in Mexico, Argentina, and Venezuela. The company was founded in 1961 and is based in Luxembourg. Upon examination of the company's financial statements in 2007, it didn't take long to realize that this was one of the most profitable steel companies in the world. The numbers literally jumped out of the page. Ternium is run by the Rocca family, which has a decades-long stellar reputation in running steel mills. Their impressive management of Tenaris, another Latin American–based steel producer, was indicative of the family's ability and competence in operating steel companies in Latin America.

At the time, Ternium had an enterprise value (EV = market cap + net debt) of $7.5 billion. In 2006, free cash flow was some $840 million. In 2005, free cash flow was over $1 billion. Earnings before taxes, depreciation, and amortization (EBITDA) for 2006 was $1.84 billion, implying that Ternium was selling for only 4.1 times EBITDA. Even for a steel company, this was absurdly low. A quick comparison of peers yielded an average EBITDA multiple of just over 7. Operating margins, at 27 percent, were among the highest in the world. Ternium boasted a low cost structure that was best in its class. Ternium's Mexican operations included access to iron ore, the main component in steel production, providing the company with a cheaper supply of this raw material.

So what was the catch that made Ternium so incredibly cheap? Simply, the market couldn't seem to get over Ternium's exposure in Venezuela. Ternium's operations in Venezuela were its interest in SIDOR, a Venezuelan steel mill. At the time, there were threats that Venezuelan president Hugo Chavez would nationalize SIDOR, which was owned 60 percent by Ternium and 40 percent by the Venezuelan government and SIDOR employees. Some careful analysis suggested that the odds of nationalization were low.

In any case, Venezuelan operations represented 25 percent of Ternium's EBITDA. So if the worst-case scenario played out and SIDOR was nationalized and Ternium received nothing from Venezuela, EBITDA would decline from $1.84 billion to $1.4 billion. At this rate, Ternium was still selling for much less than comparable international steel companies. In the end, nationalization of SIDOR would not substantially impair the overall operating profitability of Ternium. Ultimately an agreement was reached that avoided nationalization. In exchange, Ternium agreed to sell more steel to Venezuela at a slight discount (~5 percent) and agreed to make some capital investments in SIDOR.

In the first half of 2008, Venezuela had a change of heart and did indeed announce plans to nationalize SIDOR. Initially the market reacted as expected, and shares of Ternium declined. However, it didn't take long for the market to realize that it had overdiscounted the effect that nationalization would ultimately have on the long-term profitability of Ternium. Clearly, Ternium would be better off without the nationalization process, but the analysis took that aspect into consideration to account for such a scenario.

As of this writing, the nationalization outcome is still undecided. Ternium and Chavez are currently in dispute as to how much Ternium should receive for its stake in SIDOR. Ternium indicated that $4 billion was a fair price for its SIDOR assets; Venezuela countered that $800 million was fair. At one point, it appeared that both sides had agreed that $1.5 billion was a fair number, but that is now in dispute again. How long this process will take before it is ultimately resolved is anyone's guess. With Venezuela's oil-based economy facing severe budget deficits due to the decline in the price of oil, all options are back on the table. In the meantime, Ternium continues to maintain efficient operations in Argentina and Mexico. Even if the Venezuelan settlement isn't what the company asked for—a very likely scenario—the company should not be permanently impaired. In fact, with the Venezuelan cloud removed, Ternium could experience a positive revaluation in the marketplace. (Note: In May of 2009, Venezuela agreed to pay Ternium $1.97 billion for SIDOR. Ternium received $400 million immediately, the remainder to be paid in two separate payment plans. When this news was announced, Ternium shares rose by 45 percent that day.)

In the meantime, Ternium was clearly focusing its future growth outside of Venezuela. In April 2007, Ternium had reached an agreement to acquire Grupo IMSA for $1.7 billion. IMSA is a dominant steel producer in Mexico with additional operations in the southern and western United States. IMSA would add another 3 million tons to Ternium's annual finished production, bringing total capacity output to 15 million tons. The deal was closed a few months later, and in December, Ternium struck a deal with Australia's Bluescope Steel to sell off IMSA's U.S. assets for $730 million, allowing Ternium to focus on the steel industry in Latin America.

Valuation

According to the International Iron & Steel Institute, steel demand in Central and South America is expected to grow at a 4 percent clip for the next several years. In Mexico, the steel market was growing by over 6 percent. Only Asia is consuming steel at a higher rate than Latin America. The threat of cheap Chinese steel imports was minimal at best. The costs of shipping a ton of steel to Central and South America would make the steel more expensive. And because Ternium ran a very tight ship (no pun intended) with regard to operating costs, Chinese steel imports did not represent a meaningful threat.

At the time, Ternium had an enterprise value of $9.5 billion. Enterprise value is the sum of the company's market value on the stock exchange and the net debt (total debt minus cash). When looking at the numbers for the first nine months of 2007, Ternium generated nearly $700 million in free cash flow. This figure included a $300 million one-time income tax payment made as a result of the IMSA acquisition. Because Ternium will be able to use this payment as tax credits in the future, true free cash flow from operations was really close to $1 billion. As a result of the IMSA acquisition, Ternium assumed some $3.6 billion in debt, implying a $10 billion enterprise value. The proceeds of the sale of IMSA's U.S. assets were being used to pay off some of this debt. Actual free cash flow, adjusting for the one-time tax charge, was over $1 billion for the first nine months of 2007. EBITDA over the same time period was $1.7 billion.

If $1 billion in free cash flow and $1.7 billion in EBITDA over the first nine months of 2007 were normalized for the year, the annual figures for free cash flow and EBITDA would be approximately $1.3 billion and $2.2 billion, respectively, for 2007. These values would imply a free cash flow/enterprise value (FCF/EV) yield of 13 percent and an EV/EBITDA multiple of approximately 4.3 times.

FCF/EV = $1.3/$9.5 = 13%
EV/EBITDA = $9.5/$2.2 = 4.3

With Ternium's steel peer group commanding EV/EBITDA valuations of six to eight times, it appeared that Ternium's valuation was excessively low, even after assigning a discount to the Venezuela factor.

Discounted Cash Flow Analysis

In running a discounted cash flow analysis (Table 10.3), four assumptions were made:

1. To be conservative, assume that 2007 free cash flow comes to $1 billion, implying no free cash flow in the last quarter.
2. Over the next five years, if FCF growth increased 10 percent a year, the present value (PV) of this sum of money discounted back at 10 percent would be $5 billion.
3. Apply a very reasonable terminal value of 10 times 2012 FCF. A terminal value essentially serves to suggest what the business would be worth if sold based on future projected growth and cash generation. With 200 million shares outstanding, this provides an intrinsic value of $75 a share.
4. If cash flow were to grow at 15 percent, intrinsic value per share comes to around $92 per share based on 200 million shares. A 10 percent increase in shares outstanding would produce an intrinsic value of $83 a share.

Alternative Valuation

Ternium earned about $220 in EBITDA per ton of steel and was on track to sell some 10 million tons in 2007 (without IMSA) compared to 6,600 tons in 2005, a growth rate of nearly 24 percent a year.

Table 10.3 Discounted Cash Flow of Ternium Steel

Year	Free Cash Flow ($ billions)	PV of FCF at 10%
2008	$1.10	$1 billion
2009	$1.21	$1 billion
2010	$1.33	$1 billion
2011	$1.46	$1 billion
2012	$1.61	$1 billion
Sum of PV of FCF		$5 billion
Terminal value	$16 billion	$10 billion
Intrinsic value of company		$15 billion
Shares outstanding	200 million	
Intrinsic value per share	$75	
Shares outstanding + 10% increase	220 million	
Intrinsic value per share	$68	
Current share price	~$30	
Margin of safety	>100%	

This equated into 2007 EBITDA of $2.2 billion. The IMSA acquisition would add 3 million tons of capacity, but with the sale of the U.S assets, capacity will be slightly reduced. In addition, Ternium is undergoing its own capital expansion that should increase capacity by 2 million tons in three years. In five years, tons sold should easily approach 14 to 15 million, or less than 10 percent growth a year. At an average EBITDA of $160 per ton, some 30 percent less than Ternium's current level, this would produce an EBITDA of $2.24 to $2.4 billion. At 8× to 10× EBITDA, a very reasonable buyout multiple for any strategic buyer, Ternium would be worth between $17 and $24 billion, or $85 to $120 a share.

With the global economy in full recession mode in 2008 and the beginning of 2009, steel prices have collapsed, and steel companies reduced capacity in response. As a result Ternium had no free cash flow generation in 2008, but that was a result of onetime working capital changes and some disruptions in Venezuela. Table 10.4 shows a reworked discounted cash flow analysis that incorporates estimates and assumptions as of early 2009, including the near standstill of the global economy. The major changes include:

- Free cash flow for 2009 of $300 million.
- Free cash beginning to grow in 2010 to 60 percent of prior peak cycle figures.
- As the cycle bottoms out and the global economy picks up, steel prices rebound and free cash flows grow 20 percent for the next two years as Ternium's Venezuela volume is picked up by expansion in Mexico and other Latin American areas.

Table 10.4 Discounted Cash Flow of Ternium Steel: Recessionary Assumptions

Year	Free Cash Flow	PV of FCF at 10%
2009	$300 million	$267 million
2010	$600 million	$478 million
2011	$720 million	$512 million
2012	$864 billion	$549 million
Sum of PV of FCF		$1.8 billion
Terminal value	$8.6 billion	$5.5 billion
Intrinsic value of company		$7.3 billion
Shares outstanding	200 million	
Intrinsic value per share	$36.50	
Shares outstanding + 10% increase	220 million	
Intrinsic value per share	$33.18	
Current share price	~$16	
Margin of safety	>100%	
Current book value	$22	

- Discount rate of 12 percent is acceptable now that Venezuela risk is nearly nonexistent.

As you can see from the reduced figures, Ternium *is still an undervalued business at the original purchase price of $30*. And even though the intrinsic value declined in this analysis, Ternium's stock price is still below intrinsic value. In 2009, steel companies are bracing themselves for one of the worst business environments in decades, but they are responding with quick and decisive capacity cuts. Such moves should offer some price stability in the short term; in the long term, as China and other nations begin to use up their excess inventory and start buying steel again, the cycle should reward low-cost producers like Ternium. Comparing both discounted cash flow analyses verifies one very important tenet of value investing: When the stock price of a fundamentally sound business declines, the investment becomes a better bargain and is *less risky than it was before*. Figure 10.2 is the stock price chart for

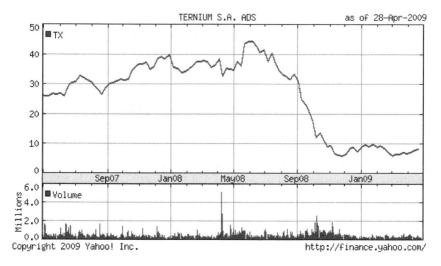

Figure 10.2   Ternium Steel: Waterfalls Lead to Rainbows

Ternium over the past couple of years. The share price perform-ance looks like a waterfall, but this waterfall likely leads to rainbows.

Academic finance will vehemently disagree and point to an increasing beta—a measure of volatility—and suggest that Ternium now poses a greater risk. I don't how that can be the case in the face of the numbers just presented. Even if the numbers continue to be grossly overstated, Ternium's shares appear still to offer a very strong margin of safety both from a cash flow and a book value perspective.

Case Study #3: A Tale of Two Shares

Mueller Water Products

Mueller Water Products was spun out of Walter Industries in 2006. Mueller Water is a supplier of water infrastructure products, such as water hydrants, valves, and pipes. Mueller is one of those companies that many people know about but don't know about at the same time. The company has the number-one or number-two market share in many of the products it sells. It has the number-one market position in fire hydrants throughout the country. Chances are good that if you live in a major urban area, Mueller is respon-sible for your fire hydrant. Mueller's businesses have been operat-ing for over 100 years, with its oldest division established in 1850. Businesses with top market shares are very intriguing to value inves-tors because a dominant market position represents an economic moat around the business.

Mueller was spun off from Walter Industries, now a coal com-pany, because Walter was in a strategic process of transforming itself to a pure-play coal company. While familiarity with Mueller's businesses and the company's history is a plus, this type of arbitrage investment was based on a mispricing of two economically identical assets. In a very elementary way, it was as if two $1 dollar bills were being valued differently.

As a result of the spin-off from Walter Industries, Mueller Water Products created two classes of common stock. Prior to the spin-off, Mueller's Class A shares were already trading in the market via an initial public offering. Subsequent to the spin-off, Mueller issued Class B shares to the existing shareholders of Walter Industries. The share structure was that 25 million A shares were floated and 85 million B shares were spun off. According to the initial corporate filings, both classes of stock had identical economic value. The only difference was that the B shares came with eight votes per share versus only one vote for each A share. The superior voting rights suggested that the B shares should command a premium to the A shares.

Historically, the A shares tended to trade at a premium to the B shares, typically at a level of 5 to 10 percent. There was no identifiable reason as to why the Class A common stock was trading at a premium to the Class B common stock, considering the superior voting structure of the Class B common. One plausible reason that explained this mismatch was the greater supply of B shares and the fact that there was greater selling pressure on the B shares from Walter Industries shareholders who wanted to monetize their Mueller stake. Additionally, unlike a Berkshire Hathaway, where conversion rights exist between the A and B shares whereby one Class A share of Berkshire is convertible into 30 common shares of Class B stock, Mueller has no such conversion rights, so there was no specific catalyst that would have prevented the shares from trading one to one.

Also, it is common for businesses that are spun off to initially experience share price declines due to selling pressure in the market by existing shareholders. Investors in Walter Industries are making a bet on Walter and not Mueller, so when the business is spun off, many investors sell the spun-off company to continue their desire to hold only the original investment. Indeed, many value investors devote ample time and effort to investigating spin-offs simply for that reason: Initial shareholders who desire to hold only the original company will sell off any spun-out entity to monetize part of their investment. As a result, many spin-offs experience selling pressure that sends prices to bargain levels.

However, around September 2008, the B shares were trading at $6 while the A shares were hovering around $9, or a 50 percent premium to the B shares. This was an absurd spread that could have been explained only by the irrational market behavior that took hold of the financial markets after the near collapse of one major investment bank, Bear Stearns, and the failure of another, Lehman Brothers.

The arbitrage investment trade was simple: Go short an equal dollar amount of A shares against a long dollar amount of B shares. Within days, the spread had closed to within 20 percent. The goal was to exit the position when the spread came close to the historical 5 to 10 percent. But as luck would have it, several weeks later, at the next annual meeting, the company announced that it would put to a vote a resolution to make the A shares convertible to B shares on a one-to-one basis. The spread closed to within 1 percent immediately. Although the 50 percent gap in the share price between the two classes of stock wasn't dependent on news of convertibility between the two shares, the announcement was icing on the cake. At a 50 percent spread, the short/long trade was like taking candy from a baby.

Fertile Hunting Ground

As of early 2009, the global economy is facing challenges the likes of which have not been seen since the 1930s. There is no quick fix to our economic problems, brought about after many years of unchecked optimism and easy credit. Faith in equities is at an all-time low as equity markets collapsed in 2008 and continued to do so during the start of 2009. It is during these moments of maximum pessimism that the seeds of fantastic investment performance are sown.

Equity prices across all industries have fallen to levels not seen for decades. Mr. Market, in his usual modus operandi, is not discriminating between healthy, solid businesses, such as many oil companies, versus severely impaired businesses, such as some in the auto industry and the financial industry. For the true value investor, this historic market sell-off has created investment opportunities of historic proportions. Forget about investments that double in price or even the proverbial 50-cent dollar. After the market sell-off in late 2008 and again in early 2009, when the Dow Jones fell below 6600, the opportunity to find multibaggers—or investments that are worth multiples of the current stock price—and 10-cent dollars was afforded to those investors willing to be patient. Given the severe depth of our economic recession, it could be 2011 before any rational recovery takes hold. But all investors realize that markets are forward-looking creatures. As Buffett said in October 2008, "If you wait for robins, spring will be over."

A sample of the fantastic bargains that Mr. Market served up to investors in March 2009 is presented next.

ATP Oil and Gas (ATPG)

This oil and gas outfit had a market value of $115 million, with a current P/E of 1.3 and a forward P/E of 4. At the end of 2008, net debt approximated $1.3 billion, so the enterprise value of the company was $1.4 billion. Management owns 20 percent of the company; they think like shareholders because they are shareholders. Most of the debt comes due in 2013. The company operates exclusively in the Gulf of Mexico and the North Sea via a hub-type concept, meaning that all of its oil platforms are clustered together. Such an operating model is advantageous because it gives the company greater efficiency over its operations.

At the end of 2008, the company had proven reserves of approximately 120 billion barrels of oil equivalent. The company's success rate has been astonishing, and in 2008, it replaced more than 200 percent of its production. At the height of the oil boom, shares overshot to $50 a share. In March 2009, they severely undershot to $3 a share for a company that earned $13.17 a share in cash flow in 2008. With 36 million shares outstanding, each share of company stock represented about 3.5 barrels of proven oil reserves with the price of oil around $50 per barrel. Factor in probable reserves, and each share represents just under 6 barrels of oil.

Horsehead Holding Company (ZINC)

Horsehead is a producer of zinc and zinc-based products. Zinc is a valuable but often misunderstood commodity. It's used as a protective coating for pipes and towers. Zinc oxide is an integral part of tire and rubber products, plastics, and pharmaceuticals. Plus, the company is the largest recycler of electric arc furnace (EAF) dust in the United States. EAF dust is an extremely hazardous waste material produced by steel mini-mill operators such as Nucor.

Horsehead was being valued by the market at $140 million with zero debt and about $60 million in cash, equivalent to about $2 per share. The price was $4 a share with $2 a share net cash in the bank and 2008 EPS of $1.43. Profits are likely to be lower in 2009. Still, Horsehead's manufacturing and recycling plants are worth $1 billion. Insiders own 16 percent of the stock.

AgFeed Industries (FEED)

Jumping over to the other side of the pond, AgFeed is the leading seller and producer of animal feed in China. AgFeed also raises, breeds, and sells hogs for use in China's pork production markets. Very few people seem to realize how important pork is to the Chinese. China actually has a strategic pork reserve very similar to the Strategic Oil Reserve here in the U.S. The Chinese consume six times the amount of pork that the U.S. consumes.

In March, AgFeed shares hit $0.90, valuing the company at $38 million, against 2008 net profits of $17 million, which were up from $6.7 million the year before. In addition the company had a net cash position of $17 million or $0.44 a share and tangible book value of over $1.70.

With overseas businesses, especially smaller ones, investors should demand a greater margin of safety. In this situation, the price—which was currently below a conservative liquidation value—was the catalyst.

Conclusion

Value comes in many varieties and forms. Only by continuous effort and intensity can an investor determine whether bargain securities exist. Contrary to popular belief, value investing is not rigid in its approach. In fact, those most successful at investing have demonstrated that investing requires a flexible and multidisciplinary mind. Because true value investors avoid the herdlike mentality that occurs in the marketplace, they demonstrate time and time again that a successful investment approach requires you to investigate all angles, even those that might not directly relate to the investment.

Where value investors don't bend, however, is in their discipline to place the process before the outcome. Value investors are always mindful of downside risk, understanding that risk represents a loss of capital and not a volatile stock price. Value investors also recognize the need for patience, understanding that investing is most successful when pursued over a meaningful period of time. Just as it is silly to think that a fundamentally sound business can lose 25 percent of its value in a single day, the same line of thinking is applied to stock prices that experience extreme bouts of price volatility.

Value investors are also skeptical. They avoid participating in market manias, fads, or any other hot investment of the day. Value investors hold dear to their hearts Buffett's notion that an expensive price is usually paid when investing alongside the crowd. Value investors are wired to avoid investment areas that are the crowd darlings. Blind faith in investing will get you killed. Such was the experience of many participants in the Internet boom of the late 1990s. Everyone felt that it was imperative to be in the stock market, regardless of valuations, because stocks could only go up. We now know what blind faith did to the many who invested this way. Like lemmings, many investors followed blindly, not knowing they were headed over a cliff. Learning to question what you are told and developing critical thinking skills are vital to successfully investing.

Key Takeaways

- Reciting value investing rhetoric is the easy part. Following it requires diligence and effort.
- As evidenced by the case studies, some investment candidates may require specific focal points in determining intrinsic value.
- Arbitrage opportunities are generally very rare in today's investment world due to the proliferation of market participants. If an arbitrage opportunity presents itself, assess it with a strong dose of skepticism. If it still turns out to be real, then jump at the opportunity.

CHAPTER

11

Avoiding Common Stumbling Blocks

I'd rather be approximately right than precisely wrong.
—Warren Buffett

Investing is by no means an exact science. In fact, a great deal of investment analysis hinges on future assumptions about a company's cash flow generation. It's not uncommon to see different investors use different methods to derive the intrinsic value of a particular business. But at the end of the day, most valuations hinge on the cash flow generation of a business. The exceptions are special situation investments, such as liquidations, spin-offs, or arbitrage.

All realistic investors realize that they will make many mistakes throughout their careers. Even though value investors are risk averse and strive to eliminate most risk by strictly adhering to the concept of a margin of safety, all investing entails risk. There is always the incalculable risk that the business environment will weaken, or as we've seen in 2008 and spilling over into 2009, the economy can come to a near standstill and affect all businesses. Business risk and economic risk are risks that all investors in all asset classes assume when participating in the capital markets. But these business risks are exactly the reason the philosophies of value investing have become such a relied-on foundation for long-term investment success.

The best value investors concentrate their efforts on avoiding avoidable mistakes, such as investing in a business they don't understand because it looks cheap on the balance sheet or income statement. Diligent investors are keen on learning from both successful and unsuccessful investments. Even more important, capable investors expend time and effort in avoiding making the same mistake twice. Value investors also strive to avoid falling in love with crowd stocks just because Wall Street continues to favor them. Value investors love businesses that are undervalued based on analytical measures of business valuation.

However, value investors will never be able to avoid buying before the bottom and selling before the top. Such buy-and-sell activities often can be misinterpreted as mistakes, but that interpretation is widely misguided and based on false assumptions. This is because often, many great investment opportunities are discovered in businesses in the midst of a company turnaround or a dip in the business cycle. Value investors aren't concerned with catching bottoms; they only are concerned with buying a dollar's worth of value for substantially less. Once the price of the security approximates fair value, value investors move on to other undervalued opportunities without any regard to whether the price is likely to rise further. A process-first, outcome-second approach to investing minimizes the likelihood of avoidable and expensive investment blunders.

Common traps include:

Investing for capital appreciation when instead you should be investing for capital preservation. Investing in this manner is like crossing the street after only looking straight ahead. The destination might be clear, but without looking left and right, the consequences can be perilous. All investors surely want their capital to appreciate over time, but the first order of business is to ensure that your capital doesn't deteriorate over time. Attention to capital preservation, first and foremost, enables the magic of compounding really to magnify the value of your portfolio over time.

Interpreting market volatility as a destroyer of opportunity when it is instead a creator of opportunity. If your approach is sound, then volatility allows you to buy that which was cheap yesterday cheaper today. In March 2009, the many market indexes were off over 50 percent since the market peak of October 2007. Interestingly, the vast majority of investors are very afraid of investing in the stock market now, while back in 2007, when most security prices were three to five times *higher in price*, people were pumping in capital at a record pace.

While it is emotionally difficult to invest money amid falling prices, successful value investors understand that exploiting market volatility helps plant the seeds for future market-beating results.

Believing you are investing when in fact you are speculating. To an investor, a stock represents a fractional ownership interest in a business. To a speculator, a stock is a symbol with price movements. Thus, investors make their buy-and-sell decisions based on the fundamental performance of the business and how the current price of the security compares with the value of the security. Investors understand that in order to make a profit from a stock investment, one of three things must happen:

1. The business must generate free cash flow to distribute back to investors or use the cash to grow the business which reflects in a higher stock price.

2. The multiple that investors are willing to pay for the underlying earning and growth potential of the business increases.

3. The gap between market value and intrinsic value narrows.

Speculators, however, buy and sell based on beliefs as to whether the stock price will rise or fall. Those beliefs are not anchored on fundamental characteristics of the business but on the behavior of others. Speculators treat stocks as tickers with little regard for the underlying business. They base their decisions on the popular sentiment of the day. Speculation involves going along with the crowd, not against it. There's great attraction in speculation as it requires no rigorous analysis of the business.

Value investors, on the contrary, pay very close attention to business fundamentals and financial reality when making investment decisions. They exert painstaking time and effort in getting to know specific businesses, industries, and various other sources of data in order to have the greatest possible edge in making their investment selections.

This chapter examines and supports the view that the difference between value investing and growth investing is in name only. A true investor, in the mold of Ben Graham, realizes that growth is an integral part of value creation. The litmus test is that for value investors, there is a limit as to how much they are willing to pay for that future growth, while speculators will pay up as long as they are in the company of the masses.

What matters most in investing is not to take what may seem obvious at face value. The attempt to separate growth from value is a case in point. Also, it would be easy to assume that because value investors like to buy a business for less than it is worth, then book value should be the yardstick by which to measure this approach. While investing in businesses at less than book value can be a very successful route, it's hardly a consistent approach. Book value is an accounting number provided on the balance sheet, and the quality of the balance sheet must be scrutinized before blindly relying on equity, or book value. Investing can yield some astronomical dividends to those who practice it successfully. Such success demands intensive effort and analysis and requires the investors arm themselves with a healthy dose of skepticism.

Growth and Value: Two Sides of the Same Coin

Value investors are really no different from growth investors. All investors, if they are truly investing, are attempting to seek out value—buying one dollar of assets for less than one dollar. The size of the markets today makes it so that most great investments are those that can grow over time. That is, the availability of other highly prized value investment situations, such as arbitrage investments, is extremely limited compared to 50 years ago. So the best investment for a value investor is what is commonly referred to as a growth at a reasonable price (GARP) business.

The most visible metric in determining whether an investment offers long-term value is its discount to intrinsic value. However, an undervalued security is not only one that must sell at 50 cents on the dollar *if your research and analysis determine that the business has a reasonable growth opportunity ahead of it.* In other words, a business that is bought at a modest discount or even no discount to intrinsic value, but with the expectation that the intrinsic value will grow substantially over a period of years, may be considered an undervalued investment. The future growth in intrinsic value implies that a discount to intrinsic value does in fact exist. As intrinsic value grows in subsequent years, then the business, at today's price, is indeed an undervalued investment opportunity and should be analyzed accordingly.

There are only two ways that a company's market price can become a greater discount from intrinsic value:

1. The intrinsic value grows.
2. The market price declines without the intrinsic value declining at a greater rate.

The obvious preference is to have intrinsic value grow; the latter situation, which is combination of a declining market price and intrinsic value, is fraught with speculative characteristics. Trying to play a seesaw game with declining market prices and intrinsic values can lead to permanent losses of capital if the loss in intrinsic value turns out to be something more than a temporary impediment. Value investors, of course, love to explore in industries currently suffering from lack of interest in the market due to a temporary set of problems. Indeed, when this is the case, investors must demand a high margin of safety to compensate for any further declines that are very likely to occur as the business adjusts itself. Just as easily as they can overshoot, it's very possible that markets may undershoot and remain depressed for a prolonged period. Witness the characteristics of the bear market that took firm hold in 2008 and continued into 2009. By November 2008, the Dow touched a multiyear low of 7,500 before rising back above 9,000 in January 2009. Less than six weeks later, the Dow was back to 6,700, a level that erased any market gains achieved during the late-1990s bubble and the 2003 to 2007 rally.[1]

In any event, companies that continue to increase intrinsic value reward the investor doubly by an accompanying rise in the stock price and a higher price to earnings (P/E) ratio multiple being assigned to the business. There is no rule in investing that a growing intrinsic value will lead immediately to a growing market value. Indeed, in periods of market pessimism, market values can continue to decline even though intrinsic values may not. That's why value investors heed Ben Graham's assertion: In the "short run, the stock market is a voting machine; in the long run, it is a weighing machine." Ultimately, a business that grows its profits and net worth will be followed by a stock price that reflects those strong fundamentals. And often, when this happens, the market assigns a higher multiple on that performance. Thus, all of a sudden a company that earns $2 per share and was trading for a P/E of 12 may now command a P/E of 15, leading to a stock price of $30 versus $24. This reasoning is not based on any formula, but it does point to another reason why value investors love growth-at-a-reasonable price investment opportunities.

The question then becomes: What determines a reasonable price for the growth? What value or parameters determine whether the investor is paying a reasonable or an unreasonable price? No definitive answer or formula determines whether the price paid for the future growth of a company is reasonable or not. The issue of whether the price paid is reasonable is more effectively answered when the question is inverted.

How Will the Growth Be Achieved?

Understanding how a company plans to grow its business and profits into the future is useful before attempting to invest in a business for growth. The options here are clear: A business can grow internally or by acquisition. While there is no ultimate preference for which way a business grows, of importance to the investor is what the business will require to achieve its desired growth. The best businesses are those that can support their future growth primarily by cash flows generated by the business, thus minimizing reliance on the credit of others. The prudent use of debt can be advantageous, but businesses that are prone to rely on the teat of a loan officer may find themselves in an unpleasant situation if the well runs dry.[2] An understanding of a business's financing ability is of extreme importance to an investor and of extreme significance to how the market will perceive, and ultimately value, a business. The ability to finance its growth needs internally suggests that the business is generating healthy levels of cash flow. This in turn implies that the business is operating soundly. That in turn suggests that most likely the business is in the hands of capable management. All of this suggests that, over time, the market will value such exceptional fundamentals with an increasing multiple, leading to an even greater value of the business.

In thinking about how much to pay for such growth, the issue depends on what metric or metrics are most useful to the investor in determining what to pay for the future growth of a business. The P/E ratio naturally stands out as the default foundational metric on which to rely. Just as the name implies, the price to earnings (P/E) ratio reflects the current price multiple investors are willing to pay for a company's earnings. On the whole, the lower the P/E, the more attractive the investment from a value-oriented perspective. Of course, a P/E alone doesn't do the trick.

First, the quality of earnings of a business should be considered. For example, a company like Proctor & Gamble, which has historically traded for around 12 to 18 times earnings, should not be immediately dismissed compared to a similar company that might be trading for 7 times earnings. Proctor & Gamble has decades of earnings history that demonstrate the quality of earnings to be as dependable as any investor might wish for. The company has also increased dividends for as many years as you might wish to go back. So, naturally, the quality and dependability of the growth *over a period of years* should weigh heavily on an investor's consideration with regard to the appropriate multiple of earnings to pay. The characteristics of an investment operation would certainly justify paying 12 times earnings for a Proctor & Gamble type business that has grown sales and profits for decades through various economic cycles rather than paying 7 times earnings for a business that could suffer a substantial decline in profits or even an operating loss during any abrupt change in the business environment.

Naturally, a value investor would employ painstaking effort in both trying to pay the *least expensive price* (i.e., low P/E) coupled with the greatest potential upside for increased growth. Proctor &

Gamble is usually afforded a fair multiple because of its decades-long record of superior earnings visibility. Value investors attempt to maximize value by locating those businesses that can produce growth while paying as little as possible. The most obvious way to do this is to buy during a period in which the company is experiencing a temporary setback, due to general economic or specific industry conditions. Doing so allows investors to pay a reduced multiple for temporarily distressed profits and benefit in the future from both increased earnings and an increasing multiple being granted on the security.

Expanding on the P/E ratio slightly, many investors also look at the PEG ratio of a business. This is known as the price-earnings/growth ratio. The PEG ratio is a valuation metric for determining the relative trade-off between the price of a stock, the earnings generated per share, and the company's expected growth.

In general, the P/E ratio tends to be higher for a company with a higher growth rate. Thus, using just the P/E ratio would make high-growth companies overvalued relative to others, all else equal. It is assumed that by dividing the P/E ratio by the earnings growth rate, the resulting ratio is better for comparing companies with different growth rates.

As Table 11.1 illustrates, P/E ratios alone may not be sufficient to determine the attractiveness of any particular investment without a closer look at the quality and growth of future potential earnings. If company C can indeed grow profits for the next several years by 20 percent, a P/E multiple of 18 may appear quite reasonable relative to the other two companies.

Consider the following basic math if these growth rates hold for the next five years and the P/Es equate to the growth rate of the earnings. Table 11.2 makes some very rigid assumptions. Unless a company is somehow manipulating its earnings, it's highly unlikely that it will grow its earnings by the same rate each year for five consecutive years. And depending on the prevailing market environment, the P/E ratio afforded to individual securities may reflect undervaluation, fair valuation, or overvaluation. There is no accepted rule in the market that suggests that a company's P/E ratio will equal or approximate the annual growth of earnings.

Nonetheless, the table is useful in illustrating once again the value of growth in any particular investment and, more specifically, the importance of paying a reasonable price for that growth. As you can see, there is no "exact" reasonable price, but what investors want to avoid is paying excessively for that growth. Both the P/E and PEG ratios help establish the parameters between excessive and reasonable. For company C, even if market multiples decline and the market assigns a P/E of 12 but 2013 earnings still came in at $2.48, the capital gain is still in excess of 50 percent. Conversely if the earnings growth stalled and earnings came in at $2 per share and the market assigned company C a 10 times earnings multiple,

Table 11.1   Examining the PEG Ratio

	Company A	Company B	Company C
P/E ratio	10	15	18
Earnings growth rate	10%	10%	20%
PEG ratio	1	1.5	0.9

Table 11.2   Value of Growth

	Company A	Company B	Company C
2008 earnings per share (EPS)	$1	$1	$1
2008 share price	$10	$15	$18
2013 EPS	$1.61	$1.61	$2.48
2013 share price (assuming same P/E as growth rate)	$16.10	$16.10	$49.60
Return on investment	61%	7.3%	175%

an investor still hasn't lost any money from the original $18 purchase price. These are not scientific assumptions, but nonetheless, they are effective in illustrating the value of growth and why value investors prize businesses with the ability to maintain sustainable growth over extended periods of time.

The PEG ratio is considered to be a convenient approximation. It was popularized by Peter Lynch: "The P/E ratio of any company that's fairly priced will equal its growth rate"—that is, a fairly valued company will have its PEG equal to 1.[3]

Businesses without Current Earnings

The price to earnings (P/E) ratio is generally a sound metric but can be useless if a business currently has no earnings. The consideration for investment in this instance is not diametrically different from a company that is actually profitable. Prudent investors realize that any business can go from being unprofitable to profitable and vice versa. Obviously since there are no earnings, reliance on the P/E ratio is out of the question. In such cases, value investors will expend their efforts on examining the balance sheet, giving careful attention to the assets and assessing whether the business can become profitable. Even more important is to determine *how soon this profitability will be achieved and whether that profitability can be sustained.* The extra focus on the balance sheet helps quantify a margin of safety in case achieving profitability takes longer than expected or, in the worst case, profits fail to materialize. Paying $5 a share against a company book value of $15 a share can minimize capital loss if a business is forced to liquidate or put itself up for sale.

In many situations, it may be far more advantageous to invest in temporarily unprofitable businesses, if you are confident after reasonable research and analysis that the business will regain and retain profitability. Unprofitable businesses may be trading at significantly depressed prices due to the short-term tendencies of many market participants to abandon ship at the first sign of trouble. As a result, the potential for share price appreciation can be significant when the market wakes up to the future profitability of the business.

As the environment faced oil refiners, Tesoro and Valero, in 2001 (see Chapter 7), many industrial and manufacturing businesses in 2009 continue to face one of the worst economic downturns in recent memory. It should come as no surprise that Mr. Market is focusing on the immediate short term and ignoring all else. For example, Terex, a U.S. manufacturer of construction and mining equipment will very likely report a net loss for the 2009 year. This poor performance is an industry-wide problem as end customers for companies like Terex are delaying and canceling orders. Some of Terex's business divisions are experiencing sales decline in excess of 50 percent. Management continues to be candid with shareholders by telling them that 2010 may also be a very difficult year for the industry. As you might imagine, shares in Terex have fallen off a cliff.

In March of 2009, shares were fetching $8; a year earlier the stock was north of $70.[4] In 2008, Terex earned $5.33 per share, likely a result of a peaking business cycle. However from 1999 to 2008, Terex has earned an average of $2.35 according to Value Line. This period includes both economic growth and contraction. So far, Terex management has succeeded at steering the ship during the storm. Anyone who believes that, at some point, the economy will improve and the need to build and repair infrastructure will pick up can bet that Terex will again start earning profits. At the then current price of $8, shares were trading for less than four times the average 10-year earnings and less than two times the average 4-year earnings.[5]

Book Value: More Than Meets the Eye

The book value of a business is defined simply as the net assets of a business. It's the value left over to the stockholder after all obligations are paid off. Book value also can be referred to as the equity value of a business.

On paper, book value looks painfully simple:

Assets	$800 million
− Liabilities	$500 million
= Equity (Book value)	$300 million

Clearly, book value is a very important figure for value investors since paying less than a company is intrinsically worth is the
cornerstone of the value investing approach. Indeed, investing in
businesses at a discount to book value is one strategy many value
investors employ, and they can be quite successful. However, to
properly appreciate and exploit businesses trading at less than
book, a clearer understanding of book value is in order.

An often-forgotten fundamental rule in business is that any asset
is worth what the next person is willing to pay for it. Market prices
aren't established out of thin air but rather are based on the supply-
and-demand mechanics of that particular asset. When equities are
rising, it's because there are more buyers than sellers, thus increasing demand, which means sellers have better prices to choose from.
The opposite is also true. When more sellers exist than buyers,
there is more supply than the market demands. Thus, sellers have
very few options and usually are forced to accept lower prices. This
pricing dynamic works across every major asset class—real estate,
cars, and commodities—not just stocks.

Value investors who have a keen understanding of this market
mechanism recognize one potential limitation of overreliance on
book value. Simply buying a share of stock in a business for $10
when its book value is $25 per share is no guarantee that a capital
gain will be realized. That's not to say that buying a business for less
than 50 percent of its book value is not an attractive proposition
but rather to say that there is no immediate catalyst in the market
that will get the share price to advance simply as result of a price-
to-book-value discount. If there are far more sellers of equities
than buyers, then stated book value might not mean much because
investors currently do not believe that the asset value will hold.

However, the book value issue is a paradoxical one, because it can reward those investors who are willing to be patient. For example, many industrial businesses, as a result of the severe economic recession that took hold in 2008, experienced such severe price declines during the end of that year that many were trading at significant discounts to book value. And unlike financial companies, whose primary assets are pieces of paper, industrial companies own plants, machinery, and tools. In some cases, these plants can be quite expensive to rebuild. Even better, regulatory hurdles may make it nearly impossible or not worth the time to try to build a similar plant. In such cases, patient investors can reap magnificent rewards from investing in these businesses.

Published 70 years ago, *The Theory of Investment Value*, by John Burr Williams, is a book that should be right up there with Ben Graham's *Security Analysis* in terms of quality and timeless value.[6] The author was certainly writing with the Great Depression in mind, meaning that the book's ideas offer tremendous value and insight for today's investors. Although much of the lengthy work is filled with dry mathematical formulas, Williams expressly states that one of the most attractive opportunities to buy equities is when the assets of the business can be bought below true replacement cost.

Williams's theory is of enormous value for two good reasons:

1. If you are really buying a company for below its true replacement costs, it's very unlikely that you will suffer a permanent loss of capital because the assets can be sold—even at a discount—and still yield a profit to the common stockholder.
2. Other businesses looking to expand in times of turmoil will find great value in acquiring assets for below replacement value via buying up other companies.

As this book went to press, a wonderful example of such an investment opportunity appeared to exist with Horsehead Holding Company, a producer of zinc-based products. A quick look at the balance sheet (Table 11.3) reveals that in March 2009, shares of

Table 11.3   Horsehead Holding Corp. Balance Sheet (December 31, 2008)

Assets	Liabilities
Cash: $123 million	Current liabilities: $60 million
Other current assets: $99 million	Other liabilities: $12 million
Property, plant, equipment: $136 million	
Total assets: $358 million	Total liabilities: $72 million
Shareholders' equity: $286 million	
Shares outstanding: 35.3 million	
Book value per share: $8.10	

Source: Company SEC filings.

Horsehead were trading for $4. Many intriguing valuation figures jump out from the balance sheet alone: The cash balance of $123 million is almost equal to the entire market valuation of the company, $140 million. And since cash can be valued with complete precision, anyone who invested in Horsehead in March was essentially getting the operating business for free.

As with any other commodity company, the value of Horsehead is based on two fundamental factors: the price of zinc and the company's production level. In the second half of 2008, just about all commodity prices went into a free fall, and zinc was no exception. As a result, Horsehead's profits began declining, but management utilized put options to provide a floor price for the price of zinc, which helped mitigate the declines. Indeed, in 2008, the company still managed to earn $1.12 per share. Unless the price of zinc suddenly shifts upward in 2009, it's likely that 2009 profits may come in below the 2008 numbers.

But to a patient value-oriented investor, the balance sheet strength suggests that Horsehead shares are very attractively priced. Aside from the cash, Horsehead owns and operates six recycling facilities and a 110-megawatt coal-fired plant. In a normal market environment, the value of these plants approximates $1 billion. And because Horsehead is the largest zinc recycler in the country with very little competition, the value of the company's assets is further strengthened.

Looking at Horsehead's balance sheet, there is no goodwill of any kind in the asset portion. While most investors are cognizant of the goodwill figure on the balance sheet, very few investors give the goodwill figure the seriousness it deserves. And as usual, the consequences of this negligence become significant when markets are declining, thus exaggerating the potential loss exposure to many portfolios.

Goodwill Basics

Goodwill is not a physical or tangible asset like cash or property. Goodwill is an accounting value that normally arises when one company acquires another. It represents the markup a company pays above and beyond the book value of a business.

To illustrate, suppose Company A decides to acquire Company B. The balance sheet of Company B is presented next.

Assets	
Cash	$20 million
Inventory	$50 million
Receivables	$60 million
Property, plant, and equipment	$120 million
Total assets:	$250 million

Liabilities	
Payables	$20 million
Short-term debt	$20 million
Long-term debt	$100 million
Total liabilities	$140 million
Equity	$110 million

Company A decides to purchase Company B for $200 million. The net assets acquired, or the value of the assets minus all liabilities, is $110 million. Once Company A consolidates its purchase of Company B, Company A will book $200 million in assets acquired, but only $110 million of that is in the form of physical or tangible assets; the difference between the purchase price and the net assets acquired, $90 million, will be booked as goodwill, an intangible asset.

Since all investors are looking to buy assets inexpensively, the obvious question is why a company would pay more than the value of a company's net assets to acquire it. One explanation is that since book value is an accounting figure, it might not necessarily reflect the real value of a given company. A company that owns a lot of land or real estate must record the value of those assets at cost. But over time, land and real estate appreciate, although that appreciated value cannot be recorded on the balance sheet. Another explanation could be that the buyer hopes that the target company will create more value as a subsidiary than it would on its own.

The Procter & Gamble (P&G) acquisition of the Gillette razor company in January 2005 is a good example. Procter & Gamble, one of the biggest consumer products companies in the world acquired Gillette for $57 billion, which was an 18 percent premium for the shares.[7] But because Gillette's balance sheet included goodwill, P&G's premium paid over net assets acquired exceeded 18 percent. The justification for the premium paid was the tremendous operating leverage that P&G's existing distribution channels would have on Gillette's products. And since Gillette was already the number-one razor company, the benefits of this increased distribution with minimal need for additional advertising expense was even more valuable to P&G. P&G hoped it would benefit from such added economies of scale in distribution and advertising and that this would lead to higher profits over time.

Goodwill is an intangible asset, and valuing intangible assets can be tricky, because their values differ from one company to the other. For example, the brand values of Coca-Cola and McDonald's are vital to the long-term success of those businesses. Coke is what it is because of the worldwide familiarity with its name, and reference to the "golden arches" is all about McDonald's.

Goodwill, however, is different from other intangible assets. While it is very unlikely that brands like Coke would ever lose value, goodwill can go away, and companies must respond by writing off its value in their financial statements. If a businesses acquisition doesn't work out, then it may write off the goodwill associated with that acquisition. Goodwill is certainly not the only asset that can be written off; inventory, receivables, and even short-term noncash investments can be written off. But while businesses usually can recover at least some value from physical assets, goodwill can end up being worthless to a prospective buyer—because it only represents how the previous buyer valued the assets of the business.

Thus, investors need to proceed with an added degree of caution and skepticism when examining any business with substantial sums of goodwill on the balance sheet. When the markets are sour, as they were in 2008 and heading into 2009, the value of goodwill should be discounted by at least 50 percent when examining the book value of a company.

Consider the situation concerning Mueller Water Products, Inc. At the end of 2007, the company's balance sheet showed an unusually high amount of goodwill.

Mueller Water's goodwill alone represented over 60 percent of shareholders' equity. Along with intangibles, these two categories exceed shareholders' equity by 20 percent. Mueller had been spun off by Walter Industries in 2004. As part of the spin-off; Mueller took on the existing goodwill of Walter's businesses that were being transferred to Mueller.

As the housing market collapsed in 2008 and the U.S. economic recession took hold, Mueller's business operations suffered as the decline in new home construction led to a decline in the company's products. In February 2009, the company announced that it was taking a $400 million impairment charge on goodwill, which served to reduce shareholders' equity by 30 percent. On the day of the announcement, shares declined by 50 percent.

Mueller's case demonstrates the potential pitfalls that excessive goodwill can create when the business environment turns sour. There is $470 million of goodwill remaining. At the present time, it's unclear if the company will require any further impairment charges. For what it's worth, Mueller is a fine company with the top one or two market shares in many of the products it supplies. But the company's capital structure illustrates the extra need for conservatism on behalf of investors, especially when the operating environment turns sour.

When comparing a company's value in relation to its assets, you have to look at the company's enterprise value as being the cost of the

Table 11.4   Mueller Water Products Balance Sheet (December 31, 2007)

Assets	(Millions of USD)
Current assets	$939.3
Property, plant, and equipment, net	$335.1
Intangible assets	$811.9
Goodwill	$871.1
Other assets	$19.7
Total assets	$2,977.1
Total liabilities	$1,666.0
Shareholders equity	$1,311.1

Source: SEC filings.

business, because debt holders come before equity holders. You can compare book value to market value, but I would look at hard book value, which excludes all goodwill and intangible assets from the calculation. Focusing on hard book value provides a crucial margin of safety; during periods of economic distress, the chances increase significantly that impairments of goodwill and intangible assets occur.

What Matters Most

Successful investing includes making mistakes. The greatest misconception in investing is that to be successful over the long term, you have to eliminate mistakes. This perception is flawed. To be successful in investing, you have to eliminate *repeating the same mistakes again.* Successful investors are the ones who study their mistakes, taking great care to learn from them, understand why they were made, and work to avoid repeating them again.

Human beings, it turns out, are innately wired to make dumb investing mistakes. Even worse, we are not wired to learn from them but to repeat those mistakes over and over again. Is there any hope for investors? The truthful answer is a resounding yes, but only if we are aware of the most common mistakes and why they are so easy to make. We can minimize them if we understand them. Warren Buffett is a brilliant human being, but his edge as an investor stems from his unwavering discipline and ability to separate the real picture from the perceived one. Unfortunately, the human mind is psychologically programmed to react in ways that can be futile to investing. The most common human psychological tendencies include:

- **Gambler's fallacy.** Humans tend to believe, incorrectly, that if a coin toss comes up tails three times in a row, it is more likely to come up heads on the next toss, thus ignoring the fact that each toss is an independent event with a probability of 50/50. Similarly, just because a stock has gone up or down for a while doesn't mean it's likely to move in the opposite direction anytime soon.

- **Self-attribution bias.** One of my favorite sayings is "If you blame others for your failures, do you credit them for your successes?" Investors like to attribute their successes to themselves but blame losses on others. This impedes investors in two ways.
    1. Investors can't learn from their mistakes because they are unable to see them as such.
    2. Investors often confuse skill with luck.
- **Conservatism/confirmatory biases.** Investors quickly form opinions and then tend to overvalue information that reinforces those opinions and undervalue information that undermines them. Going further, investors seek confirmation of those opinions by specifically seeking out supporting information.
- **Outcome bias.** Many investors love to evaluate their investment decisions based on the outcome instead of the process. If the investment was profitable, congratulations are handed out even if the choice made was speculative or without fundamental merit. As a result, investors praise themselves for making dumb choices that happen to turn out well; conversely, they reject smart investments choices that turn out bad. Many investors constantly reinforce mistakes and reject sound decisions.
- **Hindsight bias.** Hindsight bias is arguably one of the greatest flaws of investors. When investors reflect on the past, they often imagine that they knew what was going to happen. The truth is that no investor knows what exactly will happen until after it happens. Afterward, the mind thinks that it knew what was going to happen. This hindsight bias leads investors to become overconfident about their ability to predict what will happen next.

Unfortunately, humans are wired at birth to succumb to these psychological flaws. This does not make the investor's job any easier. But understanding how the mind is wired to think and working toward eliminating the misconceptions can ensure that a lot of investment blunders don't get repeated.

Key Takeaways

- Every investor makes mistakes. The key is to realize those mistakes and prevent them from occurring again and again.
- Value and growth are two sides of the same coin to value investors. The greatest creator of long-term value is earnings growth.
- Investing in growth-at-reasonable-price businesses does not always mean investing in low P/E businesses. Some of the best value opportunities lie in temporarily unprofitable enterprises.
- Businesses selling below book value are not automatic homerun investments. Unless you delve deeper into the financial statements, a company's book value may not be as sound as it seems.
- Understand that the mind is prewired with tendencies that can be hurtful to an investor. Investors should strive always to go back and ask themselves what could go wrong before making any investment.

12

Starting an Investment Partnership

The goal of this book was not simply to be another book about value investing; rather, my goal was to teach readers how to *think about investing intelligently*. Most investing mistakes are due to decisions made as a result of temperament and emotional factors rather than how smart you are.

When it comes to investment philosophies, the approach either resonates with you immediately or it doesn't. Many can learn and recite the value rhetoric with the greatest of ease. Unfortunately, merely saying something doesn't actually mean you are doing it. You're either able to remain patient and disciplined or you're not. You either view the stock market as a long-term creator of wealth or you don't. You either see the intelligence in buying a dollar for 50 cents and holding on or you don't. It's that simple.

One thing is clear. Value investing—past, present, and future— is about one thing: the practice of purchasing securities or assets for less than what they are worth. The process of investing in bargain securities provides the margin of safety. The margin of safety provides room for error, imprecise estimates, bad luck, or shelter from the surprises or shocks of the economy and stock market. As my friend Mason Hawkins of Southeastern Asset Management once told me, "Prepare to look stupid in the short run if you're value investing." I include this chapter to help those on the fence determine whether running an investment partnership is the right path to follow. I was fortunate enough to have some very gracious assistance from highly regarded value investors in setting up my investment partnership. Throughout my process I learned a lot, and this chapter is intended to help those just as I was helped when starting out several years ago.

Many part-time market participants with a value investing orientation desire to run investment partnerships similar to Warren Buffett's legendary partnerships of the 1950s and 1960s. Unfortunately, many fail to consider some key questions before starting out, and this often leads to costly mistakes and disappointing expectations. For those willing to devote the time and effort required to pursue a career investing sums of money, here are some pointers to help you launch an investment partnership.

Two Key Considerations

The first question that must be answered involves the initial capital base of the fund. Will the partnership be seeded initially by friends and family, or will it seek to attract capital from outside investors? This question is critical, especially to first-time fund managers, since it may determine how the fund is initially set up. An initial fund with friends and family may not demand all the bells and whistles needed for a partnership that will seek out investors far and wide. For instance, a very good set of legal documents can be prepared for $5,000 by a competent securities lawyer. And since your initial investor base is people you are very familiar with, the formal demands of the partnership structure may be easier to accommodate.

The second question is how much capital you can realistically begin with. A full-blown investment partnership can cost a minimum of $25,000 a year in operating expenses, and those expenses increase as the fund size increases or the investment strategy goes beyond a long/short equity fund. So if you are starting up with a few hundred thousand dollars, be aware that you may be required to spend a little time doing administrative work in addition to analyzing securities. With a smaller fund (under $1 million), it may be best to look to regional service providers to handle basic accounting and administrative efforts.

Setting up a full-blown straightforward private investment partnership can demand substantial up-front costs. These costs will include:

- Legal fees to prepare the required documents can cost anywhere from $15,000 to $25,000.
- Engagement of a fund administrator to set up the accounting of the fund: $1,500 to $3,000.
- Factor in another $1,000 or so for miscellaneous expenses, such as mailings, printings, and so on.

Service Providers

For a fully functioning investment partnership, you'll need five service providers:

1. Attorney
2. Fund administrator
3. Fund custodian (broker)
4. Accountant
5. Auditor

Attorney

You will need an attorney to draft your legal documents, commonly referred to as the private placement memorandum. These are the documents that inform potential investors of the goals, objectives, and risks of the fund. The complexity of the investment strategy will determine the ultimate costs associated with preparing the documents. Bigger, more established law firms may charge more, but it can be more efficient in the long run to use a firm that is familiar with setting up value investment partnerships. The costs might be a bit more up front, but using such a firm could eliminate additional costs down the road. Also, if investment capital is going to be sought out initially from people other than friends and family, legal documents from a well-established and recognized firm can prove beneficial and offer a sense of comfort to faraway investors.

Fund Administrator

The fund administrator handles all the essential maintenance of the investment partnership once the legal framework has been established. Legal documents must be prepared first, as the fund administrator uses them to set up the investment partnership according to its legal terms and conditions. The fund administrator is responsible for the processing of new investor subscriptions, the monthly accounting of the partnerships results, any future allocations or redemptions by existing investors, and everything in between.

Again, if the initial investment partnership is beginning with a few investors and the partnership won't initially take in new investors throughout the year, it's not impossible for the basic fund calculations to be done in-house. However, once the partnership grows and new investors decide to invest throughout the year, it may be best to assign this task to a firm.

Fund Custodian (Broker)

There are many ways to handle the brokerage needs of the partnership. Obviously, a full-service broker will incur greater costs for the partnership than using an online platform. But depending on asset size and investment strategy, a full-service broker usually can be more efficient and valuable in the long run. Value investors love special situation investment opportunities, and participating in them effectively can be virtually impossible without a broker. Also, investing in international businesses that are not traded on U.S.

exchanges can be very time consuming or impossible without the aid and infrastructure that a full-service portfolio custodian can bring. Overall, I think the benefits of a broker in running a partnership far outweigh the costs.

Accountant and Auditor

Any investment fund will require the use of an accountant and in most cases an auditor. An accountant is necessary in order to prepare the year-end tax statements for each investment partner. An audit is required for just about every investment fund because the investors will require one; more important, an audit protects the investment manager against any possible issues that can arise when dealing with other people's money. However, partnerships that are starting off with a couple hundred thousand dollars or so can probably forgo an audit for the first couple of years and just have an auditor look at the year-end figure and bless them. Again, the litmus test is the desires of the investors in the fund.

Once the partnership becomes established, an annual audit should be done. Smaller funds usually can use the services of a regional accounting firm, which often charge substantially less than national firms.

Quality Matters Most

With regard to investment partnerships and costs, never attempt to sacrifice quality in order to save a little on expenses. In the long run, the benefits of a fund that is handled by reputable service providers will far outweigh any costs savings that come at the expense of quality. Nonetheless, there are smaller service providers that perform top-quality services for investment partnerships.

Notes

Introduction

1. Benjamin Graham and David Dodd, *Security Analysis*, 6th ed. (New York: McGraw-Hill, 2009), p. xvi.
2. Benjamin Graham, *The Intelligent Investor*, 4th ed. (New York: Harper and Row, 1973).

Chapter 1

1. 2007 Berskhire Hathaway Annual Report, p. 15.
2. Robert G. Hagstrom, *The Warren Buffett Way* (New York: John Wiley & Sons, 1995).
3. Warren E. Buffett, 1969 Letter to Partners, May 29, 1969.

Chapter 2

1. John Bogle, *The Little Book of Common Sense Investing* (Hoboken, NJ: John Wiley & Sons, 2007).
2. Warren E. Buffett, *The SuperInvestors of Graham and Doddsville* (New York: Columbia University Press, 1984).
3. Benjamin Graham and David Dodd, *Security Analysis*, 1st ed. (New York: McGraw-Hill, 1934).
4. Warren E. Buffett, 1969 Letter to Limited Partners, Omaha, Nebraska, 1969.
5. Warren E. Buffett, *The SuperInvestors of Graham and Doddsville* (New York: Columbia University Press, 1984).
6. *Ibid.*
7. Eugene F. Fama and Kenneth R. French, "The Cross Section of Expected Stock Returns," *Journal of Finance* 47, no. 2 (June 1992).
8. Benjamin Graham, *The Intelligent Investor*, 4th ed. (New York: Harper and Row, 1973), p. 277.

Chapter 3

1. Benjamin Graham and David Dodd, *Security Analysis*, 1st ed. (New York: McGraw-Hill, 1934).
2. 2007 Berkshire Hathaway Annual Report.
3. Benjamin Graham, *The Intelligent Investor*, 4th ed. (New York: Harper and Row, 1973), p. 287.
4. Andrew Bary, "What's Wrong Warren?" *Barron's*, December 27, 1999.

Chapter 4

1. Warren E. Buffett, *The SuperInvestors of Graham and Doddsville* (New York: Columbia University Press, 1984).
2. Mohnish Pabrai, *The Dhandho Investor* (Hoboken, NJ: John Wiley & Sons, 2007), p. 107.
3. William Ruane and Richard Cuniff of the Sequoia Fund in 1987.
4. Warren E. Buffett, Berkshire Hathaway Annual Meeting, May 3, 2008.
5. John Maynard Keynes, *The General Theory of Employment, Interest and Money* (London: Macmillian, 1936), p. 158.

Chapter 5

1. "The Death of Equities," *BusinessWeek*, August 13, 1979.
2. Dow Jones Indexes: www.djindexes.com.
3. Warren E. Buffett, "Buy American. I Am," *New York Times*, October 17, 2008.
4. Gerald S. Martin and John Puthenpurackal, "Imitation Is the Sincerest Form of Flattery: Warren Buffett and Berkshire Hathaway," April 15, 2008: http://ssrn.com/abstract=806246.
5. Joel Greenblatt, *The Little Book That Beats the Market* (Hoboken, NJ: John Wiley & Sons, 2006).
6. Peter Lynch, *One Up on Wall Street* (New York: Penguin, 1989), pp. 19–20.
7. Alice Schroeder. *The Snowball: Warren Buffett and the Business of Life* (New York: Random House, 2008), p. 814.
8. I had the privilege of meeting Mr. Buffett over the course of two days in January of 2007. On one occasion, he actually brought the *Moody's Investment Manual* that he used to research stocks when he was younger. Buffett spent years going through the entire book, page by page, until he had gone through all 10,000 pages.
9. Buffett quoted in *ibid.*, pp. 814–815.

Chapter 6

1. Janet Lowe, *Warren Buffett Speaks* (Hoboken, NJ: John Wiley & Sons, 2007), p. 117.
2. *Ibid.*, p. 193.
3. CNN (www.cnn.com/US/9710/18/goizueta.obit.9am/).
4. In 2006, Buffett announced that he would be donating the bulk of his fortune to the Bill and Melinda Gates Foundation. Since Buffett's fortune is in Berkshire stock, his ownership percentage will slowly decline as he makes regular contributions to the foundation.
5. 2007 Forbes CEO Compensation Special Report, May 3, 2007: www.forbes. com/lists/2007/12/lead_07ceos_CEO-Compensation_CompTotDisp.html.

Chapter 7

1. I am referring to the period during the Dutch Golden Age in the 1630s when tulips reached extraordinarily high prices and suddenly collapsed. To illustrate the irrationality, at the height of absurdity, tulip contract prices traded as much as 20 times the annual income of a skilled craftsman. Fast forward to 1999. This was a lot like valuing a revenueless, profitless Internet company for billions of dollars.
2. Robert Hagstrom, *The Warren Buffett Way* (Hoboken, NJ: John Wiley & Sons, 2004).
3. Adam Smith, *The Wealth of Nations* (New York: Modern Library Edition/ Random House, 1994), p. 131.

Chapter 8

1. Geoff Colvin and Jessica Shambora, "J&J: Secrets of Success," *Fortune,* May 4, 2009.
2. Mohnish Pabrai, "Buffett Succeeds at Nothing," Motley Fool on Fool.com, October 30, 2002. Printed with permission from Mr. Pabrai and The Motley Fool.
3. Value Line Investment Survey, November 28, 2008
4. During 1997, Johnson & Johnson traded at between $24 and $34 a share (Value Line Investment Survey).
5. Between 1929 and 1932, the Dow Jones declined nearly 89 percent from the high to low points. In 1973, the bear market pulled the Standard & Poor's (S&P) 500 Index down by as much as 50 percent at one point. In 2008, the

S&P 500 lost 38.5 percent, the second worst stock market performance since 1825.

6. "Hedge Funds Lost 18.3% in 2008." *New York Times,* January 9, 2009: http://dealbook.blogs.nytimes.com/2009/01/08/hedge-funds-lost-183-in-2008-market-turmoil/.

7. Indeed, in 2008, Johnson & Johnson shares declined 10 percent versus a market decline of 38.5 percent for the S&P 500 Index.

Chapter 9

1. Seth Klarman, in Graham and Dodd, *Security Analysis,* 6th ed. (New York: McGraw-Hill, 2008), p. xvi.
2. *Barron's,* December 18, 2008.
3. The terms "bull market" and "bear market" often are used to describe the general direction of stock market prices over a given period of time. A bull market identifies a rising stock market, so named because when a bull charges, it starts with its head down and pushes up. Similarly, a declining or bear market is so named because bears attack by first rising and coming down.
4. www.sirjohntempleton.org/articles_details.asp?a = 16.
5. "Sir John M. Templeton, Philanthropist, Dies at 95," *New York Times,* July 9, 2008: www.nytimes.com/2008/07/09/business/09templeton-cnd.html.
6. John Rothchild, *The Davis Dynasty: Fifty Years of Successful Investing on Wall Street* (Hoboken, NJ: John Wiley & Sons, 2001), p. 137.
7. Graham and Dodd, *Security Analysis,* p. 35.
8. Mark Hirschey, *Tech Stock Valuation* (New York: Academic Press, 2003), pp. 1–2.

Chapter 11

1. "Stocks Hit '97 Level, Signaling Long Slump," *Wall Street Journal,* March 3, 2009.
2. Investors need to look no further than the credit crisis that engulfed the economy in 2008 to appreciate the severe consequences that can face a business when credit is restricted or no longer available. Indeed, the credit crisis of 2008 is a very severe example, but maximum severity should always be the litmus test for a value investor.
3. Peter Lynch, *One Up on Wall Street* (New York: Penguin, 1989), p. 198.
4. Value Line Investment Survey, Issue 9. July 24, 2009.
5. *Ibid.*
6. John Burr Williams, *The Theory of Investment Value* (Cambridge: Harvard University Press, 1938).
7. "P&G to buy Gillette for $57B," CNNMoney.com, January 28, 2005: http://money.cnn.com/2005/01/28/news/fortune500/pg_gillette/.

About the Author

Hesham Gad is the Managing Partner of the Gad Partners Funds, value-focused investment partnerships inspired by the 1950s Buffett Partnerships founded in 2007. Prior to managing the Gad Partners Fund, he ran the Gad Investment Group from 2002 to 2005 and delivered annual compound returns of 22 percent. Mr. Gad has written hundreds of investment articles for various financial web sites including The Motley Fool, TheStreet.com, and Investopedia. Mr. Gad received his MBA from the University of Georgia in 2007. He currently resides in Athens, Georgia, with his wife, Maggie.

Index

A

Absolute return philosophy, 64–66
    relative return approach,
        contrast, 65
Accountants, service providers, 247
Advanced search strategy, 85–88
    basic search strategy, contrast,
        85–86
AgFeed Industries, investment bargain,
    218–219
American Eagle Outfitters
    metrics, 120t
    ROIC calculation, 120
American Express
    monopolistic operations, 102
    salad oil scandal, 182
American International Group (AIG), U.S.
    Treasury investment, 51–52
Analysis
    reliance, 177
    thoroughness, 36
Annualized return, delivery, 19
Annual proxy filing, examination, 116
Apple Computer
    losses, 143
    trading value, 13–14
Arbitrage investments, 225
    trade, example, 216
Asian currency crisis, 17
Assets
    control, benefits, 170t
    purchase, 243–244
        profitability, 164–165
        value, 237
    worth, 233

ATP Oil and Gas (ATPG), investment
    bargain, 217–218
Attorneys, service providers, 245–246
Auction houses, price extraction, 184
Auditors, service providers, 247

B

Bare Escentuals, cash flow forecast, 30
Bargain securities, investment
    process, 175
Basic search strategy, advanced search
    strategy (contrast), 85–86
Bear markets
    characterization, 184
    company acquisitions, 179–180
    value investment, myth, 187
Berkowitz, Bruce (Fairholme Funds), 16,
    35, 72
    value investor, 38
Berkshire Hathaway, 6–7
    book value per share, growth, 36–37
    Buffett control, 114
    Coca-Cola investment, 104–105
    consequences, 133
    positions, price (undervaluing), 74
    shareholder letters, 24, 117
    stock price, test, 40–41
    trading level, 187–188
Board of directors, qualifications/
    experience, 116
Bogle, John, 15, 152
Bonds
    arbitrage, 154
    coupons, ROE (comparison), 121
    selection, 61

Book value, 117
  importance, 233–240
  rewards, 234
  simplicity, 233
  value investor understanding, 234
Book value per share, 118
Borrowed money, usage, 62
Brokerage firms, shares (return), 189–190
Brokers, service providers, 246–247
Buffett, Warren, 35, 67, 72
  ability, quote, 221
  approach, discipline, 86–87
  bonds investment, 12–13
  Coca-Cola investment, 104–105, 157, 170
  competence circle, reliance,
    133–134
  excitement/expenses, enemies, 173
  GEICO investment, 102, 170
  Geiger counter, usage, 156–158
  Graham impact, 36–37
  Graham perspective, 17
  Graham-schooled investors, comparison, 20
  holding period, 54
  Internet boom aversion, 40–41, 144,
    159–160
  investigation level (quote), 91
  investment
    acumen, 133
    partnership, initiation, 11–12
    philosophy, 3
    rules, 50
    track record, result, 170
  investor examination, 139–144
  Korean stock manual, 86
  margin of safety, importance, 92–95
  patience, virtue, 42
  performance, analysis, 73
  self-judgment, 179
  shareholder letter, 24
  success, 154–158
  technique, copying, 72–73
  Washington Post Company investment,
    6–7, 48, 170
  wealth derivation, 39
Buffett Partnership, 11–14
Bull markets, investment approach, 184

Business
  activity, stock price activity (separation), 51
  cash flow growth rates, reduction, 9
  cash production, 61
  CEO, association, 114
  current earnings, absence, 231–233
  definition. See Good business; Great
    business
  due diligence, 111
  earnings quality, 228
  focus, 50–51
  fundamentals, value investor attention,
    224
  future, assumptions, 8
  future cash flows, anticipation, 8
  future growth prospects, 169
  future sum, discounting, 8–9
  goodwill, investor examination, 238–239
  growth process, 227–228
  history, examination, 7–8
  inexpensiveness, purchase, 138–139
  intrinsic value, existence, 96
  long-term fundamentals, 160
  margin of safety, 93–94
  merits, 6–7
  net value, 117–118
  operations, understanding, 134
  ownership interest, 11
  ownership stakes, acquisition, 160
  publications, reading, 88
  purchase, 14
  quality, management (comparison), 112
  quantitative attributes, reliance, 19
  revenue generation, 8–9
  terminal value, determination, 109–111
  true value, determination, 29–30
  types, 21–24
  understanding
    absence, 192
    importance, 22
  value
    ranking, 183t
    stock price, separation, 3–4
  value drivers, understanding, 11
Business investment
  complication, 7

mindset, 34–35
    value, 1–2
Business valuation, 41–44
    businesslike approach, 6–11
    effectiveness, 91
    margin of safety, concept foundation, 93
    perspective, 3, 176–177
    process, importance, 44
    terminology, usage, 92
BusinessWeek, problems, 69
Buy-and-hold technique, 54–56, 148
    advantages, 164
    benefits, 162–171
Buy-and-sell activities, misinterpretation,
    222

C

Cabot Oil and Gas, value (finding), 130t
Capital
    access, 160
    allocation, 142
        judgment, 117
    appreciation, 147–148, 197
        investment trap, 222–223
    base, involvement, 244
    forms, 119–120
    influx, 144
    initial usage, consideration, 245
    losses, 52
        permanence, 51
        value investor aversion, 50
    permanent loss, 153–154
    preservation, 49–52, 61, 179
        importance, 222–223
Capital asset pricing model (CAPM), 119
Case studies. *See* Mueller Water Products;
    Sunrise Senior Living; Ternium Steel
Cash, industry viewpoint, 149
Cash flow from operating (CFFO) activities,
    106, 108
Cash flows
    growth rate, 100
    guarantees, absence, 98
    valuation, 99
Cash inflows/outflows, intrinsic value
    (impact), 106

Cheap, Greenblatt definition, 76
Cheap growth, purchase (value investor
    preference), 168–169
Chief executive officer (CEO), company
    association, 114
Chipotle, success, 44–45
Circle of competence, 133–134
    discipline, 145
Clitheroe, Paul, 91
CNBC
    digital clock format, usage, 149
    impact, 148–149
Coca-Cola
    book value, 122
    brand value, 238
    Buffett/Munger investment, 104–105,
        157, 170
    business success, 5
    discount rate, reduction, 9
    dominance, impact, 20
    Goizeuta (CEO), 112
    true value, consideration,
        29–30
    valuation, 100
Commodity-type businesses, competitive
    advantages (absence), 103
Common knowledge, investor
    underestimation, 83
Company
    bear market acquisition, 179–180
    debt, absence, 120–121
    liquidation value, example, 167
    market price, intrinsic value
        (relationship), 226
    ownership, net worth percentage,
        113–114
    performance, 116
    reputation, incompetent/unethical
        behavior (impact), 112–113
    return rates, examination, 122
    setbacks, 185
    stock, ownership, shareholder interest
        (alignment), 113–114
Competence circle
    discipline, 134
    reliance, 133–134

Competitive advantage
  existence, 103
  value, 103–104
Compounding (buy-and-hold technique),
  54–55
ConocoPhillips
  stock price, 129–130
  value, finding, 130t
Consensus, acceptance, 174
Conservatism/confirmatory biases, 241
Corporate cash flows, U.S. Treasury cash
  flow (contrast), 99–100
Credit
  extension, financial institution ability,
  131–132
Credit (abundance), exploitation, 131–132
Cuniff, Richard, 180
  investment reflection, 54
  Sequoia Fund statement, 51
Current price, intrinsic value
  (gap), 30

D
Data
  avoidance, 162
  reliance, 3
Davis, Shelby, 184
D.E. Shaw & Company, 154–155
Debt
  absence, 120–121
  capital form, 119
Decision making
  crowd, impact, 3
  importance, 158
Dell, Michael, 114
Details, attention (importance), 92
Discipline
  impact, 126–128
  importance, 140, 177–178
  maintenance, 40
    requirements, 44
  simplicity/difficulty, 145
  usage, 125
Discounted cash flows
  low-risk investment, 97t
  models, usage, 29–30

Discounted cash flows, total value
  (example), 9
Discount rate
  application, 99
  basics, 98–101
Dividend yield, increase, 128–129
Dodd, David, 35, 76, 174–175
  investment philosophy, 186
Dow Jones, trading volatility (2008),
  53–54
Dow Jones Industrial Average (DJIA), 191
  annual returns (1980-1989), 70t
  closing level, example, 69
  level, 163
  performance, 70–71
  stock purchase, example, 55
DryShips
  assets, carrying costs (reevaluation),
  171–172
  balance sheet, 167
  conservative liquidation value, 166t
  Goodwill, 167
  liabilities, impact, 167
  share price, change, 165
  stated liquidation value, 166t

E
Earnings before taxes, depreciation, and
  amortization (EBITDA), 207. *See also*
  Ternium Steel
Economic crisis (2007), 132–133
Economic recession, differences, 144
Emotional habits, expense, 128–129
Emotional misbehavior, discipline, 137
Emotions, impact, 145
Energy master limited partnerships, 119
Ensco Corp.
  cash flow statement, 107t
  CFFO, 108–109
  discounted FCF analysis, 109t
    assumptions, 109
  free cash flow, 108t
  intrinsic value, 110
    analysis, 106–111
  services, demand, 108
Enterprise value (EV). *See* Ternium Steel

Equities
  debt form, 119
  demand, decrease, 183
  prices, decline, 217
  problems, 69
  risk premium, assignation, 120
  valuations, 70
Events, six sigma types, 16–17
Executive compensation, 115

F

Fairholme Funds, filing (2008), 75f
Fairly valued business/investment, 21–24
Fama, Eugene, 23–24
52-week low lists, 78–79
Financial crisis, 62
Financial markets, price quotes, 3
Financial media, sensationalization, 147
Finova bonds, purchase, 157
First Industrial Realty, purchase, 157
Floor exchange, obsolescence, 4
Franchise-type businesses, value, 104
Franchise value, 104–105
Free cash flow
  examination, 26–27
  growth rate, 27
French, Kenneth, 23–24
Frictional costs
  impact, 55
  increase, 151
Fund administrators, service providers, 246
Fundamental analysis, 19
  depth, 154
  performing, 147–148
Fundamentals, listing, 77
Fund custodians (brokers), service
  providers, 246–247
Future returns, inadequacy, 140–141
Future sum, discounting, 8–9

G

Gambler's fallacy, 241
Gates, Bill (wealth derivation), 39
GEICO, Buffett investment, 102, 170
Geiger counter approach, 156–158
General Electric (GE), business success, 5

Gillette, competition, 105
Global economy
  challenges, 216–217
  full recession mode (2008-2009),
    211–212
Goizueta, Roberto (Coca-Cola CEO), 112
Good business, Greenblatt definition,
  76–77
Goodwill
  basics, 236–240
  intangible asset, 238
Google, investment value, 25, 67–68
Graham, Benjamin, 76
  crowd, agreement, 174
  Graham-schooled investors, Buffett
    comparison, 20
  investing course (Columbia University),
    129
  investment philosophy, 1, 175–176, 186
  investor actions, consistency, 195
  teachings, 35
  value investing, 14, 17–18
  willpower, necessity, 125
Great business, definition, 101–102
Great Depression, 132–133
Greed, consequences, 133
Greenblatt, Joel, 76
Growth
  achievement process, 227–231
  importance, 225–233
  opportunity, 225–226
  purchase, value investor preference,
    168–169
  value, 230t
Growth at a reasonable price (GARP)
  business, 168–170, 225
Growth at a reasonable price (GARP)
  investment, example, 169

H

Hagstrom, Robert, 139
Hawkins, Mason (Longleaf Funds), 16, 35,
  41, 72
  business trading examination, 95
  stupidity, appearance (quote), 173
  value investor, 38

Hawkins, Mason (Southeastern Asset
  Management), 244
Herd mentality, resistance, 147–148
High-growth businesses, value investment
  qualification (myth), 189
Hindsight bias, 242
Home Depot
  cash flow forecast, 30
  industry ownership, 102–103
Home ownership, stock ownership
  (contrast), 161
Home values, decline (2007/2008),
  160–161
Horsehead Holding Company
  balance sheet, 235t
  cash balance, 235
  investment bargain, 218
  share price, attraction, 236
  value, basis, 236

I

Ignorance, benefit, 158–159
Implied book value, significance, 165–166
IMSA acquisition. *See* Ternium Steel
Independent thinking, value, 3–4
Intangible asset, 238
Intelligence level, long-term success
  (relationship), 126–127
Intelligent Investor, The (Graham), 14, 17, 30,
  36, 42
  crowd, agreement, 174
  margin of safety, term (creation), 92–93
Internet boom, Buffett aversion, 40–41, 144
Internet bubble, 17
Internet trading, impact, 148
Intrinsic value
  analysis, 106–111
  assessments, basis, 139–140
  asset purchase price, contrast, 183
  basics, 95–101
  calculation, 99, 101, 110–111. *See also*
    True intrinsic value
  current price, gap, 30
  decline, growth rate decline
    (comparison), 226
  defining, 96–97

derivation, 93
determination, example, 141–142
estimation, 176–177
growth, 165
  preference, 226
impact, 106
market price, comparison, 165–167
price payment, contrast, 141
term, usage, 95
Inventory management, 123
Invested capital (IC)
  calculation, 118–119
  measurement, 118
Investment (investing). *See* Business
    investment
  activity, risk, 134
  acumen, development, 22
  advanced search strategy, 85–88
  analysis, 18
    market agreement, timing, 34–35
  attractiveness (determination), P/E
    ratios (usage), 230
  bargain prices, future opportunity,
    153–154
  baseball, similarity, 127, 151
  business side, 17–21
  buy-and-hold approach, 54–55
  common sense, 81–84
  conviction, 134, 136
  current price, examination, 29
  decline, 3
  discipline, impact, 126–128
  elements, 33, 39–42
    list, 41
    overview, 43–46
  flexibility, 187–192
  gains, 137
    delivery, 197
  latticework, 42–43
  luck
    impact, 3
    skill, contrast, 137
  managers, success/failure, 144
  margin of safety, meaning, 94
  mistakes, 240–241
  myths, 187–192

operations
  characteristics, 18
  Graham definition, 17, 39
  outcome, priority, 197–198
  partnership
    initiation, 243
    quality, importance, 247
  patience, 41–42
    benefits, 148
    difficulty, 45
  pessimism, impact, 45–46
  philosophy
    development, 174–175
    establishment, 47
    preference, 138–139
  process
    failure, example, 127
    manipulation, emotional decision
      making (impact), 126
    priority, 197–198
  publications, importance, 88
  reading, importance, 87–88
  sale, problems, 63
  scientific process, 35–36
  search strategy, 41, 43
    development, 67
  security, 102
  shortcuts, short-term losses, 5
  skill, luck (contrast), 137
  speculation, contrast (investment trap), 224
  starting point, 54–61
  success
    Buffett statement, 155
    defining, 186
    mistakes, impact, 240
  target price, 140–141
  timing, insignificance, 138t
  traps, 222–224
  types, 15
  value
    case studies. See Mueller Water
      Products; Sunrise Senior Living;
      Ternium Steel
    determinant, price (impact), 128–129
  value investing, comparison, 35–38
  waiting, advantages, 151–152

Investment (investing) decisions, 10
  basis, 2–3
  formulation, 53
  satisfaction, 59
Investment (investing) opportunities
  bargain, existence, 106
  comparison, 98
  existence, 185
  patience, 132
  work, 43–44
Investors
  excitement, problem, 71–72
  intelligence, 126
  investment choices, problems,
    181–182
  mistakes, recognition, 221–222
  protection, providing, 166–167
  qualitative factors, reliance, 125
  rational behavior, 180–181
  short-term orientation, 148–149
  stock market problems, 142–143
iPod, introduction, 13–14

J
Jobs, Steve, 13
  executive compensation, 115
Johnson & Johnson
  competition, 105
  intrinsic value, growth, 169
  operating history record, 190
  profits, Value Line Investment Survey
    report, 169
  progress, 112
  trading level, 228–229

K
Keynes, John Maynard, 64–65
King Pharmaceuticals, 2
Klarman, Seth (Baupost Group), 35, 37,
    41, 72
  value investing
    philosophy, 47
    requirements, 175
Korean stocks, Buffett
    investigation, 86
Kroger, cash flow forecast, 30

L

Lampert, Eddie (value investor), 35, 37
Legend, creation, 11–14
L'eggs (Lynch investigation), 83–84
Lehman Brothers, financial
    crisis, 62
Leverage
    inexpensiveness/increase, 123
    mismanagement, 123–124
Limited partners, communication, 2, 19
Liquidation value, examples, 166t
Liquidity. *See* Stock markets
    changes, 159–162
    value, 160
Long investments, margin requirement,
    191–192
Long-Term Capital Management (LTCM), 155
Long-term fundamentals, short-term
    fundamentals (contrast), 143t
Long-term investment
    results, pursuit, 147–148
    success, 127
Long-term success, intelligence level
    (relationship), 126–127
Lowe's, industry ownership, 102–103
Luck, term (usage), 139
Lynch, Peter (Magellan Fund), 83
    PEG ratio, popularization, 231
    value investor, 35, 37–38

M

Madness-of-crowds syndrome, 180
Magic Formula (web site), usage, 76–77
Management
    ability/competence, importance, 111
    business quality, comparison, 112
    compensation structure, 113
    factor, perspective, 113
    operating skill, 117
    quality assessment, 117
        executive compensation, impact, 115
    value, 111–121
Margin
    increase, creation, 124
    problems, 62–63

usage
    avoidance, 61–64
    problems, 63t
Margin of safety, 30–31, 92–95, 154
    comfort, 141–142
    concept, understanding, 94–95
    determination, 128–129
    existence, 190
    idea, derivation, 93
    increase, investor demand, 226
    occurrence, 94–95
Market
    activities, speculation, 48–49
    changes, 134–135
    correction, differences, 144
    fluctuation, 197
    investors, cash preference, 150–151
    liquidity
        changes, 159–162
        value, 160
    loss, separation, 127–128
    multiples, decline, 231
    participants, value investment
        orientation, 244
    participation, Buffett absence, 12
    pessimism, 181
    price
        decline, 226
        intrinsic value, comparison, 165–167
    volatility
        misinterpretation, investment
            trap, 223
        usage, 139–140
Market timing
    ability, problem, 185–186
    importance, 140–141
    value-oriented investor avoidance, 58–59
McDonald's
    brand value, 238
    business success, 5
    operating history record, 190
Meaningless data, avoidance, 162
Media
    information, reliance, 71
    investor avoidance, 69–72

Meridian Medical Technologies, investment, 2
Microsoft Corporation
    initial public offering, 122
    real value, 133
    return on equity (ROE)
        generation, 121–122
        understanding, 121–124
Miller, Bill (Legg Mason), 16
Milne, A.A. (intelligence quote), 15
Mittal, Lakshmi (wealth derivation), 39
Mohawk Industries, 25–29
    cash flow forecast, 30
Money making, asset purchase, 164–165
Money management, 144
Money managers, quarterly statement
    filing, 73–74
Monopolistic tendencies, 102–103
Moody's Stock Manual, Buffett investigation,
    68–69
Mortgages, sales, 131–132
Mueller Water Products
    arbitrage investment trade, 216
    balance sheet, 239t
    B shares, trading, 215
    common stock, classes (creation), 215
    goodwill, 239
        excess, 240
    A shares, trading, 215
Mueller Water Products, case study,
    214–216
Munger, Charlie, 35, 41, 72, 155
    Coca-Cola investment, 104–105, 157
    patience, virtue, 42
    process inversion, 103
Mutual funds, indices (comparison), 152

N

NASDAQ 100 Index, usage, 190–191
NASDAQ Composite Index, overvaluation,
    191
NASDAQ Stock Exchange, electronic
    exchange, 4
Net after-tax operating profit, 118
Net asset value, 117

New Stock Exchange, 181
New York Stock Exchange, floor exchange
    (existence), 4
Nifty 50, investor favorite, 190
Noninterest-bearing current liabilities,
    subtraction, 119

O

Oil companies
    valuation metrics, 92
    variables, dominance, 91–92
Operating results, examination, 113,
    116–117
Opportunistic investment, 149
Outcome bias, 241
Outlier success stories, impact, 153
Overvalued business/investment, 21–24
    stock price indication, 60–61
Ownership interests, acquisition, 152–153

P

Pabrai, Mohnish (Pabrai Investment
    Funds), 50, 72, 154
    investment returns, perspective,
        182–183
Pacific Sunwear, cash flow
    forecast, 30
Pascal, Blaise (quote), 147
Patience
    benefits, 148
    demands, 178
    development, difficulty, 45
    practice, 147
    virtue, 41–42
Patient investment approach, 149
Performance results, example,
    18–19
Pessimism
    assignation, 182
    impact, 179–181
    investment point, 173
Polaroid, operating history record, 190
Portfolio
    diversification, value, 38–39
    purchasing power, 62–63

Price
    concept, 131
    focus, problem, 141t
    impact, 24–31
    importance, 141
Price payment
    concept, importance, 129
    discipline, impact, 128–132
    intrinsic value, contrast, 141
Price-to-book ratio (P/B), 23
    groupings, Fama/French analysis, 24
Price to earnings/growth (PEG)
        ratio, 203
    examination, 229
        list, 230t
    Lynch popularization, 231
Price to earnings (P/E) ratio, 23
    discussion, 188
    expansion, 229
    foundational metric, 228
    increase, 227
    stocks, bargain qualification (myth),
        188–189
    usage, 56
Principal, safety, 18
    promise, 36
Private investment partnership,
        setup, 245
Procter & Gamble (P&G)
    discount rate, reduction, 9
    Gillette acquisition, 237
Profitability
    generation, continuation, 144
    sustaining, 232
Profit statement, impact, 123
Property values, increase (exploitation),
        131–132
Psychological tendencies, 241–242
Public companies, shares (purchase
        approach), 10

Q

Qualitative attributes, value, 20
Qualitative factors, investor reliance, 125
Quantitative measures, reliance, 125

R

Reading
    importance, 87–88
    suggestions, 88
Real estate investment trusts (REITs), 119, 157
Relative return approach, 64–65absolute
        return approach, contrast, 65
Replacement cost, asset purchase price
        (contrast), 184
Research, reliance, 177
Return
    achievement, 39–40
    adequacy, 36
    earning, possibility, 153–154
    satisfaction, 18
Return on equity (ROE)
    bonds, coupon (comparison), 121
    improvement, 123
    increase, 123–124
    understanding, 121–124
    usefulness, 120–121
Return on invested capital (ROIC),
        76–77, 117
    manager focus, 118–121
Risk
    carrying, increase, 181
    investment involvement, 134
    limitation, 153
    minimization, 147–148
    volatility, contrast, 59–60
Risk-free arbitrage, 153
Ruane, William, 21, 180
    investment reflection, 54
    Sequoia Fund statement, 51

S

Safety, conservative tests (importance),
        171–172
Safety margin, 30–31, 92–95, 153
    comfort, 141–142
    concept, understanding, 94–95
    determination, 128–129
    existence, 190
    increase, investor demand, 226
    occurrence, 94–95

Sales, margins (increase), 123
Schloss, Walter (WJS Partners), 20
Search strategy, 41, 43. *See also* Advanced
    search strategy
    basic strategies, 75–85
    development, 67
    imitation, impact, 72–75
    investor resources, 68–69
Secular bull/bear market returns (1900–
    present), 71t
Securities
    analysis, 153–154
    bargains, 149
    demand, increase, 183
    investment
        ability, 174–175
        process, 175
    price level determination, investor
        failure, 130–131
    purchase, 243–244
        example, 167
    sale, example, 126
    undervaluation, 165
Securities and Exchange Commission
    (SEC)
    documents, search, 176
    regulatory filings, 73
Security Analysis (Graham/Dodd), 17, 35,
    76, 91, 185–186
    Theory of Investment Value, comparison,
        234
Security prices, purpose, 6
Self-attribution bias, 241
Sequoia Fund, 21
Service providers, 245–247
Shareholder value, maximization, 111
Shaw Carpet, performance, 25–29
Short sales, participation, 191
Short-term fundamentals, long-term
    fundamentals (contrast), 143t
Short-term volatility, unpredictability, 159
SIDOR, nationalization, 207–208
Skill, term (usage), 139
Smart money, impact, 136–137
Smith, Adam, 145

Speculation, investment (contrast), 224
Standard & Poor's 500 (S&P 500)
    index, level, 163
    stock index (1919-2007), 57t
Standard & Poor's (S&P) index, annualized
    return, 182
Stock markets
    advantages, 158
    annual opening, hypothetical, 4–5
    closure, hypothetical, 4–5
    correction (2000), 142–143
    crash (1987), 16–17
    investment, success, 63–64
    investor problems, 142
    liquidity, 5
        advantages, 52–53
    performance (2008), 163
    returns (1900-2007), 58f
    speculative approach, 148
    value, loss, 132
    voting machine, analogy, 227
    wealth creation, 153
    weighing machine, analogy, 227
Stock prices
    activity, business activity (separation), 51
    appreciation, example, 180
    decrease, investor rationalization, 131
    fluctuation, 68
    importance, 55
        frequency, 162
    instruction, 2
    irrationality, 16–17
    noise
        ignoring, 6
        information, contrast, 4–6
    payment, discipline (impact), 128–132
    performance, 116–117
    short-term movements, 2–3
    value (control), management (impact),
        117
    zero level, 131
Stocks
    holding period, 105
    insider ownership, 114
    investment, philosophy (impact), 57–58

Stocks *(continued)*
  investor anger, 153
  management ownership, 113
  ownership, 189–190
    home ownership, contrast, 161
    net worth percentage, 113–114
    process, 114
  performance, problems, 143–144
  purchase, 1
  shorting, example, 189–190
  short-term volatility, unpredictability, 159
  trading ease/speed, 158–159
  value investor shorting, myth, 189–192
Sunrise Senior Living (SRZ)
  assisted living costs, approximation,
    199–200
  capital expenditures, 204
  company background, 199–201
  entry, barriers, 200
  EPS, growth, 202
  free cash flow valuation, 204–205
  historical real estate
    transactions, 203t
  intrinsic value ranges, 205t
  investment analysis, 201–202
  investor attraction, 200–201
  living stock price chart, 205f
  PEG ratio, 203
  residents, types, 200
  residual interest, retention, 201–202
  revenue, sources, 201
  ROI, 201
  sale-leaseback gains, 202
  start-up costs, incurring, 202
  stock buyback commitment,
    announcement, 204
  valuation, 203–204
  value (case study), 198–205

T
Target price, usage, 140–141
Technology bubble (2002–2003), 180
Technology mania (1990s), 159–160,
  190–191
Templeton, John, 24
  bull markets (quote), 173
  investing perspective, 181–182

Templeton Growth Fund, creation/
  launching, 182
Terminal value, determination,
  109–111
Ternium Steel
  alternative valuation, 210–214
  case study, 205–214
  changes, 212–213
  company background, 206–209
  discounted cash flow, 211t
    analysis, 210
    recessionary assumptions, 212t
  EBITDA, 207, 209–210
    equivalence, 211
  enterprise value (EV), 207, 209
  free cash flow (FCF), 209–210
  future growth, focus, 208–209
  IMSA acquisition, 209
  nationalization outcome, 208
  purchase price, 213
  recession survival, 206
  SIDOR nationalization, 207–208
  terminal value, 210
  valuation, 209–210
  Venezuelan operations, 207
  waterfalls, 213f
Tesoro Corporation
  investment, 143–144
  share value, loss, 232
Theory of Investment Value, The (Williams),
  96, 234
13-F filing, 74
Timing. *See* Market timing
  insignificance, 138
True intrinsic value, calculation,
  106–111
Tweedy, Browne, 33

U
Undervaluation (providing), intrinsic value
  (impact), 165, 167–171
Undervalued business/investment,
  21–24
  goal, 136–137
  stock price indication, 60–61
Undervalued securities, locating, 25
U.S. Treasury bills, yield acceptance, 149

U.S. Treasury cash flows, corporate cash
flows (contrast), 99–100
U.S. Treasury notes, yield acceptance, 149
USG, competitive advantages, 103

V

Valero
earnings per share, changes, 232–233
investment, 143–144
Valuation. *See* Business valuation
business cash flow generation,
impact, 221
metrics, impact, 60
Valuation process
importance, 44
margin-of-safety concept, importance,
93–94
operating results, usage, 176–177
Value
approach, win-win situation,
185–186
case studies. *See* Mueller Water Products;
Sunrise Senior Living; Ternium Steel
characteristics (Klarman assertion), 178
concept, 131
determination, 128–132
price, usage, 24–31
discovery processes, 195
driver, 61
finding, 130t
importance, 225–233
pessimism, impact, 179–181
receipt, price payment (impact), 52–54
Value-based approach, long-term
success, 20
Value investment (value investing), 14
analysis, reliance, 177
basics, 101–111
characteristic, 147–148
contrarian approach, 49–50
intellectual capability, usage (absence), 49
intrinsic value basics, 95–101
investments, comparison, 35–38
margin of safety basics, 92–95
philosophies
design, 154
usage, 49

requirements, 40–41, 175
research, reliance, 177
stock price, importance, 55
Value investors
business approach, 10–11
characteristics, 192
decisions, understanding, 13
default orientation, 65–66
efforts, concentration, 222
goal, 163–164
growth, perspective, 167–168
improvement, 181
learning, 38–39
least expensive price, 229
lower prices examination, 192–193
noise avoidance, 6
P/B stock investigation, 84–85
P/E stock investigation, 84–85
risk aversion, 221–222
stock selection, 41–42
Value Investors Club (VIC), 79–81
investment ideas, 80
Value Line Investment Survey, 77–78
data, subscription, 78
report, 169
website, usage, 77–78
Value-oriented business
fundamentals, 142
Value-oriented investments
approaches, discussion, 195
case studies, 196
defining, 22–23
Value-oriented investors
stock price reliance, 185
timing avoidance, 58–59
Vanguard Group (mutual funds), 15
Volatility, risk (contrast), 59–60

W

Wachovia, financial crisis, 62
Waiting, value/benefits, 151–154
Wal-Mart
equity cost, 119–120
real value, 132
share price, increase, 164
Walter Industries, Mueller spinoff,
214–215

Warren Buffett Way, The (Hagstrom), 139
Washington Mutual, financial crisis, 62
Washington Post Company, Buffett
    investment, 6–7, 48, 170
Wealth creation, 153
What if scenario, 132
Whitman, Marty (Third Avenue
    Funds), 72
Whole Foods

long-term growth prospects, 135
patience, exercise, 135–136
perspective, 81–82
Williams, John Burr, 96, 234
    theory, value, 235
Wrigley's, competition, 105

Z

Zero-sum game, investment, 15–16

Printed and bound by CPI Group (UK) Ltd, Croydon, CR0 4YY

16/04/2025

14658519-0003